Parkour and the City

Critical Issues in Sport and Society

Michael Messner and Douglas Hartmann, Series Editors

Critical Issues in Sport and Society features scholarly books that help expand our understanding of the new and myriad ways in which sport is intertwined with social life in the contemporary world. Using the tools of various scholarly disciplines, including sociology, anthropology, history, media studies and others, books in this series investigate the growing impact of sport and sports-related activities on various aspects of social life as well as key developments and changes in the sporting world and emerging sporting practices. Series authors produce groundbreaking research that brings empirical and applied work together with cultural critique and historical perspectives written in an engaging, accessible format.

Jules Boykoff, *Activism and the Olympics: Dissent at the Games in Vancouver and London*

Diana T. Cohen, *Iron Dads: Managing Family, Work, and Endurance Sport Identities*

Jennifer Guiliano, *Indian Spectacle: College Mascots and the Anxiety of Modern America*

Kathryn Henne, *Testing for Athlete Citizenship: The Regulation of Doping and Sex in Sport*

Jeffrey L. Kidder, *Parkour and the City: Risk, Masculinity, and Meaning in a Postmodern Sport*

Michael A. Messner and Michela Musto, eds., *Child's Play: Sport in Kids' Worlds*

Jeffrey Montez de Oca, *Discipline and Indulgence: College Football, Media, and the American Way of Life during the Cold War*

Stephen C. Poulson, *Why Would Anyone Do That?: Lifestyle Sport in the Twenty-First Century*

Parkour and the City

Risk, Masculinity, and Meaning in a Postmodern Sport

JEFFREY L. KIDDER

Rutgers University Press

New Brunswick, Camden, and Newark, New Jersey, and London

978-0-8135-7196-6
978-0-8135-7195-9
978-0-8135-7198-0
978-0-8135-7197-3

Cataloging-in-Publication data is available from the Library of Congress.

A British Cataloging-in-Publication record for this book is available from the British Library.

All photos in the book are by the author unless otherwise indicated.

∞ The paper used in this publication meets the requirements of the American National Standard for Information Sciences—Permanence of Paper for Printed Library Materials, ANSI Z39.48-1992.

www.rutgersuniversitypress.org

Manufactured in the United States of America

To Paul Lindsay (who taught the first sociology class I ever took),
Kenneth Allan (who inspired me to go to graduate school), and
Jim Dowd (who encouraged me to finish)

Contents

Acknowledgments

This book would not have been possible without the openness and generosity of the Chicago parkour community. I was inspired by the athleticism, creativity, and congeniality of the young people involved in the "art of movement" from my very first jam. Regretfully, as a sociologist, what interests me about the social world of parkour inevitably diverges from those in the community, especially with respect to the ways they may prefer to see their activities portrayed. While my "ethnographic gaze" may leave many practitioners of parkour disappointed (or even frustrated) with the analysis that follows, I sincerely hope that my admiration for the community and the discipline comes through the text. Over the years, I have discussed parkour with a countless number of traceurs—from the Chicago-area and beyond—and they all helped shape this project. There are far too many names to list them all here, but I owe a special thanks to Aaron Mikottis, Alex Meglei, Alex Paulus, Ando Calrissian, Angela Martin, Ben Zumhagen, Brandon Thread, Carolyn Steele, Chris Gorzelany, Chris Hal, Cody Beltramo, Dan Larson-Fine, David Yip, Eric Stodola, Evan Sink, Gerardo Carpio, Grant Lechner, Jake Markiewicz, Jaska, Jeff Strening, Jesse Anderson, Jesus Crespo, Jim Hotwagner, Jordan Oglesby, Kurt Gowan (and Parkour Ways), Luke Albrecht, Maria Von Dreele, Michael Zernow, Max Spadavecchia, Miko Vesović, Nathan Reed, Paul Canada (and Flipside Academy), Pavel Klopov, Phil Ashby, Rich Gatz, Ryan Cousins, Ryan Thill, Sam Monarrez, Sean Kalinoski, Stephan Roberts, Seth Rujiraviriyapinyo, Steve Dahl, Tommy Gilmore, Tyler

Kelly, and Zach Jarzabek. Also, American Parkour, Team Farang, and Wexin Yang were kind enough to grant me permission to reprint images and stills from videos they had posted online.

Peter Mickulas, from Rutgers University Press, is responsible for kick-starting the effort to expand my three published journal articles into a larger project. He took a chance on what was a rather slipshod prospectus and gave me the leeway necessary to gather more data and continue writing (well past the initial deadline). Paul Gilchrist and the press's anonymous reviewers were especially adept in their critiques and guidance as the manuscript progressed. Julia Ruth Dillon and the staff at Rutgers helped finesse this text into something readable. I owe a great deal to all their efforts.

As this book (slowly) developed, I had the opportunity to discuss my incipient analyses in a variety of forums. These conference presentations, guest lectures, and job talks afforded me the chance to converse with other researchers and better refine my ideas. Often it was a question asked from the audience or an informal chat with a stranger that opened up a new perspective for thinking about the social world of parkour. Simón Weffer graciously accepted the task of reading and commenting on the entire manuscript draft, and he provided much-needed feedback. I was also fortunate enough to have a graduate assistant, Patrick Dowling, to lend a hand with transcribing the final interviews. My words here are limited, but my gratitude is boundless for all those who helped along the way.

Parts of chapter two originally appeared as "Parkour, the Affective Appropriation of Urban Space, and the Real/Virtual Dialectic," *City & Community* 11 (2012): 229–253. An earlier version of chapter three was published as "Parkour, Masculinity, and the City," *Sociology of Sport Journal* 20 (2013): 1–23. Several aspects of chapter four can be found in "Parkour: Adventure, Risk, and Safety in the Urban Environment," *Qualitative Sociology* 36 (2013): 231–250. Kristen Myers, Beth Schewe, Gregory Snyder, Patrick Williams, and the anonymous reviewers for these journals aided in the process of refining my analysis for the articles (as well as what would eventually become this book). Further, all three of these journals' editors— Michael Atkinson (*Sociology of Sport Journal*), Hilary Silver (*City & Community*), and David Smilde (*Qualitative Sociology*)—showed a much-appreciated enthusiasm for the project.

Additionally, I would be remiss if I did not mention the numerous talks I had about my research with friends whose lives exist far from academia. It was on trips to the beach and hikes in the woods that I was able to candidly discuss what I was studying and to better clarify my ideas. I'm sure much of what I had to say seemed incredibly boring to my companions, and I deeply value their willingness to tolerate my babbling. In particular, Chris Gannon helped me think comparatively about parkour by offering counterpoints and insights from the skateboarding subculture. Jason George proved himself to be an interlocutor par excellence as we traipsed through Yosemite National Park. And, since college, Benji Shirley has lent an open ear to my various sociological endeavors. Finally, my indebtedness to my wife, Keri Wiginton, has only grown throughout this project. She took photographs and videos of traceurs training and meticulously pieced together a short film to accompany my *City & Community* article. Keri also read and helped edit the entire book manuscript. Most importantly, she was a champion of this project when I had doubts about continuing. *Thank you.*

Parkour and the City

Introduction

• •

Thinking Sociologically about Parkour

Jesus, whom most people called Scales, was standing on a six-foot-high wall in the northwestern corner of Grant Park in Chicago. For Scales and the fifteen or so other young people in this section of the park, it was a typical summer Saturday afternoon. Just to Scales's right, a group of teenagers were climbing up a different, higher wall. After a running start a young man would plant one foot on the wall, from which he would kick off and propel his body upward, reaching an arm as high as possible, hoping to grasp the top of the nearly twelve-foot-high structure. If successful, he would dangle for the shortest of moments—held only by the tips of four fingers—before bringing up his other arm. Once both hands had found purchase, the young man would pull his head and shoulders over the brow of the wall. Then, by pressing down on the top of the wall and straightening his arms, he would raise his torso high enough to swing a foot over the top. With one final leg thrust he would be standing on the summit. This maneuver is called a wall run, and the most skilled of the group could make it from the ground to the top in what looked like one fluid motion. Few, however, could get enough height in their initial kick off the wall to make the first hand grab. As they tried, others in the group would alternately cheer them on, offer up joking taunts, and provide sincere words of encouragement. Often someone would be using a smartphone to film the attempts.

To Scales's left—across the park benches occupied by tourists and homeless men, and past the grass where kids played games—another teenager was doing a handstand atop a seven-foot-high wall. In a show of confidence, he did the maneuver at the very edge of the structure. For nearly a minute he seemed frozen in time. As he tempted fate with his handstand, several others were running up the wall below him. Instead of trying to summit the structure, they would run a few steps up the wall and then kick out, throwing themselves into back flips. In an effort to refine his technique, one of the practitioners asked another member to film him. The practitioner did the flip, consulted the footage, and then tried it again. Frequently, members of the group made suggestions to each other: "You need more height," or "Try to rotate faster." Just a few feet to this group's right, four young men and two women were practicing their wall runs up a shorter wall, which stood about five feet high. They were beginners and not yet skilled enough to summit the twelve-foot-high wall at the other end of the grass. One of the more advanced in the group was standing watch over the novices and offering guidance.

Grant Park is a centerpiece of Chicago's downtown, popular with locals and visitors alike. The area Scales and his group were in, officially known as Sir Georg Solti Garden, lies on a slight incline in the city's topography. The tall retaining walls that border the level grass are only waist high on the other side. The variety of wall heights and the presence of shallow staircases, two electrical transformer boxes, and some interesting tree placements were the main reasons the group regularly went there. What might at first glance appear to be a tranquil (if not boring) part of the city was being used as the setting for a surprising array of stunts. Casual observers to the afternoon's proceedings often seemed confused by the total incongruence of sweaty, shirtless men gamboling over the ornate Beaux-Arts structures of the park. At the same time, the men's grace and moxie were seductive to many onlookers to whom the maneuvers appeared almost effortless—at once impossible and inevitable—like the feeling one has when watching highly trained dancers. Frequently, people passing by stopped to take photos. Sometimes they made requests of the young men: "Can you do that again?" or "Do a flip!" The week before, two police officers stopped to watch the proceedings. They observed from a distance and then continued on their way. Occasionally, passing cops offered words of support to the group.

For his part—on that day, at that moment—Scales was paying little mind to what the other members of his group were up to. And, despite his penchant for attention-seeking from bystanders (especially young women), Scales was not thinking about them either. Standing on the wall, he was staring at a nearly five-foot-high wall opposite him. Between him and that second wall was more than nine feet of open air, below which was a flight of rough, concrete stairs. His thought was to jump the span . . . *maybe*. There could be no running takeoff, and he would have to land perfectly still, lest he fall off the second wall. The distance itself was not a challenge for Scales. Even from a standstill, he could jump much farther. The angle of the jump and sculpting around the walls, though, complicated the maneuver. Seeing Scales lost in contemplation, another member of the group, Nario, walked up and stated matter-of-factly, "It looks small." With his assessment done, Nario climbed up and prepared to jump himself, but once in position he changed his mind. "It's scary; I'm not gonna lie." As Scales and Nario deliberated, others started showing interest in what was happening on the wall. Like Nario before them, most seemed to think the jump was rather basic. In turn, Nario and Scales invited any taker to come and do the jump first. A few clambered up the first wall to get a better perspective on what would be required. Despite its seeming simplicity from the ground, everyone but Scales eventually descended without trying to make it to the next wall.

After a great deal of contemplation, Scales convinced himself he could make it. As members of the group were fond of asserting, jumping ten feet is jumping ten feet. It should not matter if you are on the ground hopping cracks in the sidewalk or fifty feet in the air, leaping between two buildings. The height, the angles, the look of the walls—these did not make the physics of the jump harder. They merely produced an illusion of difficulty—creating a mental block. In varied iterations, Scales assured himself that he had done much bigger jumps in the past, that the danger today was not all that serious, and that he had fallen from higher places before without much injury. But still, to hedge his bet, he asked some people to stand below the second wall. They would be ready to catch him if his jump came up short and he started to fall backwards onto the stairs. With his spotters ready and a few more members of the group looking on (including one person filming), Scales steeled himself and—like so many times before—jumped (see figure 1). In the end, just as he had predicted—and despite what had been his almost overwhelming sense of fear—it was not that difficult a

FIG. 1. Scales jumps the span between two walls in Grant Park. Three other traceurs serve as spotters should he fall backward on the landing.

maneuver. Once complete, there was little fanfare. Scales announced it was no big deal to those who had watched, and the tiny, focused gathering around this section of the wall dissipated as group members filtered back into other parts of the park.

This was just one brief moment in the group's afternoon, occupying the attention of a handful of the participants for a few short minutes. Other members of the group were totally unaware it even took place. Aside from piquing the interest of an ethnographer, the episode is notable only in its mundanity. Before and after this moment, nearly all the young men and women present would have similar experiences that day. They would confront physical challenges and face mental struggles—culminating in periods of excitement and bouts of fear.

The physical layout of Grant Park helped allow for these events to happen. Later that same day, construction scaffolding along Jackson Boulevard would facilitate other movements, as would the benches and planting fixtures around Chase Tower. The Chicago Riverwalk had been part of the setting the week before. Months prior it had been the University of Illinois at Chicago campus and countless other sections of downtown. As they had done for years, on subsequent Saturdays, most members of the group would meet up again. Each week there would be new obstacles, new movements, and new variations of stunts done before. These young people were seeking out opportunities for adventure—what many of them commonly described as finding "challenges to overcome"—in the otherwise prosaic architecture of the city.

The Discipline of Parkour

Nario, Scales, and the rest of the group gallivanting and hurdling through Grant Park that Saturday were engaged in an emerging sport called "parkour." However, most practitioners shun the notion that the activity is a sport, preferring instead to consider it a discipline or a lifestyle. Parkour originated in France. The term "parkour" itself is a neologism derived from the French word *parcours*, which means route (as in the route of a race). Parkour is sometimes called "freerunning" (or "free running"), the "art of movement," or the "art of displacement." Practitioners of parkour often refer to themselves as "traceurs" or "freerunners." The most common definition traceurs use to explain parkour to outsiders is that it is about finding the quickest, most efficient way to get from point A to point B, using only the human body.

Experiencing Movement

In theory, parkour can be practiced anywhere. In fact, its oldest roots are in training people to move through the wilderness. As a contemporary practice, however, it is very much an urban and suburban phenomenon. In truth, in a human-built world, the most efficient way to get from point A to point B without a vehicle is almost always achieved by simply traveling on a sidewalk or street (with running on these designated pathways being the quickest method). Thus, rhetoric aside, parkour—as it is actually practiced—has very little to do with efficiency, speed or energy conservation. Instead, it is about what many traceurs describe as "experiencing movement." More specifically, it is about performing an evolving repertoire of stylized athletic maneuvers within urban and suburban environments.

When traceurs practice parkour, they call it "training." When traceurs hold a parkour event, they it a "jam." Jams are mostly informal. While some traceurs and entrepreneurs are working to formalize the discipline into a regulated sport, parkour is mostly experienced as an activity totally outside the purview of institutional control. It is mainly a discipline of young people learning from each other.[1] Because of the lack of any sort of official hierarchy, parkour jams are usually organized in the loosest of ways. There are moments of intense concentration, like Scales focusing on his jump, but there are also moments of tomfoolery. In fact, not long after Scales made his jump, he was bouncing around on all fours pretending to be an ape in order to distract another traceur from his training. Likewise, while some people might spend hours engrossed in learning a movement, others will spend hours at a jam just talking with their friends. There are, however, frequent efforts by traceurs to give parkour training an aura of seriousness. The very use of the term training underscores this point. It is hard to imagine amateur skateboarders or snowboarders describing their routine activities as training.[2] While all traceurs train because they enjoy the activity, many traceurs insist that parkour must be more than just fun and games. For them, parkour should be a true discipline—like a martial art. Not surprisingly, given the young age of most practitioners and the lack of formal organization, this is an ideal that even those espousing it rarely live up to.[3]

Over the last decade, parkour has transformed from an obscure French discipline to a global sport with mainstream appeal. In parkour's popular ascendency, Madonna hired traceurs to perform in music videos and stage acts, and in what became the famous opening sequence to *Casino Royale,* a villain used parkour to evade James Bond. In fact, the discipline now influences a variety of stunt work for television shows and movies (e.g., *The Bourne Legacy, Live Free or Die Hard,* and *Prince of Persia*). MTV produced the reality show *Ultimate Parkour Challenge* in 2009. Two years later, another youth-oriented network, G4, produced a similar parkour-themed televised competition called *Jump City: Seattle.* As interest in the discipline swelled, numerous parkour websites began popping up around the world. How-to videos became widely available online, as did documentaries. Parkour was even spoofed on NBC's hit sitcom *The Office.* While it has yet to (and may never) achieve the mass recognition of sports such as surfing or BMX, parkour's growing popularity has drawn interest from the International Olympic Committee for inclusion in future games.[4]

My goal in this book is to place parkour and its popularity within its relevant sociological context. The discipline shares much in common with other sports and urban subcultures. Skateboarding and graffiti are two of

FIG. 2. Dash vault sequence (left to right). Jordan performs a dash vault over a relatively high wall near the stairs leading to Chicago's riverfront (Photos: Keri Wiginton).

the most obvious examples. Young men dominate both, the activities are risky, and they involve reimagining how the city's built form can be used. Parkour also shares numerous similarities with the various stunts and antics young men have long been both praised and chastised for performing. One thinks of the iconic photographs from the early 1900s with construction workers precariously balancing themselves on the I-beams of unfinished skyscrapers. In sociologist Erving Goffman's terms, parkour is just one of myriad ways for finding *action* in the city.[5] It is about taking chances and testing one's character. These things said, sports, like all aspects of culture, are products of their time, and parkour represents a particular orientation to urban adventure seeking. Many of the individual components might be found elsewhere, but traceurs have given them a new arrangement. This book is an effort to map out this arrangement.

I will explore the ways that traceurs' engagement with new media can help alter their perceptions of local environments. I argue this engagement is best characterized as a dialectic between the virtual and the real world. While traceurs are not unique in this regard, they can help us understand the more general process of globalized ideas and images influencing local practices. I will also consider how traceurs use the structural resources of the city in performing their urban adventures. In particular, these young men's stunts serve as valued methods for making masculine identity claims.

Finally, I will analyze practitioners' conceptualization of danger and safety. Despite the potential for bodily harm, traceurs view their actions as affirming the self. Instead of positioning parkour as a form of thrill seeking, they insist it demonstrates an ability to successfully assess risks, manage fears, and persevere through challenges. Appreciating this unique constellation of practices is key to understanding why individuals like Scales find purpose in reimagining the architecture that surrounds them. Further still, analyzing parkour in this way enhances our sociological understanding of the city itself. If urbanism is about the lives individuals lead in the city, parkour represents a unique postmodern interpretation of that way of life.

About the Traceurs

As described above, most of the practitioners I came to know were young men. Their experience ranged from just a few hours of parkour practice to over a decade of training. The majority were white, but a significant portion of the social world comprised African-Americans, Asians, and Latinos. Class backgrounds were quite varied, but many seemingly came from middle-class families. Reflecting their class and racial diversity, members of the Chicago parkour community lived in a wide range of locations—from impoverished inner-city neighborhoods to posh exurbs. Most practitioners were in their late teens to early twenties, although some were considerably younger and a few much older. Many traceurs I encountered were in high school (or even lower grades), while some were attending institutions of high learning from city colleges to state universities to prestigious private institutions. For those working full time, occupations were similarly diverse, ranging from low-wage service workers to white-collar professionals. Young or old, working or middle class, white or minority, most people at jams had less than two years of experience in parkour.

While parkour involves an astounding degree of coordination and strength, traceurs are usually not archetypal "jocks." A few traceurs I spoke with had backgrounds in diverse sports, including gymnastics, soccer, track, and even football. Some were involved in alternative physical activities such as rock climbing and mountain biking. Most, though, described their athletic pursuits before parkour as fleeting or non-existent. Nathan provided a characteristic response: "I'll play a little ping-pong every now and then with the old man, you know. [. . .] I wasn't a high school jock or anything—more of a hacky sacker than a football player." Additionally, in distinct contrast to the stereotype of the extreme sport participant, traceurs tended to be clean-cut and mild mannered.[6] This was a point of pride for many traceurs, who often contrasted the image they tried to project with what they felt were negative public perceptions of skateboarders.

Aside from talking about parkour, a good portion of these traceurs actually spent a great deal of time discussing stereotypically "nerdy" pastimes. One group of traceurs visiting Chicago for a jam, for instance, repeatedly lamented having left their cards for Magic: The Gathering at home. Magic is a very popular (but also popularly mocked) fantasy trading card game. On another occasion Andy was nonplussed when I failed to recognize the symbol on his hat as a reference to the fantasy video game The Legend of Zelda. As such, more than one traceur referred to the community as being filled with "athleti-nerds."

When I started attending jams, there was not a clearly defined fashion or clothing style associated with parkour, at least locally. Traceurs tended to wear basic athletic attire: sneakers, sweatpants, and t-shirts. While these items were often branded with parkour-specific words or images, the cut of the clothing and the manner they were worn was not distinct. Over the years—following European trends—many Chicago traceurs adopted extremely baggy sweatpants as part of their look. Later, exaggerated drop-crotch sweatpants also became popular (again, following international trends in the parkour community).

For my first foray into the field, I was not sure what to expect, and, as I quickly found out, my preconceived notions about how parkour was practiced were utterly incorrect. Having seen edited footage on YouTube and various documentaries, I assumed traceurs would be running through the city, jumping, rolling, and vaulting over various obstacles as they traveled to some destination. On the contrary, the traceurs I studied very rarely (if ever) used parkour to traverse any sort of appreciable distance. Instead, traceurs would gather in an area well known for having structures amiable to parkour, like a particular section of a public park or a university quad. They would train on the obstacles available at one location and then move to another area—usually just by walking in the typical fashion. Often there was considerable distance between one training area and another. During these walks, traceurs would often engage in horseplay (some of which might

FIG. 3. Traceurs milling about Ogden Plaza in downtown Chicago. On display here is the popularity of baggy sweatpants in the parkour community.

be parkour related), but I never witnessed a concerted effort to have a "flow run" from one section of the city to another.

Studying Lifestyle Sports

Parkour can be considered a lifestyle sport[7]—an athletic endeavor that contrasts with traditional team sports such as baseball, basketball, and football in meaningful ways. First and foremost, while lifestyle sports are often practiced with friends, the activities themselves are individualistic. One person, on one surfboard, rides one wave. There are competitions within many lifestyle sports, but such events are often viewed as antithetical to the spirit of the activity. This is true even among many of the competitors themselves.[8] Participants feel their actions are about intrinsic enjoyment—not the money or status possibly garnered from winning competitions. Likewise, efforts to institutionalize and regulate lifestyle sports are generally viewed by participants as threatening their intrinsic enjoyment of the activity. In essence, participants in lifestyle sports tend to not consider their activities as sports at all. They see themselves participating in a lifestyle to which a certain athletic endeavor—freestyle skiing, inline skating, mountain biking, etc.—is integral.[9]

Researchers have studied an array of lifestyle sports and analyzed them from multiple angles. The original focus on these activities has tended to conceptualize them as forms of youthful resistance to the status quo. For example, if football espouses a macho, must-win ethos, then skateboarders' flippant attitude toward competitions and their outright mockery of event organizers challenges the hegemonic function of traditional team sports.[10] More recent studies, though, have been far more critical of lifestyle sports' counter-hegemonic potential. After all, these activities tend to be the purview of middle-class whites, and many are male-dominated. Thus, while participants may be undermining certain aspects of the contemporary power structure, their homogeneity inevitably reinforces other aspects.[11]

Over the last several decades, lifestyle sports have also become big business. Some researchers, therefore, have reoriented academic attention to how previous forms of resistance have been co-opted by corporations. Alternatively, others have stressed that while lifestyle sports involve a great deal of consumption, participants are not just cultural dupes. Their purchases are selective and their understandings of advertisements highly nuanced. In other words, lifestyle sports participants can be understood as simultaneously resisting and embracing corporate influence.[12]

Most of the previous social research into parkour has focused on traceurs' appropriation of the city, especially as it relates to what Marxist philosopher Henri Lefebvre calls "abstract space." For Lefebvre, abstract space results from the conceptions of urban planners and architects. In the neoliberal city, for example, the environment is cleared out and built up for the generation of profit.[13] Against abstract space, though, is the lived experience of the individual. As people actually inhabit the material world, there is the potential to challenge the capitalist production of space. As Lefebvre writes, "The user's space is *lived*—not represented (or conceived). When compared with the abstract space of the experts (architects, urbanists, planners), the space of everyday activities of users is a concrete one, one which is to say, subjective." In other words, those who design and build urban environments cannot perfectly dictate how its denizens will use them.[14]

Organization analyst Maria Daskalaki and her co-authors offer a good example of how previous researchers have analyzed parkour as a subjectively lived production of space. "Parkour is about the inhabitants' ability to take control of the given space and transform it into a landscape of possibility. [. . . T]he philosophy of parkour continues to offer lenses for seeing the corporate spaces differently [. . .]. This is because parkour was conceptualized not as a reactive movement but as an expressive medium of individuals who view the city as a playground." Or, as literary theorist Paula Geyh writes, "Parkour effectively remaps urban space, creating a parallel, 'ludic' city, a city of movement and free play within and against the city of obstacles and inhibitions." Likewise, sociologist Michael Atkinson writes, "Free running is a mode of bringing forth or revealing dimensions of the physical and spiritual self through a particular type of urban gymnastics. It destabilizes and disrupts technocapitalist meanings of the city's physical and social landscape for its practitioners."[15]

The Affective Appropriation of Space

There are two essential points to be made about traceurs' appropriations of the city. First, parkour is not only happening *at* some place: it is enacted *through* space. This is Lefebvre's most critical insight into what he describes as the production of space. "Space is at once the result and the cause, product and producer [...]."[16] To this point, architectural historian Iain Borden offers an especially adroit study of skateboarding. He shows that the landscapes of possibility produced by the sport are about more than the reinterpretation of space. Instead, it needs to be understood that skaters' embodied practices can only happen through an engagement with space. "In terms of skateboarding's relations to architecture, its production of space is not purely bodily or sensorial; instead, the skater's body produces its space dialectically with the production of architectural space." That is, the skater finds lines of movement through the material world, and his body interfaces with the physical structures—"a dynamic intersection of body, board, and terrain." According to Borden, it is at this interface (and only at this interface) that skaters appropriate space. In other words, spatial structures enable and constrain skaters' actions.[17]

This social dialectic of spatial structures is no small point. Sociological theories are typically aspatial. To the extent that sociologists even consider the material world, they are apt to rely on concepts of place.[18] Space involves abstract geometry (direction, distance, shape, size, and volume). Place, on the other hand, is about the cultural significance attributed to spaces. For example, a researcher may focus on the meaning of Fenway Park to baseball fans or how housing project residents feel about patronizing local businesses catering to the middle class.[19] Alternatively, sociological studies of space involve what psychologist James Gibson calls "affordance"—that is, what can be done *in* and *with* the physical environment.[20] Grant Park's Sir Georg Solti Garden, for example, affords wall flips and wall runs (see figure 13 in chapter two). The wooden playground in North Side Chicago's Oz Park affords swinging movements (called "lachés") and "precision jumps" (see figure 7 in chapter one). The city, in this sense, provides structural resources that individuals use agentically, but their agency is only possible because of the structures.

The appropriation of space, of course, helps define and redefine places[21]—a point that will be touched on throughout the book. My theoretical and empirical emphasis, however, is on traceurs' actions within space itself, not the meanings practitioners attributed to the places in which they train. In other words, in this book, I focus on how traceurs come to reimagine what type of movements the city affords. Admittedly, most sociological inquiries are probably best complemented by thinking about place rather than space. Some social worlds and subcultures, though, need to be analyzed in terms of how they use space—the dialectic between individual agency and physical structures.[22] I contend that parkour is one of those social worlds, and I argue that to think sociologically about parkour requires a serious consideration of the activity's spatial aspects and how they relate to the meaning of the discipline for traceurs.

Second, spatial appropriation must be understood as an embodied practice. To be in the world is a visceral experience.[23] This is highlighted in the opening vignette. At various moments, the traceurs became engrossed in their training. This was necessary because to lose concentration would be to risk personal disaster. Psychologist Mihaly Csikszentmihalyi refers to such engrossment as being in a state of flow. Flow is about becoming totally immersed in embodied practices. It is about losing oneself in an activity.[24] In essence, flow involves straddling the threshold between boredom and anxiety. The tasks being performed must perfectly match the abilities a person possesses. To illustrate this point, consider paid labor. Work is generally described as unpleasant precisely because it lacks this balance between skills and requirements. If jobs are too easy or mindless, they feel boring; when jobs are too challenging or stressful, they create anxiety. The same holds true for games. Games are fun when talents are stretched to the very limit, but not beyond it. At this threshold, an individual's attention is focused in the moment and—unlike normal, reflexive thought—*only* in the moment.

FIG. 4. Kong vault sequence (right to left). Seth performs a long kong vault over a picnic table in Cummings Square in the suburb of River Forest, Illinois.

In thinking about flow, we must continue to be attentive to the fact that such experiences can only happen through an engagement with the physical spaces in which they are embedded. Thus, it is traceurs' appropriations of space that generate flow. Further, it is in seeking out the flow experience that they appropriate space. In geographer Stephen Saville's study of parkour, for instance, he notes that "through intimate play with place, the practice of parkour is a good example of how people can explore, refine and even enjoy fearful emotions. They become a key through which place can be engaged." For Saville, those fearful but enjoyable emotions are about flow.[25] This can be seen in the description of Scales as he readied himself for his jump. He was scared of the jump, but immersing himself in the challenge was viewed as a positive experience. And, this was only possible in and through his interface with the physical structures of the city. Taken together, this is what I call the affective appropriation of space—the intersection of embodied practices and lived experience within the material world.[26]

Postmodernity and the Neoliberal City

Inherent in all sociological studies of sport is the assumption that play and games have a significance that extends beyond the activities themselves. As Norbert Elias writes, "[S]tudies of sport which are not studies of society are studies out of context." His point is that whatever a person does, it must be understood as one part of the ongoing process that constitutes society.[27] This does not mean that any practice or outcome is the inevitable result of a given set of social conditions, but it does mean that certain social conditions make certain practices or outcomes possible.

In this book, I argue that parkour is quintessentially postmodern. Following geographer David Harvey, I understand postmodernity as a particular cultural form bound to changes in the global flow of capital.[28] This involves a general incredulousness toward meta-narratives, an increasing exposure to mediate images, and the breakdown of stable identities. Further, neoliberal discourse is hegemonic within postmodernity.[29] Whether this cultural condition really represents something that is *post*modern or whether it is better conceptualized as part of a new phase of modernity is less relevant for my argument than the fact that the term "postmodernity " has come to encapsulate these cultural changes.[30]

Ultimately, the sociological study of parkour enhances our understanding of the city within the conditions of postmodernity. New media, by which I mean the coupling of the Internet with personal computers, smartphones, and social networking tools, have changed how individuals experience reality. Sociologist Jean Baudrillard goes so far as to argue that reality itself has been supplanted by simulacra.[31] To speak of postmodern culture, therefore, is to speak of the proliferation of new media in everyday social life. As I will show, traceurs are engaged with the real world, but their engagement cannot be separated from what anthropologist Arjun Appadurai calls "global ethnoscapes"—the worldwide circulation of ideas and images.[32] These mediated forms are intertwined with traceurs' affective appropriations of the city.

The self in postmodern culture is predicated on performance. Identity is no longer understood as something purely ascribed by one's characteristics; it is something that must be individually developed. To quote philosopher Judith Butler (1990), "[A]cts, gestures, and desire produce the effect of an internal core or substance, but produce this *on the surface* of the body.

[. . . They] are performative in the sense that the essence or identity that they otherwise purport to express are *fabrications* manufactured and sustained through corporeal signs and discursive means."[33] The urban adventures of traceurs exemplify such performances. Parkour allows for tests of character that sociologist Michael Schwalbe refers to as "manhood acts."[34] In other words, traceurs' affective appropriations of space are a way for young males to lay claim to the valued identity of manhood within the ever-shifting culture of postmodernity.

Sociologist Pierre Bourdieu describes neoliberalism as a "Darwinian world" that substitutes public trust in the democratic state with faith in the free market. Individuals are charged with being personally responsible for their physical well-being and financial success. As political scientist Earl Gammon writes, "Unlike Fordist man, who conceived welfare as a right, neoliberal man saw reciprocal relations with greater society as incompatible with the new vision of selfhood."[35] Postmodernity is the culture of neoliberal man, and risk taking in parkour must be understood within this context. Far from seeing themselves as daredevils, traceurs see themselves as risk assessors who manage their fear and avoid potential harm. In contrast to pushing the edge of survival—à la sociologist Stephen Lyng's lauded concept of "edgework"[36]—traceurs' actions can better be conceptualized as attempting to make a *hedge* on their bets. Such actions are symbolic, and they affirm a self prepared to live in the neoliberal city, which shifts collective risks onto the individual.[37]

Overview of the Book

Parkour and the City is the product of several years of participant-observation among traceurs in Chicago and the surrounding suburbs—which is to say, I spent time with these young men and women as they trained and jammed, and, occasionally, I practiced parkour maneuvers with them. I also spent a lot of time talking with traceurs and asking them questions about their discipline. More information on my qualitative approach to researching parkour can be found in appendix A. We have already come across many parkour terms in the course of this introduction. Moving forward with the book, though, readers may find it helpful to consult appendix B. There I provide a quick and easy reference for some common words in the social world and how I am using them.

My argument in this book is broken into four substantive chapters. In chapter one can be found a history of the discipline and efforts to develop it into a commercialized, regulated sport. This broader overview is interspersed with specific connections to the past and present of the Chicago parkour community. Chapter two links simulacra and global ethnoscapes to the situated, embodied practices of traceurs. I emphasize how the virtual worlds of the discipline (made possible through new media) are dialectically connected to engagement with the tangible, real world of the city. Chapter three shows parkour as a form of urban adventure, allowing for performances of manhood acts. This chapter highlights the structural resources of the city and the ways traceurs utilize them in masculine identity construction. Chapter four contains an analysis of the dangers of parkour in relationship to the traceurs' conceptions of safety. In symbolically prioritizing risk assessment over thrill seeking, I posit the discipline as a form of "hedgework"—resonating with the rhetoric of personal responsibility abounding in the neoliberal city.

1

Developing the Discipline and Creating a Sport

● ● ● ● ● ● ● ● ● ● ● ● ● ● ● ● ● ● ● ●

When writing about parkour, it is routine to mention David Belle and Sébastien Foucan as the progenitors of the discipline. Belle and Foucan were both born in the early 1970s, and they grew up in Lisses, a suburb south of Paris. What would eventually become known as parkour—it is said—evolved out of their adolescent games. This evolution, however, is much more complex than one or two charismatic individuals creating a *sui generis* sport. Beyond Lisses, Belle also spent significant amounts of time in the northern Parisian suburb of Sacrelles with his cousins, Williams Belle and Châu Belle Dinh. In this mix were several other friends as well, including Yann Hnautra, Laurent Piemontesi, and, eventually, Stéphane Vigroux. Hnautra's family lived in Évry, a town neighboring Lisses. During the friends' teenage years, the Belle and Hnautra homes were regular hangouts for the group, and it was in the woods and on the playgrounds and rooftops of Évry, Lisses, and Sacrelles that parkour slowly developed.[1] At that time, the word "parkour" did not yet exist. Their activity was referred to as *parcours*—referencing military obstacle course training (*parcours du combatant*).

The group's interest in parcours owes to the influence of Belle's older brother, Jeff, and his father, Raymond. Both were firefighters, and in the service they were exposed to the ideas of Georges Hérbert.[2] Hérbert was a physical fitness advocate and former French naval officer at the turn of the century. Like many of his contemporaries, Hérbert worried that life in an industrial metropolis weakened the body and tarnished the soul. Based on his experiences watching indigenous populations in Africa, he argued that the solution to modernity's malaise was to eschew the comfort and safety of the city. Through what he called the *méthode naturelle,* individuals were taught to move fluidly through untamed environments.[3] In short, the goal of the "natural method" was to hone the mind and train the body to agilely traverse over rocks, through thickets, across streams, and over other obstacles normally absent in the urban landscape. Alternatively, if training in nature was not an option, purpose-built courses—parcours du combatant—could be designed and built.

Hérbert's intention with the natural method was for citizens of the republic to "be strong to be useful."[4] Raymond Belle's use of parcours skills throughout his career as a firefighter exemplified Hérbert's fitness philosophy. And, within the Belle family, Raymond was discussed as a figure larger than life. He was described as a man of incomparable agility and strength who used his talents to protect others. David grew up in awe of his father but spent most of his life estranged from him. However, practicing parcours was a way for the younger Belle to try to impress Raymond and live up to his legacy.[5] Taken together, Hérbert's natural method and the heroism of the firefighting Belle family form the origin myth of contemporary parkour. In varied iterations this story has been retold at jams, recounted to inquiring reporters, and asserted in books, documentaries, and websites.

It must be pointed out, however, that what parkour became is *not* the parcours of the natural method. The elder Belles trained parcours to navigate burning buildings for their own survival and to save those trapped inside. This was the utilitarian purpose Hérbert envisioned for his physical regimen—being strong to be useful. Conversely, the younger Belle and his friends applied what they learned of parcours as a form of play. They integrated their bodily practices with youthful fantasies inspired by comic books and superheroes.[6] For these teenagers, the activity was noninstrumental. It was not about utilitarian labor; it was about the joy derived from spontaneous, creative actions.[7]

There are three factors that stand out about the young men's adaptation of parcours. First, there is the sheer athletic prowess of what they were doing. The combination of balance, coordination, speed, and strength involved in their incipient discipline was remarkable. This aspect of their revision to parcours was perfectly in line with Hérbert's intentions. The members of the group were certainly strong, and their skills had the potential to be useful. However, Hérbert did not envision people incorporating the quotidian structures of the city into their training. The purpose of the natural method was to counter the immoral sloth promoted by urbanism, not to transform hand railings, park benches, and staircases into objects for playful risk taking. The second thing that stands out about the revised parcours, therefore, was the group's affective appropriation of space. Third, working in tandem with their raw physical skill and their reimagining of their everyday environs was their stylized movement. In this adaptation of parcours, form became more important than function. As with other lifestyle sports, practitioners' look and attitude defined the activity.[8] More than anything else, navigating their surroundings was a matter of style.

When put together, these three factors (athletic skill, spatial appropriation, and kinetic style) eventually resulted in a sporting practice the media wanted to cover. Advertisers were also eager to exploit it. In turn, young people around the world began to emulate it. In essence, Belle and his friends were skateboarding without boards; they were graffitiing without paint. And, as with these other urban subcultures, this new discipline contained a sense of youthful aggression and mischief. It was edgy, and it produced an image of personal freedom and self-expression.[9]

The French Originators

Before parkour was "cool," it was a more or less unknown activity conducted on the outskirts of Paris, and, in many ways, the group's adaptation of parcours was made possible through the particularities of French urban development. It was the nation's government policies and social realities, after all, that configured the physical spaces in which the teenage boys roamed. In the 1950s, when the boys' parents were quite young themselves, foreign workers began flowing into France to find employment in the postwar rebuilding effort. A severe housing shortage for these migrant laborers and their families quickly ensued. In response to the growing crisis, suburban construction boomed for two decades. Towns like Sacrelles saw their populations explode. Others, like Évry, were more or less created from scratch during the 1960s to house the nation's expanding workforce. At the same time, the decision to locate much of these new residential areas outside the nation's cities was not entirely benign. As immigration among non-Europeans rose (especially from former French colonies), policies were enacted that sought to physically isolate these populations from the heart of the republic.[10]

From the *Banlieues*

The French word for suburb is *banlieue*. However, within the French context, banlieue has a very different meaning from the quintessential American image of large, single-family homes amid idyllic surroundings. According to one French philosopher, "The sociological equivalent would rather be inner cities, owing to inverse urban logics." While some suburban districts are quite posh, since the 1980s the French imagination has come to associate the banlieues with crime, poverty, and a resistance to assimilation. In other words, during the latter half of the century, the spatial exclusion of immigrants was complemented by an increasing social exclusion of immigrants from mainstream public life. Further, since the 1990s this "fear of the banlieues" has become manifest in concerns over Muslims and Islamic terrorism.[11]

Beyond immigration—and the racial and ethnic stigmas associated with it—France, like many Western nations, experienced the shocks of economic restructuring that began in the 1970s. During this time, much of what was once stable, domestic industrial production became globalized.[12] However, as in the United States, media pundits and politicians often couched these structural problems in individualized terms. Banlieues, like American ghettos, were described as the home of hoodlums raised without a proper work ethic. Of course, the social strife and moments of spectacular unrest that have flared up in the French suburbs over the last several decades are expressions born of severe economic inequalities that cannot be reduced to the personal failings of banlieue residents.[13] In rather stark terms, scholar Graham Murray writes of suburban French youth, "Globalisation means that factories that once employed their parents are disappearing; racism means that the remaining jobs are given to whites." Further, Murray notes, "With a few notable exceptions, *les banlieues* [. . .] are, more often than not, dull and isolated places where unemployment can reach 40 per cent. Scattered through the towns themselves are the ubiquitous post-war apartment blocks—rather ugly edifies, whether they be council or privately owned."[14]

The reality of France's growing ethnic and racial diversity in the postwar years was reflected in the original parcours group itself. The Belle family was French-Vietnamese, Foucan's family originated in Guadeloupe, and Hnautra's family was from New Caledonia. While there is little reliable information about the class upbringing of the group, Hnautra describes Évry in the 1990s as a rough place to live. "If you wanted to just walk certain streets, you had to be a man, but a man with a big 'M.' You had to be able to cope with anything that could happen to you."[15] In more recent times, Sacrelles has been in the international news regarding tensions (and occasional violent outbreaks) between North African Jews and Muslims. Lisses, on the other hand, is usually characterized as a mild-mannered, middle-class suburb.[16]

Regardless of the specifics of their families' finances, the social experiences of members of the parcours group were undoubtedly shaped by the inequalities and economic uncertainties rumbling through the French republic during their childhood and into their adult years. While Évry, Lisses, and Sacrelles were not at the epicenter of the infamous riots in the 1980s and 1990s, many in the group were non-white and of non-European origin, and they inevitably wrestled with the stigmas associated with being young men from the banlieues. This more than likely included difficulties finding employment, a lack of adequate social services, and police harassment. In fact, when members of the original parcours group eventually ended up in acting roles, these challenges were recurring plot lines in the films in which they appeared.

The feature of the banlieues that had the most obvious impact on the group was their physical design. Known as new towns, postwar developments (along with the changes being implemented in older settlements) were products of modernist urban planning. As writers like Jane Jacobs would famously critique, planners during this time were enamored with zoning laws. Cities and suburbs, which had often grown in rather organic ways, were segmented into regions: industrial zones, commercial zones, residential zones. In the parceling of social space, the vibrancy of many public places was squelched. Recoiling against such development in another French new town built in the 1960s, Henri Lefebvre claimed,

"Whenever I set foot in Mourenx I am filled with dread."[17] Perhaps most important for the evolution of parkour was that an architecture style known as Brutalism heavily influenced the postwar building boom. This style relies on dense concrete structures shaped into basic, often repetitive, geometric forms. Brutalism was particularly prominent with state-sponsored construction projects at the time. These were the kinds of structures France used to help house, educate, and administer to the growing populations channeled into the banlieues. As one journalist noted, "That parkour originated in Lisses is unsurprising once you visit the place. [. . .B]ored teenagers like Belle and Foucan saw extreme possibilities in their lackluster environment."[18]

Modernist urban planning often involves what Iain Borden calls "reductive architecture." It leaves much of the built environment feeling sanitized of meaning—a spatial "degree zero." While this degree zero can invoke indifference (or in Lefebvre's case, dread), it also has the potential to invite resistance—which is to say, it can be appropriated for new purposes. In particular, Borden discusses spatial appropriation by skateboarders. Referencing places like Milton Keynes in England (a new town outside of London), Borden notes, "[Skateboarding] is not an activity which could take place in medieval, renaissance, or early industrial cities [. . .]. It requires the smooth surfaces and running spaces of the concrete city [. . .]."[19] In essence, Borden claims that skateboarders redefined the reductive, utilitarian aspects of modernist architecture. In Lefebvre's terms, skaters take the abstract space of city planners and make it a lived space—a site of joyous, risky play.

Free from the dependence on small wheels that get stuck in the cracks and cobbles of older urban forms, parcours, perhaps, may not have *required* smooth surfaces. However, Borden's larger point remains. Reductive architecture that produces spatial degree zeros can encourage individuals to try to infuse their environments with meaning, and, like skateboarders, the original parcours group took otherwise alienating environments and incorporated them into personally agentic practices.[20] Building on these themes, Nathan Guss, a professor of French, writes, "Parkour, an art whose main themes are escape and spatial appropriation, is a response to these feelings of claustrophobia created by recent French urban policy."[21] Thus, in considering the history of the discipline, it is important to note that the built environment—in conjunction with a social environment characterized by spatial marginalization along the lines of class and race—inevitably shaped the lives of its originators.

Into the Limelight

There is very little record of Belle and his friends' athletic progression during their initial years of training. In fact, the discipline might never have expanded beyond their original circle of friends had Jeff Belle not intervened. In 1997, Jeff encouraged the group to put on a demonstration at an annual firefighter event. This attracted media attention to the young men's adaptation of parcours. Reflecting their interest in fantasy, the group dressed up as ninjas and labeled themselves the Yamakasi.[22] The term, while sounding Japanese (which is one of the reasons they liked it), borrows from the Lingala language (*ya mákasi*). It means a person "strong in body and spirit," or as Hnautra himself defined it, "strong man."[23] That year, in a television interview, Foucan used the phrase *l'art du déplacement* ("the art of displacement" or "the art of movement") to describe their activity.[24] Following their initial television exposure, commercial opportunities quickly opened up for the Yamakasi and their discipline. Various organizations wanted to hire the group for performances. Most significantly for the future of the sport, film directors and companies looking for new ways to sell their products took notice. Like skateboarding before it, what the Yamakasi were doing looked to many people like the next big thing in youth marketing.

Although the explanation remains opaque, it is clear that by the late 1990s relationships between the friends in the original group were frayed. Belle and Foucan left the Yamakasi soon after the firefighter event (before any of the group's subsequent performances). In 1997, in an effort to claim ownership of his version of the activity, Belle coined the term "parkour" and stopped using the terms "parcours" or "l'art du déplacement."[25] The next year he started a new group called the Tracers, with whom Foucan was briefly associated. However, as time went on, Belle and Foucan grew apart as well. In fact, during the waves of media hype in the early to mid-2000s, the two rarely acknowledged the existence of each other or of their connection with the Yamakasi. While their subjective motivations may have been more complex, from an outside perspective it is easy to view the original group splintering into three distinct franchises: Yamakasi and "l'art du déplacement," Belle and "parkour," and Foucan and "freerunning" (a phrase first used in 2003). And, all of these franchises were battling for public recognition and roles in advertisements and movies. As explained in appendix B, following the discursive norms of most contemporary practitioners, I use the term "parkour" as a generic reference to *all* variations stemming from the original group's adaptation of parcours.

The remaining members of the Yamakasi, building on the continuity of their name, had the first major commercial success with the discipline. They played ninjas in the French action film *Taxi 2* (released in 2000) and then starred in *Yamakasi: Les Samouraïs des Temps Modernes* (released in 2001). The latter film casts the group as modern-day Robin Hoods, trading Sherwood Forest for a banlieue. In the movie, the Yamakasi use their parkour skills to rob from the rich to pay for a poor child's heart transplant.[26] Both *Taxi 2* and *Yamakasi* were brokered through the group's connection with French director, writer, and producer Luc Besson (most famous in the United States for *The Fifth Element*, starring Bruce Willis). Besson had seen the Yamakasi during one of their first television appearances and immediately reached out to them.[27] In 2001, the Yamakasi were also featured on American television in an episode of *Ripley's Believe It or Not!*

Soon afterward, Belle and Foucan started making even bigger names for themselves. Nike used parkour in 2002 for its Presto running shoe campaign. Spoofing foreign-language documentaries, the ads feature rapid-fire narration in French with dry, truncated translation into English. In one, Belle appears as the suitor of a young woman—using his skills to retrieve items she drops from the upper levels of a banlieue apartment. The most famous ad from the Presto series, one that traceurs still reference today, stars Foucan (accompanied by the same French-English narration) frantically running through a new town of concrete high-rises—desperately (and comically) fleeing from an "angry chicken." This visually spectacular ad would garner Wieden + Kennedy an Emmy nomination for Outstanding Commercial, and it undoubtedly exposed a wide American audience to parkour. Despite the exposure, though, there was no context: the ads gave no information about what Belle and Foucan were actually doing and no indication that other people practiced in the discipline.

The same year as the Nike campaign, the BBC used Belle in one of its station promotions. Playing a bored office worker at the end of his day, Belle gets up from his desk, strips off his shirt and tie, climbs out a skyscraper window, and runs across London's rooftops in an awe-inspiring display of parkour. British audiences were stunned, and it created a sustained public response qualitatively different from the industry-insider appreciation of Wieden + Kennedy's work. A writer from the *Evening Standard* wrote, "TV viewers this week have been spellbound by the new BBC

1 promo showing [a] real-life Spiderman [. . .] performing a series of stomach-churning stunts over the rooftops of a busy city." Or, as another journalist put it:

> You may not think you know what Le Parkour is, but believe me, if you have a TV, you do. The apotheosis of Le Parkour can be seen in that new 90-second BBC promotional film, in which a young man with the torso of Apollo [. . .] leaves work via the window of his multi-storey office and proceeds to get home by the apparently effortless method of somersaulting across rooftops, leaping 30-foot gaps between buildings and doing handstands on railings 120 feet above street level—among other death-defying acrobatics. Like me, you might have thought that this was computer enhanced, but no. Le Parkour is for real.[28]

Spurred on by the widespread public interest in the BBC promo, in 2003 Channel 4 aired *Jump London*, a one-hour British documentary in which Foucan and two other French traceurs perform parkour on iconic structures in the city.[29] This feature and its sequel, *Jump Britain* (aired in 2005), had an immeasurable impact on the popularity of parkour across the world.

British and American Parkour

The *Jump* series marked the end of parkour being a primarily French discipline and the ascendency of British and American parkour.[30] In contrast to its previous media iterations outside France, parkour's portrayal in the *Jump* series was buttressed by the existence of Urban Freeflow (UF), an English-language website offering information about the budding parkour community in the United Kingdom. And, the growth of UF can be directly traced to the popularity of the *Jump* series.[31]

From the Television to the Streets . . . to the Internet

UF went live in 2003 (after Belle's BBC ad), and its following was under 300. After *Jump London* aired, UF's membership ballooned into the thousands. After *Jump Britain* aired, UF membership hit 10,000.[32] Further, during the filming of both films, the director of the *Jump* series, Mike Christie, helped make valuable social connections between the English traceurs associated with UF and the French traceurs within Foucan's orbit.

On the other side of the Atlantic, the *New York Times* ran one of the first American newspaper articles on parkour in 2003.[33] The focus of this article was exclusively on French traceurs and the corporations courting them. That same year, Toyota launched an ad campaign featuring Foucan and other traceurs doing stunts throughout a parking garage. A year later, several other American papers were publishing features about the growing popularity of parkour within the United States. To put this in perspective, there are no English-language articles about parkour, l'art du déplacement, or the Yamakasi in LexisNexis's database before 2000. In the following three years, at least thirty-five articles were published, mostly in the British press. In 2005, the year *Jump Britain* was released, there were over forty articles on the topic. In 2006, the year *Casino Royale* opened in theaters—featuring Foucan doing a series of death-defying leaps in the opening sequence—there were more than fifty (without counting movie reviews that mentioned the discipline). And, by the middle of that decade, parkour and freerunning became household words in the United States—at least among homes with teenage boys.[34]

As various media images showed parkour to the would-be traceurs of Chicago in the early 2000s, Urban Freeflow became *the* social networking hub all of them turned to. For example, Ryan C., one of the first traceurs in Chicago explained, "Yeah, there were two French forums too, but those were exclusively French. [. . .] So pretty much we defaulted to the UK website for information." Likewise, Michael, a Michigan traceur who became a prominent figure in the formation of the Chicago parkour community, explained, "[. . .T]here was really only like a few websites or information at all about it, like in France and they hated Americans and they didn't even like people that spoke English. I remember seeing French parkour forums where they would just be like, 'You can't have jams in the US,' or say things you didn't understand [. . .]."

Several of the first generation of Chicago traceurs referenced the Yamakasi's appearance on *Ripley's Believe It or Not!* as sparking their interest in parkour. For example, Michael explained, "[T]he Yamakasi had done a feature for *Ripley's Believe It or Not!* [. . .] I was immediately obsessed with this idea: just seeing these guys picking two places on the map and just like figuring out how to get from one place to the other. And, the way that they did it was just so mesmerizing that I wanted to do [it]." However, going from being mesmerized by parkour to actually learning the discipline was not an easy task. Most would-be American traceurs did not speak French, and many perceived disinterest (or even hostility) from French traceurs on their Internet forums. Therefore, Urban Freeflow, far more than the teachings of the French originators, was what helped shape parkour in the United States. Of course, even with UF as a resource, information was sparse, and online technology was far more limited than it is today. As Ryan explained, "[A]t the time, you know, there was no one to teach us, it was just us learning off of each other and together. You might go online and see somebody do a movement that might look interesting. We'd have no idea what the name was, but we saw them do it in a video or someone maybe described it in a forum post. So then you just try to recreate that just based on what our knowledge of the movement was, which was very limited. But, at the same time, it's how we progressed—through trial and error."

Eventually, more information became available online. Most importantly, in those early years, UF's message boards helped connect individuals scattered across the world. Andy, Ryan's brother and a pivotal member of the nascent Chicago community, explained, "We started going to Chicago [from the suburbs] and met up with [lots of different traceurs]. [We met] though the forums [on] Urban Freeflow. [...] In the beginning we had guys come out from Indiana, and eventually we met up with [Michael] from Michigan [...] and then everyone from New York, from the first national jam in New York [in 2004]. We started making a lot of connections nationally."

Because the creation of the American parkour community was so heavily mediated through UF's message boards, screen names became a quintessential part of the social world. As Ryan explained, "[A]t the time nicknames were a huge trend over at Urban Freeflow. Pretty much every person and thing had a nickname." For example, the original English traceurs were almost exclusively known by aliases: EZ, Livewire, Sticky, etc. Following this practice, American traceurs adopted their own on-screen monikers. In Chicago, Andy became known as Ando. Ryan took the name Cloud. Michael was called Frosti. To this we could also add an array of colorful appellations that became part of the Chicago parkour community: Fresh Face, Psycho, Scales, Wolf, and so on. And, like their English counterparts, Americans interested in parkour hastily formed "crews" or "teams"—essentially just a name denoting a collection of friends. In Chicago, the local network of practitioners christened themselves Aero. In a move not widely emulated, Aero—instead of being confined to those personally close to the original group of Chicago traceurs—morphed into a synonym for the overall Chicago parkour community. Thus, anyone who regularly comes out to jams in Chicago is part of Aero. In recent years, the popularity of personal nicknames has waned. Conversely, the practice of forming teams is still prevalent.

Parkour versus Freerunning

During the growth of the discipline beyond France, English-speaking traceurs started making a distinction between parkour and freerunning. Issues of terminology are discussed in appendix B, but in this chapter it is relevant to go into more detail on the history of these two terms. "Freerunning" was a term created for *Jump London* to help translate the meaning of parkour to British viewers. However, it seems that Foucan and his manager were less interested in clarifying a term and more interested in placing their brand on the movement—just as Belle had done with changing "parcours" to "parkour."[35] While the use of different terms was nothing more than a semantic sleight-of-hand on the part of Belle and Foucan, American and British practitioners quickly began imputing philosophical and kinetic distinctions between parkour and freerunning.[36] Belle's parkour came to be understood as a style whose singular concern was efficient movement. Along with this assumption came ancillary beliefs about Belle's parkour requiring physical asceticism and a disavowal of competition. Foucan's freerunning came to be understood primarily as a style focused on aesthetic movements: maneuvers were incorporated simply because they were visually pleasing and subjectively fun to perform (like flips). Freerunning also came to represent the competitive, sports-oriented side of the discipline.

The assumed division between parkour and freerunning was certainly exacerbated by Foucan's and Belle's different temperaments, especially as revealed in their interviews. Foucan, for example, often peppered his discussions of the discipline with the metaphysical. Practicing freerunning, he said, is to "discover the forests from the top to the bottom," or that it is "about the expression of human beings with their environments." Alternatively, Belle was more reticent in the media spotlight and prone to a bit more machismo. For instance, in an interview regarding his BBC ad, Belle commented, "Parkour is a battle between confidence and fear, and at the moment my confidence is stronger than my fear." Perhaps most famously, Belle said that parkour is "a training method for warriors."[37]

Despite the philosophical and kinetic differences others attributed to them, Belle has also stressed an interest in aesthetic movement; he incorporated flips and other non-"efficient" stunts into his BBC ad. To this point, the director of the BBC spot, Tom Ewart, recalled, "It is an art form for him; it's about the graceful movement and the shapes he can make in the air. [...We] only had to do a second take if David was not satisfied with his shape." And, for his part, Foucan has been critical of competitions, stating, "Competitions and my discipline is not a good combination."³⁸ Of course, in many respects, the actions and intentions of Belle and Foucan are beside the point. Within the global parkour community, parkour and freerunning came to represent two related but different practices, and making distinctions between parkour and freerunning became important for many traceurs.³⁹

A good example of the boundary work some practitioners draw between parkour and freerunning can be seen in this 2011 quote from Phil:

> There's parkour, and there's freerunning. A lot of people confuse the two, and there's [...] an ongoing [debate about it]. [...] Parkour has a definition [...]. It is getting from A to B, quickly and efficiently as possible, using the human body. That is my definition. I think it is a defined practice. [...] Freerunning is moving through your environment more expressively—getting from A to B as [expressively] as possible. What ticks me off, though, is I see people with videos and they say, 'I'm doing parkour,' and then it's all flips. They're flipping everywhere. I'm like, 'No, that's not really parkour. You're doing freerunning. It's a little bit different. Nice try, though.'

Toward the end of my fieldwork, members of the Chicago parkour community seemed less inclined to fret over the supposed differences within the discipline. For example, in 2014, Cody told me, "The whole thing is just stupid. I've gotten into so many arguments with people on this. It just comes down to me saying, 'I don't really care.' [... For me] it was the same [...] as [with] everyone else. You look it up online. You see, 'Oh, there's a difference,' and you're defensive about the difference. Then you really start to realize that, 'No, no there is no difference.'" Likewise, Zach explained, "I understand the difference, but at the end of the day, it's movement. [...] I don't make a distinction." This notion—that parkour and freerunning are just "movement"—represented the way many Chicago traceurs came to feel about the debate.

Practices in Space and Meanings of Place

Over the years, Lisses, France has become something of a parkour Mecca. Media accounts often leave out the significance of Évry and Sacrelles. The most iconic parkour spot in Lisses is the Dame du Lac (see figure 5). This massive climbing wall looks like an abstract sculpture, with numerous ridges and protrusions providing brave traceurs with ample opportunities to creatively ascend its vast surface. Citing its dangers, however, authorities fenced off the structure in 2000.[40] Regardless, the Dame du Lac has been featured in countless photographs, stories, and videos about parkour since its closure, and numerous foreign traceurs—having seen the climbing wall time and again—still relish the chance to train on it.[41]

Meanwhile, much of Chicago's built environment predates the "smooth surfaces and running spaces of the concrete city" popularized by modernist architects. Regardless, Chicago traceurs were drawn to the city's reductive architecture. That is, traceurs made use of spaces seemingly devoid of meaning. These were the areas leftover in the creation of something else. In the case of Grant Park, a grand example of nineteenth-century urban green space, it was not the statues or fountains that captured the imagination of the traceurs. It was the forgotten crevasses of two walls meeting,

FIG. 5. The Dame du Lac (Photo: tongeron91). This image is available on Flickr, https://www.flickr.com/photos/tongeron91. Courtesy of the Creative Commons License Deed.

the hidden stairwells, and the random ledges where much of the action was (see figure 6 in this chapter and figures 11 and 13 in chapter two). These places seemed insignificant until they were brought to life through parkour. Like skateboarders, therefore, traceurs offer a lived critique of the built environment, asserting playful creativity in the dead spaces of the city.

Chicago is filled with countless places for training in parkour, but none of the local spots is remotely comparable to the social prestige given to sites like the Dame du Lac. At the same time, many parts of Chicago are very important to local traceurs: the "Nacho" sculpture at the University of Illinois, "the Wall of Death" at the intersection of Monroe and Columbus, the grass terraces at the Vietnam Veterans Memorial by the riverfront, and many more. These places are ingrained in the lore of the community. Max, for example, described how he and his friends branched out and started training at other spots and traveling to other cities. "But, we always thought back, 'Man, there's nothing better than Grant Park.' I went to St. Louis for a week, and parkour was okay over there [. . .]. It was okay. I'll always go back to Grant Park. [There is] nothing better."

FIG. 6. David prepares for a jump in a stairwell at Grant Park. He found a way to use the slanted wall of the stairwell as a personal challenge.

As Max's remark indicates, many of the traceurs in the group traveled, usually to attend jams hosted by practitioners in other cities. Likewise, traceurs from other places traveled to Chicago for jams. Most of the traceurs spoke very highly of these opportunities. As Cody explained, "There [are] always jams going [on] somewhere. [. . .] The main appeal [of traveling for a jam] is the spots. [. . .G]oing to a different state can give you a completely different environment. That's why I don't mind traveling to different gyms or different towns around here [too]. It gives you a fresh environment to train in." That said, traceurs are generally ambivalent about the specifics of these new environments. Unlike an iconic site like the Dame du Lac, most destinations in the United States are exciting to traceurs simply because they are new to them or will involve meeting new people or reconnecting with old friends. As for the actual physical details of these places, Steve told me, "It's all the same." Or, in Zach's phrasing, "At the end of the day, [we] all do parkour. [. . .] It was pretty similar. [It was] a different place with different people. [. . .] The spots [we went to in Boston] weren't that much different [from Chicago]. It was just bigger versions and smaller versions of what you have everywhere else. [. . .] It wasn't that much different."

To be clear, Steve and Zach were not saying that everyplace is actually the same. Chicago has certain features that separate it from Boston or

FIG. 7. Traceurs train on the wooden playground at Oz Park.

St. Louis. Instead, their point was that in all places, traceurs work to find a satisfying interface between their bodies and the material world. For example, Frosti contrasted Los Angeles with Chicago. "So, like in a place like LA, where there are like hills and traffic and bullshit, things are isolated [but] you get great moments. [...] Chicago has like these long parks and huge plazas where it is just open and there's a bunch of random things there: ledges, stairs, rails [...], random drops [...], and benches. Its space and its style create very unique pathways." In the end, as Steve said, "I find all the spots first, and I adapt to them. [...] I think about adapting my own spot my own way." Or, as Eric insisted, "Regardless of where you are, if you look and you're creative, you will find something to move over."

Commercializing the Discipline

Since the original parcours group's initial media coverage, various individuals have worked to find ways to profit from the discipline. Filmmakers and companies have incorporated parkour movements into movies and advertisements. For their part, established traceurs have been generally eager to court such attention. We have already discussed the Yamakasi's early commercial success in Luc Besson films and briefly touched on some of Foucan's and Belle's paid work. In terms of understanding both the spreading popularity of parkour, as well as the development of the discipline into an organized sport, it is necessary to look more closely at how parkour was commercialized.

Performance for Pay

While Belle's BBC ad was pivotal in first exposing parkour to audiences in the UK, he is probably most famous for his starring role in *Banlieue 13* (or *B13*), another parkour action film written by Luc Besson. *B13* was released in France in 2004. It would get a limited US release in 2006 with the title *District 13* (often referred to as *District B13*). While none of the original Chicago traceurs I interviewed claimed to have seen this movie in the theater, the opening chase sequence (viewable on YouTube) was frequently mentioned as an exemplar of the discipline.[42] For example, Eric reflected back on his first exposure to parkour by explaining, "It was something I'd seen videos of on the Internet [...]. Namely, there's David Belle's scene in *District B13*, where he's escaping his apartment complex, and it's probably one of the most popular parkour clips on the Internet. That was probably the first clip I saw. [. . . He] was really doing some really impressive physical feats."

Beyond his famed part in *Casino Royale* and his well-known Nike and Toyota ads, Foucan did various other commercial works as well. Madonna hired him to help her incorporate parkour into the theatrics of her *Confessions Tour* in 2006. One year later, K Swiss used him as a model and actor in the marketing of their Airake freerunning shoe. In 2008, Foucan authored *Free Running: Finding Your Way*, a book mostly filled with stylish, staged-action photographs accompanied by pithy motivational quotes. He also co-starred in the British B movie *The Tournament* (2009). As is often the case with lifestyle sports stars, Foucan's mainstream success came at some cost to his legitimacy among other traceurs. While still respected for his role in developing the discipline and for his outright talent, Foucan has often been derided for being too eager to accept commercial work.[43]

As the portfolios of the original parcours group demonstrate, the first people courting traceurs were those in advertising and the entertainment industry. This represents what sociologists Bob Edwards and Ugo Corte define as the mass-market form of commercialization.[44] The emphasis on *mass* marketing involves using a lifestyle sport to sell products to consumers unassociated with the sport. A good example of this type of commercialization is the Wheaties cereal box featuring mixed martial arts fighter Anthony Pettis's image. Most Wheaties buyers do not participate in MMA (or even follow the sport), but they may know of Pettis as the UFC lightweight champion. Likewise, a moviegoer can find the action of *Casino Royale* riveting without knowing anything about parkour.

In an effort to capitalize on such mass-market opportunities—and to generate new demand for their services—entrepreneurial traceurs outside France started creating performance teams. These teams were part of larger business ventures. Most prominent in the UK was Paul "EZ" Corkery's Urban Freeflow. Not only was UF the source for social networking and tutorials in the early days of English-language parkour, it was also a clothing brand, online magazine publisher (*Jump Magazine*), and talent agency for a stable of traceurs who could be hired out for promotional events, stunt work, and advertisements. Writing for the *Independent*, Kate Burt noted, "There are also commercial opportunities to exploit. Everyone wants a slice of the brand of urban cool associated with parkour, and Corkery has assembled 'the Krew'—a crack team of core UK traceurs [. . .] to deal with the demand. They have already been hired by Siemens [an engineering and electronics company] and O2 [a telecommunications company] and appeared in music videos."[45]

The stateside equivalent to Urban Freeflow was American Parkour, commonly referred to as APK. Mark Toorock, who lived in London during the early 2000s, was originally affiliated with Urban Freeflow, but he went on to found APK in the middle of the decade. Like Corkery in the UK, Toorock established a one-stop website for social networking, online tutorials, and parkour-themed clothing. Toorock also opened America's first parkour gym, Primal Fitness, in Washington, DC. And, like UF, American Parkour had its associated performance team, the Tribe. Toorock, a former stockbroker, was always quite blunt about his business interests in parkour. As he told the *Washington Post*, "From the beginning, I realized it could be lucrative [. . .] I figured if I could make a lot of money by helping a lot of people get fit and have a lot of fun, I'd be a very happy man."[46]

Some of Chicago's original traceurs were part of Toorock's Tribe. Just as the Krew—through the prominence of Urban Freeflow—was well positioned to attract UK business interests, the Tribe—through the prominence of APK—was the American go-to for parkour performers. Thus, when Madonna (via Foucan) was looking to incorporate parkour into the act, the Tribe supplied a lot of the talent. Likewise, when the *Survivor* television series wanted a traceur on their show, they contacted Toorock.[47] Toorock's suggestion for *Survivor* was Frosti—an Aero founder who had graduated to become a Tribe member. Frosti had previously been on the *Confessions Tour* as well. While he was not part of the *Confessions Tour*, Ando was another Tribe member from Aero. Referencing Chicago's prominence in the formative years of parkour in the United States, Cody lamented in 2014, "There's so much [parkour] history [in Chicago]. Aero's one of the first communities in the United States. It's one of the oldest communities. [. . .] It's kind of fizzled out over the last few year. [We] haven't been so involved, but there's a lot of history a lot of people don't know about anymore."

During the research for this book, performance teams were still an important part of the professional side of parkour. When I interviewed Frosti in 2015, for example, he had just returned from filming for a Chinese action movie. Frosti did this as part of Team Tempest—a performance team based in Los Angeles that is part of Tempest Freerunning (a clothing company and parkour-specific gym). Tempest exemplifies the diversified parkour business model that includes performance, apparel, and training facilities.

Parkour Commodities

One of the appealing aspects of parkour for many practitioners I met was its technological simplicity. Pasha, for example, told me, "I would say parkour is the cheapest [sport], and it's fun. Skateboarding is really popular. [So is] mountain biking and BMX [. . .], but you have to spend money [on equipment]. [. . .] All you need in parkour is shoes and pants. [. . .] Sometimes you don't even need shoes [e.g., training barefoot is popular among some traceurs]." As Pasha intimates, lifestyle sports are, in many respects, commodity-driven.[48] To be a participant in most sports, you need to buy certain things: boards, bikes, pads, shoes, etc. And, every year companies "improve" on existing models, enticing regular turnover of their goods. Parkour requires no special devices for training. Pads, gloves, and helmets are universally eschewed by traceurs, making those objects complete nonstarters for marketing (at least for now). Thus, shoes were the main equipment that could be sold to traceurs, but despite some companies' efforts to the contrary, most traceurs continued to train in shoes not specifically developed for parkour.

In 2005, Adidas became the first major company to seriously attempt to court the parkour market with its Hyperride shoe. Adidas also sponsored Urban Freeflow's Krew. However, the Hyperride's lifespan was short and its popularity limited. Old APK message board posts, though, reveal a few promotional pictures of the Krew modeling the shoes. K Swiss's efforts to develop a parkour-specific shoe in 2007 were more successful.[49] The Airakes were available for several years, but they too were eventually discontinued. However, when I first started studying parkour in 2010, several Chicago traceurs wore Airakes and spoke very highly of them. After major retailers ran out of supplies, persistent traceurs turned to Internet sites hoping to find sellers with new old stock. Five Ten, primarily known for its rock-climbing shoes, also produced parkour-specific designs for a brief period.

In recent years, as traceurs seem decreasingly interested in the relevance of high-end sneaker technology, major companies appear to have lost interest in developing parkour-specific shoes. Instead, many practitioners swear by low-tech options like Onitsuka Tigers (an Asics retro brand) and Feiyue

FIG. 8. Traceurs look through merchandise being sold at the 2011 Colossal Jam in Chicago. Slogans on the shirts include "Gravity is overrated."

martial arts shoes. The latter are made of lightweight canvas uppers atop a thin, gum rubber sole. At the same time, parkour companies and organizations have begun producing their own niche-market shoes. In contrast to mass marketing, this represents the "movement" form of commercialization. Whereas large corporations like Adidas are only interested in lifestyle sports if they can offer sizable (and expanding) sales potential, companies from within the parkour community (who represent the "social movement" of lifestyle sport participants in Edwards and Corte's conceptualization) have a vested interest in the growth of their sport (even if the growth is slow), and they are willing to operate with much lower profit margins.[50]

While shoes are the only major piece of performance-related equipment traceurs might currently be interested in purchasing, there is a great deal of money circulating in parkour-themed clothing. Beyond UF's and APK's clothing brands, parkour merchandising trickles down from prominent organizations to mid-level teams and local communities like Aero. At all the jams I attended, for example, a significant portion of traceurs were wearing t-shirts and sweatpants emblazoned with some term or phrase related to parkour. Further, at larger jams, there was always at least one entrepreneurial traceur hawking parkour-themed gear. Sometimes this involved selling "official" shirts to commemorate the jam; other times the shirts were just various designs the seller had come up with (see figure 8).

Belinda Wheaton is certainly correct to observe that despite the conspicuous consumption of lifestyle sports, individuals cannot simply purchase their way into social acceptance by acquiring the right commodities.[51] Miko, for example, complained that with parkour's growing popularity came some people not truly dedicated to training. "They're not just there to practice. They're there to look cool with their clothes and stuff. That can get kind of annoying because it's misrepresenting what we are to everybody else." While the emphasis on merchandising may rub some practitioners the wrong way, it represents a major prong in the now-dominant business model for parkour organizations. Further, the professionalism with which parkour-themed apparel is marketed (e.g., expertly lit fashion spreads featured in "lookbooks") highlights the sincerity of these entrepreneurial efforts (see figure 9). More importantly, the ubiquity of these commodities underscored the integration of consumption into lifestyle sports participation.[52]

FIG. 9. Image from Farang Clothing's website for its fall 2015 lookbook. Courtesy of Team Farang.

The New Parkour Business Model

Throughout this chapter, Urban Freeflow and American Parkour have come up repeatedly as pivotal to the history of the discipline. To this list we must add the World Freerunning and Parkour Federation (WFPF) and Parkour Generations (PKGen). These four organizations have been at the forefront of what Norbert Elias calls the process of "sportization."[53] That is, they have worked to institutionalize and regulate parkour—transforming it from a loosely organized, grassroots activity to a bonafide sport.

Merchandise, Competitions, and Corporate Sponsors

UF's role in the early promotion of parkour to the English-language world cannot be overstated. Important here is the fact that Corkery used UF as a platform for developing parkour into a profit-oriented sport. Beyond his promotion of the Krew in commercial advertising and performance work, *Jump Magazine* was filled with photographs of traceurs wearing UF merchandise. There were also advertisements with traceurs modeling various products (such as wristwatches). Of particular importance was UF's overall editorial emphasis on sponsored athletes and promoting competitions (which were also underwritten by UF). In other words, UF used its various media outlets and social network prominence to assert its vision of parkour's future—a future similar to the model of incorporation followed by snowboarding.[54]

By the time I started studying the Chicago parkour community, UF's relevance was already eclipsed by organizations including American Parkour and the World Freerunning and Parkour Federation. Further, UF's image within the larger parkour community was always somewhat divisive. Many viewed its overt emphasis on competitions and corporate sponsorships negatively, and Corkery's more traditional male bravado ran counter to much of the parkour philosophy found outside of UF's domain. In 2012, UF ceased its affiliation with the sport of parkour—briefly operating as a fitness and bodybuilding company before dissolving.[55]

At the height of its influence, UF developed the World Freerunning Championships, which were sponsored by Barclaycard (part of Barclays financial services) and filmed by one of Britain's premier television networks, Sky Sports.[56] Despite strong corporate backing for its inaugural competition, these championships only lasted from 2008 to 2009.

Interestingly, UF was not the first organization to sponsor formal parkour competitions. Energy drink company Red Bull launched an event called the Art of Motion in 2007. It has been held every year since and has grown in prominence within the global parkour community.[57] Not only does the Art of Motion serve as a spectacle to drum up interest in Red Bull's products, the event has also exerted a great deal of influence on the social world of parkour—helping change how traceurs understand the discipline.

One unintended consequence of the Red Bull Art of Motion was the creation of the World Freerunning and Parkour Federation. Brought together by Red Bull for the first time and seeing potential for even greater interest, several of the competitors decided to capitalize on the possible financial opportunities to be made with the sport. To this end, these entrepreneurial traceurs collaborated with three other investors, one of whom was a producer for MTV. Using their connections, the WFPF's first major undertaking was the creation of the reality show *Ultimate Parkour Challenge*. The show lasted for two seasons and helped solidify the careers of several traceurs.[58]

Initially, very few traceurs I interacted with talked about any of these competitions. To the extent they were discussed at all, they were often viewed negatively. For example, back in 2010, Aaron stated, "I started watching the first episode of [MTV's *Ultimate Parkour Challenge*] and I just got bored. [. . .] I don't know why I was bored. They were doing cool stuff. I don't know; I think it was just over-commercialized. I just did not like it." Hearing this, Brandon chimed in, "That was the problem I was having with it. [. . .] They took the discipline out of it." Sociologist Robert Rinehart makes a similar point regarding lifestyle sports participants' feelings about the original X Games on ESPN: the coverage perverted what participants most valued about their activities.[59] And, it is worth noting that Aaron and Brandon were only discussing the MTV show because I brought it up. For the most part, this mass-market commercialization did not appear as a pertinent concern for the people training and socializing at Chicago jams in the early part of the decade.

By 2014, though, the pendulum was swinging in the other direction. To a degree, the difference simply represents a changing of the guard. The older traceurs—steeped in the original Belle-inspired parkour rhetoric against competitions and commercialization—were cycling out of the community. Younger traceurs—many who watched shows like *Ultimate Parkour Challenge* or G4's similar *Jump City: Seattle* before they ever started training—were rising to prominence in the community. For example, one of this new guard, Alex, told me:

> Oh yeah, I grew up watching those. [. . .] Before I was really into [parkour], those kind of came on. [. . .] I'm thinking, "Oh, these guys are awesome," because I watched *Ninja Warrior* [an obstacle course competition that occasionally featured traceurs] all the time. I watched that. I watched *Jump [City:] Seattle*. [. . .] When you're first watching it, when you're a kid, you're thinking, "Oh, this is the coolest thing ever" [. . .] I'm, in a way, grateful that MTV did [their show] because [. . .] it got more people exposed to it. [. . .] In a way it gave [parkour] a bad name, because of the competition aspect, but in a way it got more people exposed to it. It kind of brought it out to more people.

While traceurs—especially in prior years—worried that competitions and overt commercialization denuded parkour of its meaning (in Brandon's words, its "discipline"), increasingly, traceurs like Alex saw them as necessary for the sport's growth.

Even the older traceurs who remained in the community started adopting favorable attitudes toward competitions and other forms of commercialization. Grant, for example, started training in the mid-2000s. Reflecting back, he claimed to have been very critical of companies like Red Bull. Years later, he felt differently. "Let Red Bull do what it wishes with [parkour]. [. . .] I'm all for it. Their product sucks, but they at least know how to market it." Grant went on to explain, "It gives [highly skilled traceurs] the potential to devote their life to [their training]—literally devote their life to it—and not have to partially devote their life to it and then go to their nine-to-five [job] that doesn't excite them. [. . . Commercialization] offers a lot of potential to the people who are taking it really serious to make a living. People like Jason Paul [a famous traceur], sure he sports Red Bull attire [. . .], but whether the parkour community likes it or not, [Red Bull] is doing a great job of [marketing parkour]. You have to accept it." In other words, traceurs like Grant began to emphasize the opportunities corporate involvement could bring to the parkour community.

Grant's hope that corporate sponsorships could liberate serious traceurs from workaday drudgery is similar to political scientist Douglas Booth's historical observations on surfers' support of a professional competition circuit to provide a livable income riding waves. Likewise, while many in the skateboarding subculture were once highly critical of competitions and corporate sponsorships, they eventually became more accepting of commercialization and sportization.[60] However, as with the consumption of commodities, traceurs' contentment with corporate involvement and formalized competition did not represent an uncritical co-option of the discipline by the interests of capital. As with other lifestyle sports, the involvement by outsiders and efforts to mold the sport into a television-friendly event were treated ambivalently.[61] This can be seen in Grant's negative views of Red Bell's actual merchandise ("Their product sucks, but they at least know how to market it"). Thus, commercialization represents a contested terrain, with authenticity to the discipline on one side and the potential benefits offered by the mainstream on the other.

Revising the Business Model: Certification and Gyms

Films and commercials were the first ways the original parcours group tried to profit from the discipline. These opportunities, of course, proved to be quite limited. Competitions, therefore, were the primary means for the second generation of practitioners to try to make a living with parkour. Entrepreneurial traceurs like Corkery wanted to professionalize the sport. The intent was to turn it from an avocation to a vocation by changing it into a contest-driven activity with corporate sponsorship. As it turned out, though, competitions were not the only route to sportization or a sustainable business model. Parkour Generations (PKGen), for example, was founded in 2006 with the explicit aim of countering the more extreme sport imagery propagated by UF and WFPF. To this end, they have lobbed invectives at what they call the "Red Bullion" crowd—referring to the profit-driven focus of companies like Red Bull.[62] Their public statements aside, PKGen has been just as focused as the other organizations with branding itself and capturing market share. Like UF before it, PKGen has a performance team and offers a variety of services from stunt work to modeling to exhibition shows. But, whereas UF saw the future of parkour in competition, PKGen has worked to establish a governing body for the training of parkour in the United Kingdom. They have done this through a public outreach organization called Parkour UK. Instead of governing competitions, PKGen has tried to institute regulations for the instruction of parkour—on which they are primed to corner the market.[63]

PKGen's certification program is called A.D.A.P.T.—Art du Déplacement and Parkour Training. The semantic emphasis on l'art du déplacement underlines PKGen's affiliation with the remaining members of the Yamakasi. Once an individual completes level one of A.D.A.P.T. certification, he or she is qualified to teach parkour at gyms affiliated with PKGen and Parkour UK. Following PKGen's lead, WFPF also offers a certification program in conjunction with its affiliated organization, USA Parkour. Both organizations proffer liability insurance for certified instructors as a selling point for their programs. APK also has a competing certification program. While differences exist between them, all of these certification programs span about three days, with tuitions of several hundred dollars.[64]

The rise of formalized certification for parkour "coaches" (as PKGen refers to them) goes hand in hand with the success of paid instruction and purpose-built spaces as a business strategy. In contrast to the early years of parkour's global expansion, the public face of parkour is increasingly connected to parkour gyms and coaching services. This training includes advanced classes, but the focus is mostly on beginners. PKGen is exemplary in instituting this new profit stream. They have a network of affiliated gyms in London and also offer classes outside of gyms. Further, PKGen has expanded beyond the UK, with PKGen Americas, PKGen Asia, and PKGen Brasil. I attended one day of an A.D.A.P.T. certification in Chicago in the summer of 2014. Several of those enrolled worked at or owned gyms themselves and hoped that having official certification would add legitimacy to their enterprises.

While American Parkour originally splintered off from Urban Freeflow, it has recently followed a business trajectory more aligned with PKGen. For example, as discussed above, Toorock opened the Primal Fitness parkour gym in Washington, DC in 2007. This has now morphed into the APK Academy, with affiliated gyms in other states. Following this trend of parkour-specific gyms, in 2009, renowned American traceur Ryan Ford opened Denver's Apex Movement, which also offers a certification program, and in 2011, Team Tempest opened the Tempest Freerunning Academy in Los Angeles. Meanwhile, in 2009, WFPF began partnering with Equinox Fitness Clubs to offer classes.[65]

For my first few years studying the Chicago parkour community, there were no parkour-specific gyms in the area. Some Chicago traceurs (like traceurs elsewhere) developed relationships with gymnasiums, and there were frequently meet-ups and jams at certain gyms. These connections persisted, but entrepreneurial traceurs in the region began trying to establish spaces that would allow them to set up the bars and boxes in a manner conducive

FIG. 10. Flipside Academy in Forest Park, Illinois.

to parkour maneuvers (but not to gymnastics training). Most of the efforts never got off the ground or were short-lived, with little participation from core members of the community. By the end of my study, however, two parkour-specific gyms had opened (see figure 10). They appeared to be developing stable client bases and making connections within the local, national, and global parkour communities.

In sum, second- and third-generation traceurs have continued to evolve the business model for the discipline. As of this writing, parkour-specific gyms and certifications represent the current focus for making a living from the activity. This is on top of the previous model's commercial performances and commodity production. These strategies still continue, but the revised business model depends on a more rationalized version of parkour's discipline and training. Coaching provides more opportunities for more practitioners, and there is quite a lot of potential for expansion in the market. Gyms and purpose-built facilities also provide (comparatively) safe, controlled environments. This opens up training to younger—as well as to more timid—clients. It also limits insurance liabilities for paid instructors. Finally, instructors are increasingly expected to have some sort of formal certification. A key form of legitimacy, this certification is a source of revenue for organizations.

Ultimately, this commercialization and sportization helps to shape the larger social world of parkour. Today, would-be traceurs might first be exposed to parkour through an advertisement or film clip. Their first actual training experience may come in the form of a paid class at a purpose-built gym. Further, beginners and experienced traceurs alike are apt to read blog and Facebook posts from organizations such as American Parkour, Apex Movement, Parkour Generations, and Tempest Freerunning. In fact, gyms, organizations, and their affiliated performance teams constitute a significant portion of the parkour social world's new media presence.

At the same time, the daily practices of most traceurs are generally far removed from such routinization. Organizations like PKGen (or UF before it) influence the content and character of the global parkour community, but they do not unilaterally define it. In practice, most traceurs may borrow from these organizations' ideas and imagery, but they mix them together with other ideas and images, then alter everything to fit the particularities of the dynamics within their own social context. The meaning of parkour, therefore, must be understood as embedded within seemingly disjointed perspectives and practices that are experienced in nuanced ways. In this chapter, for example, we have seen how the instrumental fitness goals of Georges Hérbert were revised by a group of teenagers in the banlieues as a form of playful, stylized spatial appropriation. Seeking to capitalize on a new form of urban chic, advertisers and filmmakers took interest in the activity during the early 2000s. Media attention helped the discipline spread beyond France. Would-be traceurs in America and Britain wanted to emulate what they saw the French originators perform, but in the process the discipline changed. Some of these changes were the result of translation problems (e.g., confusion over parkour versus freerunning), but the activity mainly evolved as traceurs applied and practiced the discipline within a changing social context. In the next chapter, we will explore how the virtual worlds made possible through new media intertwine with real world practices—transforming the way local environments are conceptualized.

2

New Prisms of
the Possible

• •

Sherry Turkle, a renowned professor who studies human-computer relationships, famously characterizes the integration of new media within society as living life "on the screen." Sociologist Manuel Castells refers to this as
a culture of "real virtuality." Both theorists emphasize the ways communication and information technologies are changing sociality.[1] The Internet,
portable electronics, and social networking tools facilitate the rapid transmission of ideas and images from around the world and connect individuals separated by vast physical distances.[2] As Arjun Appadurai writes,
"[Ordinary life] no longer occurs within a relatively bounded set of thinkable postures but is always skidding and taking off, powered by the imagined vistas of mass-mediated master narratives."[3] This results in researchers
observing local activities that are not necessarily local products. Instead,
with the advancement and proliferation of new media, daily practices are
increasingly manifestations of a hybrid, globalized culture. This unbound-
ing of thinkable postures is what Appadurai calls global ethnoscapes. To
put it simply, the fantasies of on-screen life can result in reimagining what
is actually possible offscreen.[4]

In this chapter, I analyze the global ethnoscape of parkour, with a focus on how virtual worlds become *emplaced* in the real world—that is, the ways traceurs' use of new media influences their perceptions of the physical environment. I propose that by thinking about parkour in this way we can better grasp how diffuse, globalized interactions become realized in specific locales by unique local actors. In particular, I will show a dialectical connection between the ideas and images circulating within the virtual worlds of parkour and the real-world practices of traceurs in the city.

The Global Ethnoscape of Parkour

Chapter one of this book contains numerous illustrations of parkour's global ethnoscape. Appadurai writes, "More persons throughout the world see their lives through the prisms of the possible lives offered by the mass media in all their forms. That fantasy is now a social practice; it enters, in a host of ways, into the fabrication of social lives for many people in many societies."[5] This is to say, in a culture of real virtuality, on-screen lives blur into offscreen activities and vice versa.

Traceurs' Lives On the Screen

The role of fantasy is particularly apparent in the recollections of Ando. His retelling of the Chicago parkour community's history is filled with references to the formation of local, national, and international connections, all of which were mediated through different on-screen lives:

> Back when it first started getting popular in Britain, that's when [Cloud and I] heard about it. [...] We saw it on TV. We saw Yamakasi on TV. [...] They had their own movie for parkour [...]. It just looked like they were jumping and moving really uniquely. They're jumping really high, moving really swiftly. It seemed kind of like they were super-human. We didn't know people could jump that high. We never thought of tic-tacs getting you higher like that. They had everything down and coordinated. All the moves were really tight. We just watched all [the videos available on] Urban Freeflow. We mimicked it. We went on the forums and talked to them. It was really helpful, but it was very unorganized back then. [... There was] only Urban Freeflow. [There was a] French website [... but] everyone spoke French. Barely anyone spoke English. [...] It was

just very inspiring to see how they moved, to be able to move like them. [. . .]
It was just fresh and new, and exciting to see something new like this.

It is clear how media images redefined what Ando and Cloud thought
was possible: "We didn't know people could jump that high. We never
thought of tic-tacs getting you higher like that." Frosti made the same point
in the previous chapter: "[T]he Yamakasi had done a feature for *Ripley's
Believe It or Not!* [. . .] I was immediately obsessed with this idea: just seeing these guys picking two places on the map and just like figuring out how
to get from one place to the other. And, the way that they did it was just
so mesmerizing that I wanted to do [it]." Thus, for Ando, Cloud, Frosti,
and many more, it was a television show featuring a mysterious group of
Frenchmen that altered what had been a relatively bounded set of thinkable postures for urban movement. The BBC promo featuring David Belle
had a similar effect in the United Kingdom. This was followed by the
broadcast of the British documentaries *Jump London* and *Jump Britain,*
featuring Sébastien Foucan. These documentaries in particular had a profound impact on both sides of the Atlantic. Taken together, mass-media
coverage of various French practitioners provided a new prism of the
possible for the lives of would-be traceurs throughout the world.

Today, the most significant aspect of parkour's global ethnoscape is the
proliferation of online videos. Unlike when the original Aero members
were first exposed to the discipline, most young people have now heard
of parkour, and there are hundreds of practitioners in the Chicago area.
Regardless, even as more people have started training locally, most beginners still learn about the discipline through the screen. Like Ando, Cloud,
and Frosti, third-generation traceurs occasionally cite film or television as a
source for learning about parkour. However, the most common answer to
the question "How did you learn about parkour?" is "Videos on YouTube."
As Cody told me, "[How I got into parkour] is actually kind of lame. I saw
some videos of it online, and I was like, 'Oh, that's cool.'" Almost identically, Counsel told me, "I came across it the way everyone else did: on the
Internet." While Cody might have wished he had a less "lame" answer to
my question, his response was highly representative. Parkour knowledge is
produced, altered, and consumed online.

Beyond allowing individuals to learn about the existence of the discipline, new media are crucial for the transmission of parkour skills and
styles. In particular, there is a wealth of information about parkour on the

Internet. Like all social practices, parkour is continually evolving—new maneuvers are created and old ones fall out of favor—and the Internet is the means by which parkour training is codified and explained. These aspects of the discipline can also be found in traditional forms of media, such as books, but none of the traceurs in my study indicated that they used or read them. For example, when I told Grant that I was planning to eventually write a book about parkour, he told me that a few such books already existed. He then told me that he had never read any of them because "you can learn everything in them and more with fifteen minutes on the Internet." Likewise, while every traceur I talked with had watched countless online tutorials and had seen at least segments of documentaries about parkour, only one person told me he had purchased a physical DVD. Moreover, this individual seemed rather embarrassed to admit his acquisition, and those within earshot were surprised to learn anyone would buy such a thing. Likewise, a few traceurs told me they read parkour "magazines," but upon further inquiry, it was revealed they were referring to online resources—not the product of a printing press. As a recent phenomenon, parkour has matured with the Internet, and more traditional mediums of knowledge transmission have been disregarded. In their place are web-based articles, blogs, forums, and, most importantly, videos.⁶

The traceurs in the Chicago group watched all sorts of parkour-themed videos online—from documentaries to feature film clips to self-produced showreels and samplers. As Eric noted in the last chapter, he learned about parkour watching the opening chase scene from *District 13*. Similarly, Jaska became interested in parkour from watching samplers put out by Oleg Vorslav, originally known as the Russian Climber. As Jaska told me, "If I had to nail it down [. . .] there's a video called 'Russian Climber.' That's it. That's the video. [. . .] I saw it. 'Oh, we should do that. It's pretty cool.'" Or, in Max's words, "'Hey, look at this video of these crazy dudes jumping off of buildings.' 'Oh, that's so cool. We should do that someday.'"

The usage of such videos in the transmission of bodily skills deserves special attention. In particular, both beginners and experienced traceurs in the group regularly consulted how-to videos posted online. Often, YouTube tutorials served as beginning traceurs' introduction to proper parkour techniques. Recounting his initial method of training, Ryan T. explained, "I'd look up a new vault [on Urban Freeflow], I'd do it, and, [. . .] like a true beginner, I'd be like, 'Okay I have this vault now' and I'd go to the next one [. . .]." Max described a three-part process of first seeing a movement in a sampler video, asking someone to label particular movements, and then looking up tutorials for those movements. "At first I used samplers. 'Oh, what's that trick?' I'd YouTube it. Sometimes it helps because [. . . it shows] an example [. . .] of the proper way to do it." Likewise, Alex told me, "YouTube is huge. You can just search 'parkour' and millions of hits come up. [. . .] When I was learning [how to] cork [i.e., a type of aerial rotation], I would write on YouTube 'cork tutorial,' and fifty hits come up. I usually watch four or five of them, just so I can get different views on it and different methods, [and I would] kind of mix them together." As these examples make clear, parkour—as a local practice—derives from knowledge filtered from across the globe.[7]

Further, many of the traceurs shaped their personal training experiences around their own production of videos. To this point, Luke exclaimed, "Man, I got to tell you, after training all day, and when you come back home and just collapse on the couch, it's just so fun to just watch everything you did. It's fun to edit videos. I love that process of making videos. It's there then. It's there forever. [. . .] When I'm fifty years old, I'll be able to watch and see what I was doing back in 2007." Reflecting the same sentiment, Cody told me, "I'm just [filming myself regularly] so I don't bitch out of [training]. If I have to put a video out every week and film a bit everyday, it makes something more out of [my training]." (see figure 15 later in this chapter). And, Cody's persistent filming throughout 2014 garnered him frequent praise from his peers. Speaking of this consistency, he also added, "It's also nice getting everything on video, in case something like [an injury] does happen." This last comment referred to a point earlier in the interview when Cody was able to queue up footage of his recent ankle sprain for me on his smartphone.

Cody's comments in particular underscore the interactive aspect of traceurs' on-screen lives. That is, videos played a significant role in the traceurs' social interactions with each other. Cody's filming was influenced by considerations of what others would think. In his case, he felt a sense of expectation to regularly post updates on his training ("so I don't bitch out"). Additionally, Ryan explained, "I get inspired by videos." In more detail, Strafe stated, "Before, I'd only seen the videos that were really good, and as a beginner [. . .], those would really discourage me [. . .]. But, I saw a [. . .] sampler [of] someone after their first year [. . .], and I realized there was an intermediate step. You didn't have to be that good right away. So, I thought, this is at least worth a try. That's how I got into it." In short, traceurs are not passive consumers of new media.[8] Take, for example, the previous quote from Max. It ends with a call to action ("We should do that someday"). Likewise, ZK recalled, "Oh, wow. They're running, jumping, flipping. I enjoy watching this. I could probably do this if I put in the time." Videos are essential to the infusion of parkour into traceurs' lives.

When a video is made available online, viewers are usually able to post comments about it. Again, we can see that this aspect of Cody's on-screen life was integral to his offscreen training. Likewise, Ryan remarked about reactions to videos he had posted of himself, "Sometimes it's nice to hear people say, 'Ryan, your training's been awesome lately.' Sometimes I'll post it, [. . . and I'll] get criticism, and it's like, 'I hadn't thought about that [technique or movement] before'" (see figure 11). Thus, videos not only serve as instructional tools, they also become incorporated in symbolic interactions with the self and others.

Ultimately, the virtual worlds of parkour function like numerous online communities. They are part of what danah boyd calls "networked publics"—virtual places to post questions and provide answers, as well as to express thoughts and feelings. For young adults, in particular, on-screen

FIG. 11. Ryan T. jumps the gap between two electrical boxes in Grant Park.

life can offer a sense of autonomy and freedom from the constraints of family, school, and work.[9] Outside of parkour-specific virtual spaces, Chicago traceurs were also on Facebook and other forms of social media, and their experiences with the discipline made up a significant part of their online identities. For example, many of the traceurs in this study used photographs from their training (usually a maneuver captured in midair) as their profile pictures for various sites. Like Cody and Ryan, many also frequently posted pictures, videos, or comments about their training. Some traceurs also used Google Maps to share knowledge about various training spots. Jake, for example, grew up in northwestern Indiana. He explained, "My buddy and I would start going out on our own, and finding spots and stuff. There used to be this Google Map with spots all across [the area]. We'd go out and check all these other spots, and, of course, look out for our own new spots." Aero maintained a similar Google Map for Chicago. As Jake intimated, these maps were a way to share valuable information within the community. They were especially useful for beginners and traveling traceurs.

Parkour as Simulacra

The global ethnoscape of parkour is part and parcel of the postmodern culture in which it arose. Historian Daniel Boorstin argues that public life is now defined by staged performances intentionally designed for mediated consumption. Real events have been surpassed by what he calls "pseudo-events." In other words, people think less about what they are actually doing—what it means within its current context or how it subjectively feels—and think more about what it will *look like* when shown to others. French writer Guy Debord refers to this phenomenon as the "spectacle"—"a social relationship between people that is mediated by images." Most famously, Jean Baudrillard describes reality as totally subsumed by simulacra.[10] For example, instead of listening to live music—complete with the idiosyncrasies of each rendition—people now listen primarily to recorded music. These renditions are often pieced together from multiple takes. Such production processes create a finished work that never actually existed in its entirety. The result is an approximation of reality, an unreal verisimilitude that is something more than "virtual." It offers up an enhanced version of reality—hyperreality. To the extent that interactions become permeated with such simulacra, real events become secondary to the interplay of signs (images of images, simulations of simulations).

The mediation of social relationships by images is quite apparent in parkour. As we have just seen, nearly all of the traceurs in the group first learned about parkour through the screen. In this sense, the ideas and images that the parkour ethnoscape comprises are a spectacle of pseudo-events. Their production is contrived, and, once posted, the photographs and videos are divorced from the reality in which they were produced—which is to say, to watch Vorslav (the Russian Climber) train on the remnants of Soviet architecture from the comforts of a Chicago apartment is very different from being there with him. The mistakes and missteps have been edited out; the moves are shot from the most dramatic angles; and the events have been spliced together with a music soundtrack to help set a particular mood. Thus, even though traceurs are not passive consumers of new media, their interactions on the screen are removed from the real world in which the events actually took place.[11]

Further, the virtual world of parkour is a collection of simulacra. It is a hyperreal version of the world that traceurs actually confront in their training. Parkour, of course, involves direct experience. It is also subjectively meaningful. However, a traceur's experience may be shaped by a desire to produce images for mediated consumption. Stacy, for example, explained that unlike training done when no camera is around, "When you're filming you repeat the same things over and over again." Likewise, Frosti described his recent training as being defined by the camera. "[I do] one-off tricks, like skateboarders. You know, like hit it, film it, hit it, film it, hit it, film it." Sam provided a particularly instructive example. Sam had a great deal of skill and style, and, like Cody, he was a studious documenter of his training. "I have a lot of footage [. . .] because I didn't like the way it looked. I didn't like the way I saw myself performing a trick." In other words, as he trained, Sam consulted his footage and routinely reshot maneuvers he felt did not demonstrate the right image. Like many traceurs, Sam also felt filming improved his performance. "When I'm filming I feel like I get more creative. 'All right, I'm filming. I got to film something kind of cool.' [. . .] I want to impress myself." In this way, parkour maneuvers are reduced to objects for consumption—not real life but the interplay of signs.

Most notably, knowing their footage will eventually be edited together in videos radically alters traceurs' actual performances of parkour. This was what Frosti expressed when he said traceurs "hit it, film it, hit it . . ." Practitioners repeatedly film one maneuver over one structure (or maybe a sequence of a few tricks over a few obstacles) until they are satisfied with how it looks on screen. They then move on to something else, repeating the process. The final product of this type of training is a video of separate maneuvers from a variety of locations edited into a cohesive stream of images. To this point, one parkour website gave novice filmmakers the following advice: "Most people fall foul [when] making their first parkour video [because it] consist[s] of lots of walking to and from camera etc. [...] Start your clip after the traceur has started to move, and stop it just before they have finished. This will ensure to give your video a sense of urgency and pace."[12] Practitioners inexperienced in performing for videos will often stop moving immediately after a maneuver is completed. This is normal in training when not being filmed, but it ruins the "sense of urgency and pace" of the final product because it implies a halting in the action. When filming, therefore, traceurs have developed techniques to help give the *illusion* of continued movement when the clip is spliced with another segment.

The relevance of simulacra in lifestyle sports can be seen in Robert Rinehart's analyses of ESPN's X Games. Rinehart argues that broadcasting the event involved learning how to adopt music video editing styles into sports coverage. Instead of long shots of entire events, footage "became choppier, results-oriented, and non-linear." Take the BMX freestyle competition. As experienced from the spectator's bleachers or the

FIG. 12.   Dan performs a massive side flip at Ogden Plaza during the 2014 Colossal Jam.

stationary angle of a single camera, the live action is far less emotionally intoxicating than an edited version fusing multiple angles, varied speeds, and replays of key moments. And, this "MTV style [of] quick-cuts [and] choppy, handheld camera work" has become the norm in the mediated presentation of numerous lifestyle sports (as well as many other forms of entertainment).[13]

Cultural critic Susan Sontag writes, "Instead of just recording reality, photographs have become the norm for the way things appear to us, thereby changing the very idea of reality, and of realism."[14] This is apparent in the way traceurs base their athletic practices around performing disjointed tricks in order to edit them into an approximation of reality that never actually existed. As Eric explained, "I post videos of myself partially because there's an artistic element. [...] One of the things I engage in when I edit a video is having a directional logic. In one shot, if I go to the right side of the screen, I'm going to come from the right side of the screen in the subsequent flip. [...] I'm trying to create what I find aesthetically pleasing, and hopefully other people find aesthetically pleasing too. But, that's just kind of a [...] style thing." In other words, as Eric was training, he considered how different pieces of footage could be spliced together to create an "aesthetically pleasing" video segment. Pseudo-events take precedent over the actual event.

So far, the analysis of this chapter has emphasized two points. First, new media are essential to the development of the discipline. The virtual world of parkour exposes individuals to the activity and provides traceurs with the opportunity to learn from and interact with other practitioners. Thus, traceurs' on-screen lives reveal new prisms of the possible. The global ethnoscape of parkour can be understood as being part of a culture of real virtuality. Second, these new prisms are also a form of simulacra—the consumer- and image-based foundation of postmodernity. Edited hyperreality shapes how traceurs understand their discipline and alters their very practice of it. That is to say, their otherwise very real actions are considered in relation to how they can be transformed into pseudo-events for the screen. These points notwithstanding, in the following sections, I will emphasize the offscreen aspects of the discipline. The parkour community I studied was far more than simulacra bouncing through cyberspace. The discipline is still very much about embodied practices. This should go without saying because, quite clearly, traceurs are performing actions in the real, tangible world.

Appropriating the Real World

Like most (if not all) athletic practices, parkour is enjoyable precisely because it allows individuals to experience what Mihaly Csikszentmihalyi calls flow.[15] As with other lifestyle sports, the physical exertion required in parkour combined with the potential for bodily harm (if not death) means that traceurs must become engrossed in their movements. "The point is to survive, and most people feel no ambivalence about the value of this goal."[16]

The Flow of Parkour

Eric's explanation of what he enjoys about training was particularly poignant. He also perfectly articulated Csikszentmihalyi's concept:

> A lot of different religions have a word for this. [...] The Hindus call it moksha. The Zen Buddhists call it a state of Zen awareness [...]. When you are engaged in parkour [...] you are envisioning your route. Everything else goes quiet for a moment. You feel the wind on your face. You feel the sweat dripping down your body. You feel muscles in your body moving, and in that moment you are completely aware of your environment. Then, when you take off, it is complete [and] utter [...] focus. [...] You know when the moment is right. I don't want to say succumb because that's a negative word, but you succumb to these instincts. It's a very, I'm going to say, spiritual [experience]— not in a religious context, but in a context that has to do with understanding the self in a manner that creates [...] great joy and relaxation. [...] I don't want to call it nirvana, because that's not technically correct. I'm going to use the term "moksha"—awareness of the universe. That's a goal that's been sought after by many ascetics [...], just to feel at one with the universe [...]. Parkour grants that to me in a sense that I've never felt with any religions I've studied or tried to practice.

Similarly, Luke stated, "It's like the marriage of mind and body. Your mind has to work perfectly in sync with the rest of your body. [...] Everything has to work perfectly in sync. You have to go through the methods in your mind to visualize, to process, to figure out how to do it, and to figure out what you need to do. Your body needs to be capable [of doing the maneuver] as your mind sees it. [...] Somehow you know. That's always fascinated me." Likewise, Ando captured the imagery of flow in his description

FIG. 13. Steve does a wall flip in Grant Park.

of enjoying of parkour. "The feeling you get from [training parkour] really feels like you're moving through the world in a unique way. It feels more like you're experiencing it. You can feel the gravel on your hand, and the stone under your feet, and air, and you move through it smoothly. It's really nice. It's got a real energetic feeling. You're transferring the energy [from] your feet to the ledge, to the wall. It's all being used equally. It's like going down a rapid on a river. You can feel the push and the pull."

In chapter four these flow experiences will be reconsidered in relation to how traceurs deal with the dangers of their activities. For this chapter, though, what matters is simply that training can and does engross practitioners, and that such engrossment is considered positive—"optimal experience" in Csikszentmihalyi's terms.

From a sociological perspective, the most important aspect of the flow produced in parkour is that it is frequently experienced in conjunction with others. It is not only a subjective, inner state. To the contrary, it tends to be overtly social. Consider, for example, the vignette from the introduction about Scales's jump in Grant Park. As Eric, Luke, and Ando remarked, Scales was working within himself to do the maneuver, but he was also among friends. His fear and his excitement were not felt alone. In this sense, jams are parkour rituals that generate a collective sense of flow.[17] In explaining his training with others, Sam told me, "Sometimes I see things I haven't seen before. Some people can be pretty creative. I [. . .] just walk around. You see people just playing with different objects [and] playing with different techniques. [. . .] It [is] nice just walking around and seeing [other traceurs]." It is these social aspects of flow that make the group experience feel more significant than solitary training. As Emile Durkheim observed long ago, moving in unison with others makes actions feel objectively real and meaningful.[18]

Referencing a particular training session he had with another Chicago practitioner, for example, Sam said:

> I['d] been training alone [. . .], and I'd made a lot of progress, but [. . .] when [I] train with other people I'm more motivated to try other things. I get more creative. [. . .] I saw [my friend] maybe twice last year. [. . .] We were at Grant Park [. . .] and we were [. . .] both trying things we'd never tried before. [We were] thinking of things we'd never thought of until we were together. [. . .] We were just throwing things around and playing with them. He saw what I was doing and I saw what he was doing and we were getting ideas off each other. [. . .] It's always interesting when you start mashing [people's different styles] together and see[ing] what happens.

Distinguishing between the serious training he did alone or in small groups, Ando emphasized the social aspects of being at larger jams (see figure 7 in chapter one, figures 12 and 14 in this chapter, and figure 19 in chapter three). "[S]ometimes you [train seriously at jams], sometimes you don't. Sometimes you just go out and have a good time with your friends. That's a lot of what I'm doing now: going out with all the guys, meeting new people, having a good time, not training too hard, helping people, helping make everything organized. It is what you make of it. You can train really hard at a jam, but at the same time you cannot train as hard and learn from other people and really enjoy it."

The point here is that parkour is more than a collection of pseudo-events and simulacra. The individual and collective flows generated through training are real, embodied practices. At the same time, traceurs' embodied experiences are wrapped up in parkour's virtual existence. And, this virtual existence is, again, integrally intertwined with its material practices. For Ando it was not simply that parkour has "got a real energetic feeling." His ability to have these sensations was dependent on his particular interface with the built environment of the Chicago suburbs. Further, his personal interface with physical space was only possible because of his social network and their collectively mediated exposure to what the Yamakasi had done in Paris's banlieues. Taken together, this is all part of a dialectical relationship between the virtual and the real. Thus, looking now at the material world, we need to attend to how the dialectic between the real and the virtual is integrated into the ways the built environment constrains and enables traceurs' actions.

FIG. 14. Attendees at the 2012 Colossal Jam pose for a group photo in Grant Park.

Overcoming Obstacles

Traceurs appropriate physical space in order to transform it into something useful from their perspective. Handrails become balance beams; ledges become launch pads. This appropriation, however, cannot be performed willy-nilly. The material world itself (as a structure) is intertwined with the actions that can be performed within it. Sam, for example, explained, "You can't do a wall trick in an open field. You have to go find a specific obstacle. With these creative movements [. . .], sometimes they are specific to this one object. For example, there [are] a few tricks that people have done with a vertical pole. You can't find those everywhere. Those are actually kind of rare. [. . .] It's really hard to find [a bar to swing on] in Chicago, unless there's construction [scaffolding on a building]. I've seen a lot of tricks with those, but you can't really find a nice set randomly." This is what James Gibson means with his concept of affordance.[19] Certain environments allow for certain types of actions, but only to the extent that individuals can perceive these possibilities.

Various parts of Chicago, like all urban areas, afford the movements of parkour. That is, there are objects and structures available to be used as obstacles, but as Sam's comment highlights, some sections of the city are better than others for some things. More to the point, despite their discursive claims about the efficiency of movement, traceurs are really interested in finding the path of *greatest* resistance between points A and B. For example, a video of a man running down a paved path—no matter how flawlessly efficient from an abstract, scientific point of view—would probably not inspire too many YouTube viewers. To train in parkour, therefore, a traceur must develop routes that will be difficult—scaling a wall, vaulting over a railing, or walking up a staircase on one's hands. Generally speaking, traceurs are lauded for overcoming obstacles other people cannot, or for doing so in a fashion too difficult or frightening for the non-traceur.[20]

Traceurs discuss their training in terms of personal progression. Sync described it well. "When you do something that you've never done before, or you've been trying so long to be able to do, and you finally do it, it's like an adrenaline rush when you finally do it, and it just feels really good, but then it goes away so you have to do something else." Similarly, Strafe stated, "In that moment, you are the king of your own little world in which this was the obstacle and you overcame it. For that obstacle at that time, you own it. And, then you go on to another obstacle. To me, that's what's so great about parkour." Or, as Max explained:

I'd say that parkour became *the* thing to do when we [i.e., a small group of Max's friends] all [...] got good. We would endlessly waste time training, and we just didn't feel like we were going anywhere, and then one day I got the kong [vault], and then [soon after my friend] got the kong. [...] After that it kept on going, getting better and better. And, you just wanted to get better. You felt tired at the end of the day, but there's a sense of accomplishment at the end of the day that you did something [...]. Like today was [...] different than yesterday—[one] step better. I used to have a fear of high drops, and I love them now. It's like a night and day thing for me with parkour. It's just awesome.

The progression being described in these quotes is about flow—balancing skill with task. Max's frustration arose from feeling outmatched by even the simplest techniques, but once he learned a few basic maneuvers, his outlook changed dramatically. For all traceurs, training starts with relatively small jumps and climbs, and they then work toward riskier, more difficult maneuvers. Traceurs' understandings of progression will be discussed in much greater detail in chapter four.

PK Vision

To successfully train parkour (regardless of one's skill level), practitioners must develop their bodies and minds to be able to perform the required movements. This is rather obvious. To engage in any physical activity, individuals must condition themselves for it. As traceurs develop their mental and physical capacities, however, they must concurrently refine the way they see the world.[21] In other words, traceurs do not just need to be able to jump a certain height or to keep a level head while balancing on a high platform. They need to be able to perceive the environment as affording such stunts in the first place. This is one of the main things that distinguishes traceurs from gymnasts. The latter perform amazing feats on purpose-built equipment; the former reimagine their everyday environment as presenting the necessary conditions for performing their amazing feats. This reimagining is generally referred to among traceurs as "PK vision." It is through the development of one's PK vision that the global ethnoscape of parkour becomes localized. PK vision, therefore, is a dialectical product of the global (virtual) and the local (real) embodied within the traceur.

An aimless walk with a group of about fifteen traceurs through downtown Chicago provided instructive examples of PK vision. The traceurs had left one of their usual training spots near the Shedd Aquarium and set out to find construction scaffolding to train on (which we never did find). As we walked, Strafe pointed upward to the top of an apartment building where several floors were staggered in setbacks. Being many stories up, the setbacks were certainly unreachable. However, Strafe was still awestruck: 'You wish you could climb that. I love that building. Wall run after wall run after wall run.' Later on the walk we passed a large building with a long protruding ledge under its windows. The ledge was about eight feet off the ground. Seeing this, one of the traceurs got really excited about getting on top of it. A second tried to dissuade him, telling him it was a bad idea because it might attract attention from the police. The first traceur retorted, "So climbable." The second traceur agreed, and then, despite his previous advice, they conspired to try to climb it.

Echoing these same points, Pasha stated, "I would say parkour's a lifestyle. [. . .] It doesn't matter where you go. [. . .] You see the roofs [of buildings]. Your imagination creates ways [for] how you would go through these roofs by using parkour. People who don't know what parkour is, they would just look at these roofs, and their imagination wouldn't do anything with that. People who do parkour, they have [a] completely different [. . .] imagination." Likewise, after I first started attending jams and training in parkour (as limited as my training might have been), I began developing PK vision, although it was not until sometime later that I would learn about the term. An excerpt from my early field notes is interesting in this regard:

> I've definitely noticed myself evaluating [. . . how places] could be used for PK [. . .]. Yesterday [my wife] and I went [. . .] to the downtown [. . .] park, and even before we left the house I was excited about the options (remembering that there were some interesting structures there from my last visit). [. . .] I made a point of having us walk over to the amphitheater area [to try wall runs]. [. . .] I half-heartedly tried a kong vault over a weird concrete ball thing, but it didn't really work. [. . .] I [spent] some time looking around for things that maybe I could try to do—to no avail, but it was interesting to want to look at the environment this way [. . .].

Around the same time as these field notes, I remember walking by another park. I had been by this park countless times in the past, but then, suddenly, the low and wide wooden posts that lined the parking lot jumped out at me. They were about two feet off the ground and five feet apart, forming an ideal setup for practicing precision jumps.[22]

The imagined potential that PK vision creates was perfectly summed up by a traceur who chimed in during my interview of someone else, "The way you perceive objects around you changes *a lot*. You'll never look at the world the same way again. [. . .] Instead of challenges you begin to see opportunities where challenges are. [. . .] You can't help it. You just see stuff and you're like, 'Oh man, I want to do parkour.'" More accurately, non-traceurs see neither challenges nor opportunities. The urban environment is not filled with "obstacles" at all; the forms and shapes they see are largely devoid of the potential for any creative human use. The environment may afford vaults and wall climbs, but most people fail to perceive such possibilities.[23]

To this end, Micca stated, "You learn to appreciate things in life that most people never see. When somebody walks into a building with a stairway and a bunch of rails around it, they're walking into a building. They don't even see what's in front of them. When I walk in, I'm *excited* instantly. I don't even know what's in the building or why I'm going there, but I know that in [. . .] the building is exciting stuff." Expressing the same sentiment, Cody asserted that as a traceur, "you're never bored." He went on to explain, "[Parkour] just helps you get over mental boundaries. After training it for probably about six months you start to see things kind of differently. [. . .] I'm driving; I'm constantly looking around for a new spot. [. . .] 'I wonder if I can make that wall run?' [. . .] You just see everything as an obstacle to overcome—instead of just a boundary or a border you cannot cross. [. . .] 'I wonder if I can do this to get to that?' [. . .] You just start thinking more about what's in your grand spectrum of abilities. You just start thinking different[ly]."

It's important to note that this PK vision does not solely reside in the eye of the individual traceur. Just as flow is experienced collectively, so are traceurs' reimaginings of the built environment. The social aspect of PK vision has already been hinted at in several of the earlier excerpts on flow: "You can [. . .] learn from other people and really enjoy it" (Ando) and "He saw what I was doing and I saw what he was doing and we were getting ideas off each other" (Sam). In the same vein, Stephan explained, "If we both stare at this tree, you might be thinking, 'climb it.' I might be thinking, 'spin off of it.' Someone else comes, 'Oh yeah, wall flip it.' Someone else can go, 'Tic off of it into a roll.' Everyone gives you a different perspective to train on a single object." Likewise, Aaron said, "[. . . S]omeone will [do] something you've never thought of before and you can do it [too], and you wouldn't have seen it if it weren't for them." In rather dramatic terms, another traceur told me, "I hate training on my own. I need people to suggest things to do." Ryan summarized these sentiments by describing jams as less about "training" and more about "discovering other movements with people."

PK vision, though, is also more than just a collective phenomenon. It needs to be understood as something trans-local. That is, it is not only shared with those who are physically present. Instead, it arises out of the discipline's global diffusion through new media. Without the virtual world of parkour, the imagined possibilities of the traceur would be truncated. As the previous quote from Ryan indicates, he was "inspired by videos," and these videos came from around the world. At the same time, this virtual world of parkour is only possible because it is emplaced in the real world. *The local is globalized and the global is localized.*[24] New media facilitate this dialectic, but it is equally dependent on the individual traceur's emplacement of these practices. Thus, yet again, what might—especially from a cynical, postmodern eye—be derided as pseudo-events and spectacle are shown to be very real moments. Hyperreality is incarnated back into the flesh, if only to be

FIG. 15. Cody tic-tacs off a tree onto a picnic table at Cummings Square in the suburb of River Forest, Illinois.

turned into yet another image for mediated consumption later. The next step, therefore, is considering the implications of this dialectic.

The Emplacement of a Global Ethnoscape

As already discussed, traceurs in this study recollected their first virtual exposures to parkour with awe. Mediated through the screen, they saw people performing seemingly impossible actions. "Hey, look at this video of these crazy dudes jumping off of buildings" (Max); "[David Belle] was really doing some really impressive physical feats" (Eric). This helped inspire them to begin their own training, and their involvement in the discipline usually progressed from individual practice (or practice with a few equally inexperienced friends) to eventually attending jams. At all times, even after they became seasoned traceurs, the virtual world of parkour was continually thrust into the real world of their parkour practices. Whether they were inspired by someone's sampler video, posting their own videos online, learning a new movement via a YouTube tutorial, or reading a Facebook post about the discipline, the traceurs' on-screen lives fed into their offscreen lives, and vice versa.

There are important sociological points to be made of this relationship between parkour's virtual and real worlds. First is the mere fact that it is a dialectic and not an either/or proposition. Second, and more importantly, the relationship helps us better understand the city and our place within it. Through the traceurs' descriptions of PK vision and of their creative and risky exploits within the urban environment, we can see how the profit-oriented intentions of urban planners do not necessarily dictate how urban spaces are actually put to use.[25] This is to say, through parkour, individuals reimagine the city. The abstractions of capitalism can be turned into something joyfully lived in ways never intended by their designers. For example, for non-traceurs, the slanted concrete walls beneath Chase Tower in downtown Chicago serve simply as the backdrop for the employee lunch crowd on a sunny day. But for traceurs, they allow for playful thrills that have no connection whatsoever to Chase, let alone its financial bottom line. As described in the introduction, this has been one of the main interests of previous researchers of the discipline. The sociological analysis of parkour, however, can go even further.

Following Appadurai, parkour is unbounded from the local at the very same time it is put into localized practice. Traceurs remake the city—turning reductive architecture into meaningful objects via the flow of play. These real, embodied practices, though, are also instantiations of far-off, ephemeral worlds lived on screen. We have already seen this in the original Aero members' inspiration from the Yamakasi. "We mimicked it" (Ando); "it was just so mesmerizing that I wanted to do [it]" (Frosti). In doing so, the outskirts of Paris were brought to downtown Chicago.

In very specific terms, practitioners can explain how they search through their local environments in order to replicate what they discover is possible through the virtual worlds they inhabit. For example, when I asked Luke about trying maneuvers he learned by watching videos, he replied, "One [instance] that stands out [is when] you have a ledge or a railing and you go kind of sideways at it [...], and, because you go in sideways at it, when you do your flip, you land on the other side. [. . .] I'd never thought to do anything like that [before]. I saw it in a video, and I'm like, 'That is sweet, I've got to do that.'" Similarly, Tommy told me, "I started watching videos of Daniel Ilabaca [a world-renowned traceur from England]. 'I want to do that.' [. . .I watch videos] all the time. [. . .G]uys from Europe, I watch a lot of that. [. . .] Whenever I see a video of theirs, 'Oh, I want to do that.' So, I go out and try to do that."

Despite the eagerness expressed by Luke and Tommy to go out and perform the movements they had seen on screen, it was not always easy to replicate these actions in their offscreen worlds. To this point, Eric said, "Some of [the buildings featured in Russian videos] have multiple tiers. [. . .] You don't find that as often in [the United States]. Sometimes you have to improvise. For instance, there might be a terrace-type structure [. . .] with a man-made hill on one side. You'll have to figure out, 'How will I drop from here to here to here?' [. . .] There are a lot of architectural differences that have an impact in parkour [. . .]. That does influence what you can do, but you can find things and you can improvise on a lot of this stuff [. . .]." Nearly identically, Tommy insisted, "You try to adapt [the moves] to [the environment] you have [locally]."

But, as Eric's comments intimate, the maneuvers one can watch in the virtual realm are not always ones the local environment affords, regardless of one's skill level. As Tommy would go on to explain, the desire to replicate what he was seeing performed elsewhere sometimes took added effort. "I could never find anything to do [a double kong vault on]. I drove around for a day until I found something." In other words, Tommy learned about double kong vaults virtually, and he wanted to enact them offscreen. This took effort—driving around his midwestern suburban town searching for a spot that contained just the right kind of obstacle to afford the movement. Likewise, David told me that he had come across an online discussion about the utility of using the railings on handicap access ramps for vaulting practice. After learning about the potential of such railings, David said, it got "a little bit obnoxious." By this he meant that he found himself continually scanning the environment for such structures, and he was exceedingly eager to use them when he came across them.

As we have seen, the various forms and shapes in Chicago's urban landscape were given new life by traceurs. And, by studying parkour we see how these embodied practices were dialectically woven into individuals' on-screen lives. On the one hand, traceurs' imaginations were inspired by ideas and images circulating within virtual worlds. Such on-screen activities require little in terms of embodied practice. At the extreme, they can be nothing more than passive consumption. In this sense, postmodern urban life can be thought of as ephemeral and imaginary—as simulacra lived only in mediated form. Turkle, for example, worries that our culture of real virtuality has made us too reliant on approximation and simulations.[26] Indeed, it often seems that as a society we are increasingly plugging in and tuning out. From this perspective, the city itself is reduced to little more than a container for biological beings cognitively transported somewhere else. Immediate experiences are forgotten in the seductive glamour of hyperreality. On the other hand, with parkour, we see the intertwining of the real and the virtual. Traceurs are plugged in and tuned in to the world around them. In fact, the former is dependent on the latter. Thus, traceurs are not naively escaping into a virtual world disconnected from their corporeal selves and the physical spaces they inhabit. On the contrary, parkour represents a visceral engagement with reality. Its joys, its pains, and its risks are not simulations of action; traceurs' bodies are really moving through the built environment of the city.

At the same time, while parkour is not merely simulacra, these embodied practices are possible only through the traceurs' replications of action found in their virtual worlds. In this way, virtual lives can (in certain respects) actually enhance a person's engagement with the real world. In particular, by studying traceurs we see how reimaginings of the city can arise out of and feed back into the virtual domain. This dialectic is perfectly illustrated when Tommy finally found a place to try the double kong or when Eric adapted the movements he had seen performed in Russia to his local college campus. Moving forward, researchers need to consider other ways in which the virtual and real intertwine. Numerous participants in various art worlds, lifestyle sports, and subcultures inevitably transpose on-screen lives into their inhabitations of specific physical spaces.[27] Further, the dialectic of the virtual and the real extends beyond the practitioners themselves. In the case of parkour, traceurs' actions also altered how other residents and tourists experienced the city. Take for example, Grant Park, which, among many other things, became a place where young men flip off walls.

In the next chapter, I will analyze the city as a series of structural resources composed of the built urban form and the people within it. Traceurs make use of these structural resources as they seek out the fateful actions of adventure. Whereas this chapter considers the relationship between on-screen lives and traceurs' embodied practices, the next chapter will examine parkour training in relation to culturally valued performances of masculinity. In both chapters, the emphasis is on expanding our understanding of the affective appropriation of space and how it relates to postmodern urban life.

3

Young Men in the City

● ●

In sociologist Georg Simmel's classic essay on the subject, he describes adventure as a particular form of experiencing in which individuals give themselves over to uncertainty. "[I]t is just on the hovering chance, on fate, on the more-or-less that we risk all, burn our bridges, and step into the mist, as if the road will lead us on, no matter what." In this sense, adventure represents a symbolic break with the mundanity of modern life.[1] This extraordinary aspect of adventure is what increasingly drives recreational pursuits.[2] Mountain climbing is a paradigmatic example. It pits individuals against the challenges of vertical rocks and the wilderness, allowing them the opportunity to develop and use their skills to cope with risk in ways markedly different from those found in typical daily routines.[3]

Adventure, however, does not necessitate forging into the untamed wild. The city can also offer adventure. Crowds of people hustle to and fro. Unfamiliar sounds and unique sights abound. Encounters with strangers occur unexpectedly. For these reasons, the "hovering chances" found in urban life are fundamentally different from those of the village. Indeed, this is what inspired philosopher Walter Benjamin's interest in the *flâneur*— the strolling people-watcher of the modern metropolis. Urban adventures can be as exotic as spelunking in sewers and abandoned subway tunnels, or as commonplace as taking a bicycle ride or a leisurely stroll.[4] The only requirement is for individuals to give themselves over to uncertainty and let the mysteries of the city lead them on.

Ultimately, adventure—whether it takes place in the backcountry or the central business district—comes down to the creation and testing of one's character. Erving Goffman famously describes this as "action"—that is, taking risks and pushing one's luck just for the sake of it. Goffman's definition of action, like Simmel's of adventure, involves potentially fateful consequences. And, when individuals engage in action (for its own sake), who they are in the eyes of others, as well as their own, is put on the line. Does the person buckle under pressure, or can he maintain a cool composure? As Goffman writes, "On the one hand, [character] refers to what is essential and unchanging about the individual [. . .]. On the other, it refers to attributes that can be generated and destroyed during fateful moments. [. . .] Every time a moment occurs, its participants will therefore find themselves with another little chance to make something of themselves."[5]

In the previous chapter we saw that architectural forms can be reimagined by traceurs to afford fateful moments. To quote Goffman again, "The social

FIG. 16. Stephan walks down stairs at the Chicago riverfront on his hands (Photo: Keri Wiginton).

world is such that any individual who is strongly oriented to action [...] can perceive of potentialities for chance in situations others would see as devoid of eventfulness [...]. Chance is not merely sought out but carved out."[6] The PK vision discussed in chapter two enables such a "carving out" of chance. As Micca said, "You learn to appreciate things in life that most people never see. [...] When I walk in [a building], I'm *excited* instantly. I don't even know what's in the building or why I'm going there, but I know that in [...] the building is exciting stuff." In other words, Micca claimed to see potential for action in situations that non-traceurs would feel were devoid of eventfulness. The next chapter will address the meaningful frames given to the dangers such action entails. This chapter, meanwhile, considers the built environment as a set of structural resources for enacting urban adventures and presents an analysis of such action as a gendered performance for traceurs.

Manhood Acts

Goffman's concept of action is distinctly masculine, couched in terms of bravado and risk taking.[7] Goffman's masculine bias is fitting for this chapter because while women participate in parkour, men dominate the discipline. Even the most dedicated female traceurs are unlikely to do the fast, powerful, and risky stunts that tend to capture the attention of onlookers and the praise of other practitioners. Moreover, as a sport, parkour is not unusual in this regard. Numerous researchers have made connections between masculinity and leisure-time risk taking. For example, decades ago, writer Janice Kaplan quoted a male cliff diver's indignation toward a highly skilled female competitor. "This is a death-defying activity. [...] The men are taking a great gamble to prove their courage. What would be the point if everyone saw that a woman could do the same?" While the explicit chauvinism described by Kaplan is less apparent in most contemporary lifestyle sports, there is little doubt that adventurous action is ingrained into men's understandings of themselves *as men* and is integral to their presentation of self.[8]

The masculine attributes of adventure align with sociologist Michael Schwalbe's concept of manhood acts.[9] From this perspective, masculinity is not something inherent or innate in the individual, nor is masculinity the sole province of males. Instead, manhood is something that must be asserted (and reasserted) through one's actions. By behaving in certain ways, an individual can make claims to the "appropriate" gender identity.[10] The social significance of these behaviors, of course, is historically situated within a given culture, and the resulting identities are neither static nor totalizing. They must be continually renegotiated. Further, this negotiation is disrupted by the conditions of postmodernity, which undermine taken-for-granted characteristics and predefined social roles. This makes the astute performance of gender all the more important to identity claims.[11] In contemporary Western societies, manhood acts are often buttressed by the fateful moments of adventure—which is to say, carving out chance is one of the premier ways for individuals to test their masculine character.[12]

My analysis of manhood acts as embedded within the affective appropriation of space focuses on two key ideas. First, the city can function as an environment with the potential for experiencing adventure. Second, participating in parkour allows traceurs to transform such environments into structural resources for asserting gender identities culturally coded as masculine. Of course, not all traceurs (much less all men) pursue masculinity in the same ways or with the same goals in mind.[13] In fact, most traceurs are unlikely to meet—or aspire to—the standards of hegemonic masculinity.[14] Regardless, most men engage in some form of manhood acts to distinguish themselves as masculine, as separate from women and children.[15] Put simply, through parkour, young males learn to perceive new types of affordances within the urban landscape, and these adventurous actions can be interpreted by themselves and others as "manly."

Not Your Typical Jocks

As with most lifestyle sports, the difference between parkour and traditional competitive team sports is readily apparent. As Colby told me, "You can just be yourself and not have anyone tell you what's right or wrong. […] In different sports, like basketball [and] baseball, there [are] rules you have to follow. Parkour is just free. [You can] do what you want." As discussed in the introduction, some traceurs in the group had athletic backgrounds, but many others recalled only a passing interest in other sports—often mentioning activities more akin to youthful play than to competitive athletic pursuits. And, in stark contrast to what might be expected of a nearly all-male social world, talk involving the objectification of women or sexual exploits was strikingly infrequent. This is very different from the tone reported to be typical of conversations in other sports, and it is even more surprising given that almost all the traceurs in my study were teenagers or men in their early twenties. Additionally, when spending time with male traceurs, I rarely heard disparaging remarks about the sincerity or dedication of female traceurs. This, too, can be contrasted with previous research in the sociology of sport.[16]

Because of the generally welcoming atmosphere at jams, the few female traceurs who routinely attended were quickly integrated into the parkour community. Carolyn, for example, recalled her first jam three years earlier by telling me, "It was so scary. I'm not someone who talks to people. I'm shy. To go [to that jam] was scary. [. . .] I saw some of the things other people were doing and I want to do some of those things too [but was too scared to try]. [...] The people there were really nice. [... A more experienced traceur] walk[ed] up to me and he's like, 'What are you doing? You come out to a jam and just sit there? No, you're coming with me and you're going to [train].'" By the time I met Carolyn, she was leading various training sessions at parkour events and traveling with other Chicago traceurs to jams around the country.

In fact, all the women I interviewed were adamant that the community treated males and females equally. For example, Angela insisted, "I think guys encourage the girls to train. They really like to see girls training." Similarly, Mercede contrasted traceurs with video gamers—another social world in which she was a core participant: "[In] gaming, yes [I am treated differently because I'm a female. I was] never treated differently [in the parkour community]." Likewise, Miko, a graduate student in mathematics who also trained in boxing and martial arts, said, "Boxing is very male dominated, and I study math, which is male dominated. So, maybe I'm used to [being around guys], but I think [other female traceurs I train with] would also have the same response. We never really noticed [being treated differently]."

These things said, because there were few women in Aero, I formally interviewed only four female traceurs. By definition, these were women who were willing to be part of a male-dominated parkour community. I do not have data on the women who *might* have had interest in the discipline *if* there were more females to train with them, nor do I have data on the women who trained outside the purview of Aero. Regardless, the perspective of the young women I interviewed highlights just how far removed the participants of the parkour community were from the defensive boundary work epitomized by Kaplan's sexist cliff diver.

Admittedly, there were occasions when a male traceur talked down to a female practitioner. As Angela described, "I tried giving a guy a tip on doing something once, and he [was] just like, 'No, you're a girl. What are you telling me? Girls do that small jump. Guys do the way bigger jump.' [. . .] Because I'm a girl, he didn't take me seriously [. . .]." Likewise, there were times I witnessed young men tease each other to "stop being a pussy" or cajole someone to "be a man." But, these were exceptions. Even if individuals trained timidly or lacked obvious athletic talent (male or female), they were still treated as welcome participants at jams by simply showing an interest in the discipline.

For these reasons and more, traceurs, regardless of gender, were cognizant and proud of the fact that they were part of a social world not composed of stereotypical jocks. At the same time, for all the progressive aspects of the community, young men used the discipline to bolster their masculine identities. To be clear, though, my point is not that parkour is *more* gendered than other sports or recreational social worlds. If anything, it appears to be the opposite. All the same, in critically analyzing how parkour allows for manhood acts, we can better understand why young men are drawn to the discipline.[17] And, we can better conceptualize the city as a dialectic part of this process—a set of structural resources from which traceurs can carve out chance through their affective appropriations of space.

The Adventure of Parkour

To be at a parkour jam is to be in a chaotic swirl of activity. Jams are held in areas that have multiple sections conducive to parkour training. Even at small gatherings, the traceurs in attendance rarely have a unified focus. Instead, they break off into ever-fluctuating groups based on friendships and momentary interests. Some people will be vaulting in one section; others will be jumping or swinging in another section. Integral to the enjoyment traceurs get from their training is the continual evolution of movements that can be practiced over obstacles. As discussed in chapter two, jamming allows for "discovering other movements with people." Thus, a jam is chaotic not simply because at any one moment some people want to train vaults while others want to train precision jumps. It is chaotic because as one person adds a new variation to how an obstacle is being surmounted, or combines unique movements to get over a structure, the attention (and imagination) of other traceurs is piqued. The result is an erratic flow of people with continuously evolving training goals as the jam progresses.

Training, Jamming . . . and Mischief

Some of the traceurs in this study took their training very seriously. They viewed parkour in a way that aligns with more traditional forms of athletics. For example, Ryan T. expressed frustration over what he felt was a lackadaisical approach to training on the part of others. "In my perfect world everyone would be drilling things. Everyone would be doing repetitions. I'd really like to try to get people to do it [. . .]. We have beginners' jams and I try to show people repetition there. If they're not going to take it home and do it there, there's not a whole lot I can do about it." Ryan was particularly concerned with how this made the parkour community look to outsiders. "If people walk by and they see people drilling precisions over and over in a straight line, they're like, 'Okay, these guys are serious.' But, if they come by seeing people doing poor flips and landing them poorly [. . .], they are more apt to say, 'These are just kids messing around.' I think that's what most people think when they see a group training like this [motioning to the people doing parkour around us]."

As will be detailed in the next chapter, most people involved in the Chicago parkour community seemed to agree with Ryan's general sentiments about the value of regimentation and repetition in training. During informal discussions and formal interviews, traceurs stressed the inherent seriousness that they felt *should* accompany parkour training. Most were also quick to disparage others for slacking too much at jams. However, few of these individuals consistently followed through with their own training. At times, their participation at jams was focused on improving their athletic skills, but at other times, their concentration on training broke down. Time and time again, I witnessed as the chaotic swirl of activity that characterizes a jam was twisted into something that had nothing to do with the codified maneuvers of parkour. Instead, the city became a resource for other types of adventure.[18]

Sometimes, more outlandish feats of strength and bravery substituted for the finesse and technique required in parkour. To this end, play fights and wrestling were commonplace, as were various exercise challenges, such as one-arm pull-ups, or push-ups performed with someone seated on the traceur's back (see figure 17). Now and then, the group's attention turned

FIG. 17. During their weekly jam in Berwyn, Illinois, Wolf and another traceur challenge each other to see who can balance longer on a column using only one arm for support.

to purely thrill-seeking stunts. Goaded by a crowd, Arnold once intentionally flipped into the Chicago River. This water is notoriously polluted, and with his jump Arnold literally took a plunge into the unknown.[19] Several others claimed that had the police not responded in seconds, they were also prepared to follow suit. Most frequently, training was sidetracked as traceurs became more interested in socializing than in honing their skills. They would talk and goof around among themselves—and also seek the attention of onlookers. Young women in particular were a sought-after audience for many of the male traceurs. As will be described a bit later in the chapter, parkour stunts were often used to intentionally capture such attention.

Cops and Traceurs

Chicago traceurs frequently complained of police and security guards harassing them. As Miko told me, "[In Chicago] if you tell someone you're having a jam, [the authorities are] going to make sure the police are [there] to kick you out." Likewise, Eric lamented, "We would try explaining our movement and our philosophy to the police officers [breaking up our jams]. The police officers would not make much of an effort to listen. They'd make more of an effort to judge. They'd say, 'Well, you're going to break you neck,' or 'You're going to hurt yourself.' To me, that's offensive because it is judging someone's physical abilities." Conversely, Cody, one of Aero's more senior members, described a much more ambivalent relationship with police and security officers. "It's really mixed. I've actually gotten a lot of cops that were cool. [. . .] We've had cops drive by and stop and they'll just enjoy the show. We've had [good] conversations. Then we've had some [cops] kick us out. I think that some [of the cops] that kick us out [. . .] don't really want to. Usually they're understanding and cool, but there are those situations [when they aren't]. Even then, at the very least, it's just a shitty part of their job. I don't think they like doing it." The feelings of a few disgruntled traceurs notwithstanding, most practitioners in Chicago echoed Cody's mixed impressions of police enforcement. And, like Cody, many tended to stress the positive experiences they had had with authorities.[20]

Having spent a great deal of time with traceurs in downtown Chicago and the surrounding suburbs, I can attest that parkour is (for the time being) far less regulated than skateboarding, which is frequently banned outside of designated areas.[21] I have certainly been with countless groups asked to move along by police or security. Alternatively, I have witnessed a nearly equal number of encounters when police or security, as Cody described, approvingly watched members of Aero train. The general tolerance the Chicago police showed traceurs can be contrasted with studies of suburban police officers, who often treat the mere presence of young people in public space as a social disturbance.[22] The most aggressive runins with authorities (in the city or the suburbs) occurred when traceurs climbed on top of buildings. No traceurs were ever ticketed or arrested in my presence, but I talked with several traceurs who claimed they had been formally charged with trespassing at least once during their training. This had occurred most frequently in the suburbs.

The racial dynamics influencing the police response to parkour is an unavoidable issue. Chicago is infamous for its racial segregation.[23] Just as the original French practitioners inevitably grappled with the stigma of the banlieues, black and Latino traceurs enter downtown marked by prejudiced assumptions of where they live and what kinds of individuals they might be.[24] I have been with majority-minority groups training in the predominantly white spaces of downtown that went unmolested. I have also been with all-white groups that were pushed out of areas by the authorities for no clear reason. These things said, if Aero comprised mainly young black or Latino men instead of clean-cut white boys, it is hard not to imagine a much sterner response from the powers that be as traceurs gallivanted through the city. In this sense, parkour training is an expression of white privilege. At the same time, it is important to remember that Aero is quite diverse in terms of race and class. For many members, training sessions were probably among the few instances in the traceurs' lives (outside of school and work) when they had the chance to socialize with people from markedly different backgrounds.[25] Conversely, where the parkour community most clearly lacks diversity is in terms of age and gender. It is a social world composed primarily of young men, and the adventures of parkour tell us something about contemporary masculinity.

Traceurs' ambivalent relationship with authority involves, on one hand, a desire for social acceptance of their discipline. That is, they want parkour to be a respected activity. For this reason, most traceurs are committed to not overtly defying requests from police or security.[26] The traceurs I talked with viewed this position as a valuable countermeasure to what they saw as the negative public image of skateboarders. For example, Zach explained to me:

> It's not like skateboarding [...] The way they treat cops and the way we treat cops is completely different. We're nice, "Oh yeah, we're going to leave." [...] We were [at the Chase Tower] recently and there were some skateboarders there [too]. Security came over the intercom and kicked them out, and just told us to be careful. They know we're nice about it. [...] Some people don't talk to cops well. [...] Most of the time you can defuse the situation by getting out of there. [...] There's more of a "Fuck the police" [...] mentality [among skateboarders]. [...] When you do that, it makes cops hate you more, and you get more run-ins and [tension] keeps building.

Likewise, Ryan told me:

> From my experience the whole culture is different from the fact that skateboarders tend to be rebellious. If security comes they're like, "Oh, fuck you," or whatever, "We'll do what we want," and they'll just keep skateboarding [...] and they'll fight with security. Generally, traceurs are extremely respectful, and if they're asked to leave they will. I think that's because a lot of people saw what

happened with skateboarding. The "no skateboarding" and "no rollerblad-ing" signs got put up, and we don't want that to happen. [. . .] It's definitely great. I think [traceurs] do it more to keep the image of parkour looking good. [. . .] There's just not the rebellious nature to it. Like skateboarding, there's the whole counterculture type thing.

True to these words, even when I could discern no grounds for their removal, I never witnessed Chicago traceurs argue when they were asked to leave an area.

On the other hand, and in spite of the nearly universal position in the community to "keep the image of parkour looking good," many traceurs in this study were also drawn to the fateful moments that could be found when taunting authority. They tended to do this passive-aggressively, never engaging in the head-on confrontations that Zach and Ryan attributed to skateboarders. However, the Chicago traceurs did occasionally train in location with the intention of courting run-ins with security guards.

Millennium Park was the most popular destination for this type of "training." A newer section of Grant Park, Millennium Park is one of the crown jewels of downtown Chicago's tourist attractions. It boasts an amphitheater designed by Frank Gehry as well as extremely popular outdoor artwork, including *Cloud Gate* (by Anish Kapoor) and *Crown Fountain* (by Jaume Plensa). The park also has its own security detail, which is quick to quash any untoward behavior, including violating the strict bans on skateboarding and on climbing on structures. At the same time, few of the park's features are well suited for parkour training. The park's forbidden status, therefore, was not much of a loss to the traceurs in this study. Regardless, practitioners often entered Millennium Park. One reason was the large crowd (which I will discuss below). Another rea-son was that within minutes (if not seconds) of traceurs doing any stunt, security would swoop in and tell them to stop.

The traceurs' goal was less about *challenging* authority and more about *invoking* it. Not being police officers and therefore possessing rather lim-ited powers, Millennium Park's security guards were perfect candidates for the traceurs' passive-aggressive taunting. For example, on one occa-sion, a security guard—instead of kicking the group out of the park, as was normal—told a group of traceurs merely to avoid climbing on the park's walls. Had the traceurs been sincere in their desire to train, they would have executed their most benign tricks in the guard's presence and waited to do anything flamboyant until she left. Instead, upon discovering they were not yet banished, several members of the group immediately started taking turns doing flips and spins from the sidewalk directly in front of the guard. After each progressively outlandish maneuver, they would look in the guard's direction and ask if "that" was allowed. In other words, the goal was to get kicked out, and they seemed genuinely deflated that this particular guard was willing to tolerate their antics. After a while, the traceurs got bored and left the park of their own volition.

The games traceurs played with security enabled them to transfer risk out of the corporeal realm and into the social realm. In place of uncertain physical consequences (such as broken bones and bloody knees), when traceurs entered Millennium Park they were stepping into the mist of uncertain *social* interactions. Given the guards' limited powers, the risk of formal repercussions was low. These interactions, though, provided traceurs with a different type of opportunity for testing their character. It made their training seem a little taboo, and, thus, the adventure seemed a little more worthwhile.[27] In the end, whether they were testing their athleticism or taunting security guards, the traceurs were engaged in the fatefulness of action. These practices added to their buzz from urban life. While the methods may have fluctuated, the adventure (in one form or another) remained. The analysis that follows will focus on parkour-specific activities. Parkour, however, was actually one part of a broader set of adventurous actions that could be had in the metropolis—by this I mean the ways the city could become a setting where uncertainty was experienced. In the case of parkour, this uncertainty most commonly pertained to the potential for physical harm, and this sort of risk taking was valuable because it tested masculine character. By putting it "on the line" (whatever "it" might be at that moment) young men could show (to themselves and others) what they were made of.

Performing Risks

All sports involve potential dangers to the self, but one of the defining features of many lifestyle sports is the emphasis placed on such threats.[28] The next chapter will expand on these matters. Like skateboarders, traceurs take otherwise safe environments and transform them into places of risk by appropriating architectural features for new purposes.[29] These transformations are primary to the traceurs' adventure. As numerous gender researchers have argued, such risk taking is distinctly masculine.[30]

It involves physical power and control. In order to train, traceurs must have the strength and speed to do the maneuvers (power), and through their actions, practitioners show they have mastery over their bodies (control). Further, with their physical power and bodily control, traceurs demonstrate a sense of agency over the material environment as well. That is, instead of being controlled by the environment, they appear to be in control of it.

As discussed in chapter two, traceurs' risky appropriations are collective achievements. This underscores the performative aspect of their masculinity. The parkour community provides an opportunity to see and be seen by one's peers in the midst of conducting manhood acts. An afternoon I spent with three traceurs in the Chicago suburbs provides a useful example of young men taking risks together and performing in front of each other. Throughout the afternoon, Aaron, Blade, and Flux each pressed the other two into doing maneuvers they were clearly nervous about doing. They would offer encouragement by assuring each other. "You've got that. You just need to commit to it," was a common refrain. At one point Aaron attempted to pump himself up for a front flip by getting Flux to agree to do it next. They were both scared of doing it, but Aaron found comfort in knowing Flux would follow him, and after Aaron succeeded in doing the flip, Flux did not renege. There were also times when one of the young men would even ask another person in the group to give a countdown to help spur him into performing.

Similar to Scales's jump described in the introduction, Voigt's effort to precision jump a gap outside the entrance to Millennium Park provides another useful example of risk taking and peer influence in parkour. Voigt practiced the distance required for the jump at ground level several times and then moved onto a wall. The traceurs gathered around him to watch. Standing on the wall, Voigt said, "This is scary." More than once he explained to the group, 'I don't want to do this.' People just continued to stare up at him. It was apparent to everyone in the group that, as long as he could get over his fear, he could make the jump from the wall. As he stood above us trying to build up his nerve, ZK came up to him and said, 'Don't think about it. On the count of three, just jump.' Voigt replied, 'I don't want to do that.' But, ZK counted, and Voigt jumped. The jump lacked commitment, and, as a result, he missed his mark, but he did not get hurt. Voigt got back up, hesitated some more, and jumped again. He almost made it. The whole process was repeated several times, until—finally—he nailed it.

Had Voigt committed fully the first time but missed the landing, this particular maneuver was still extremely unlikely to have critically injured him. It could, though, have easily resulted in broken bones, sprained joints, or torn flesh. Knowing that such contingencies were possible is precisely what allowed Voigt's jump to serve as adventurous action and function as a manhood act. The same can be said for Aaron, Blade, and Flux's training in the suburbs. Further, injuries would be almost certain for a non-traceur who attempted the maneuver, and this heightened the significance of the acts. While the traceurs knew they *might* get hurt, they were able to push through their doubts and jump. In doing so, they demonstrated a power and control over themselves and the environment others would not or could not perform. These were tests of character, and despite their initial fears (and occasional failings) they all showed themselves to possess the traits of manhood.

Additionally, the goading traceurs gave each other shows how practitioners work together in their performance of potentially dangerous actions. As I was told multiple times, the joy of jamming in parkour is having an opportunity to push and be pushed by other traceurs. For example, when I asked Ando about whether jams increased the risks people took, he replied, "Yeah. Some people feel that sometimes. That's only natural when there's pressure from other people, when they're like, 'Yeah! Do it.' [...] It's good and bad. You can surprise yourself, 'Wow, I actually could do that' when the pressure's on [...]." In other words, jams were the setting for more than "discovering" movement. They also provided audiences to witness manhood acts and to motivate traceurs to engage in them. As Sync told me, "It's more like, 'I can do this. Let's see if you can do it.' [...] You push each other a little bit. By yourself, it sometimes gets to that point where you kind of lose your own motivation, and then when you see someone do something you've never seen before then you go to try it, there you go, you've got something new to try."

As with other lifestyle sports, a traceur's position in the social hierarchy of the community was largely the result of the risks he or she took.[31] However, as we will see in the next chapter, very specific symbolic criteria must be met to validate the risks taken in training. Regardless, seeing and being seen by other traceurs as one acts in a "manly" way is an essential part of what gives parkour its meaning. It allows young men to test themselves in relation to their peers through adventurous action, and it is by putting their bodies on the line that traceurs make claims to the valued gender

identity of manhood. In this chapter, we will see how performing dangerous stunts in view of strangers was even more important for practitioners
in this study. In this analysis, the adventure of parkour is linked to traceurs'
use of the urban environment as a structural resource—which is to say,
traceurs' risky actions are not performed in a spatial void. The city is
dialectically connected to this gendered process.

The Structural Resources of Adventure

Emphasizing the "lifestyle" component of being a traceur, numerous practitioners told me about ways they routinely trained parkour as they went
about their everyday lives. JimthePirate, a college student, said he balanced
on handrails and vaulted over walls as he walked to class. Jake, another college student, said he did the same thing, adding in, "You'll have people stop
all of the time—including professors. They'll watch you, and they'll clap."
David told me, "On the way to work there is this wall. [. . .] Everyday, going
in, I've [vaulted over it], and I keep going." Or, as Jaska said, "Whenever
there's one of those little scaffold things, I can't help but under-bar through
it and then go back to walking like I'm a normal person." Attempting to
instill these practices in beginners, Counsel advised those in his parkour
classes to continually look for ways to train in everyday life. 'If you see a
gap, jump it. If you come to a staircase, precision up forty stairs.'

Opportunities in Public Space

The point here is not simply that the traceurs exercise in public. Runners
and bicyclists are also dependent on public space for their fitness. More
than merely working out, parkour training is inexorably connected to
appropriating the environment in risky ways.[32] That is, while urban adventures can take many forms, parkour training is tied to corporeal danger,
and for the traceurs in this study, carving out such actions served as poignant manhood acts. The remainder of this chapter will describe the direct
connection between the traceurs' uses of the city and the masculinity of
parkour.[33] As we will see, quotidian spaces became proving grounds for
masculine gender identities, and the result was a cityscape redefined in
terms of those with the power to control the risks of the discipline and
those without.

That the traceurs' action played a signification role in the construction of their gendered identities became especially apparent when they discussed what they liked about parkour. A frequent refrain was that, as traceurs, they could do things other people could not. Of course, this is true for most sports. Someone who routinely plays basketball can make shots that others cannot, and someone who spends a lot of time rock climbing can ascend routes too tricky or arduous for novices. Because of parkour's enactment in the quotidian regions of the city, though, the distinction between traceurs and non-traceurs was routinely put on public display. And, it was this public display of parkour that also brought to light the dynamic nature of the city as a structural resource for traceurs.

First, as has already been discussed at some length, the built environment is necessary for parkour maneuvers: there must be obstacles that can be transformed into opportunities. Different spaces afford different types of movements. This was the most obvious way that the city functioned as a structural resource for traceurs. As described in the introduction, previous research has focused on this aspect of the discipline. Second, beyond the physical possibilities of its architecture, the city provided an audience

FIG. 18. Two traceurs put on a performance for onlookers along Chicago's crowded Michigan Avenue.

of strangers to witness the traceurs' activities. Such non-traceur observers serve as another type of structural resource offered by the city. Whereas the built form affords particular movements, a crowd of onlookers—who are generally unambiguously impressed with the traceurs' athletic prowess and risk taking—affords the possibility of positive social appraisal.

To be clear, social status within the parkour community is derived from other traceurs. It is only traceurs who are capable of evaluating the technical nuances of the discipline. Moreover, such evaluations come from community members with whom practitioners have reoccurring contact—again, making their judgments far more significant in identity construction.[34] In part because they do not fully comprehend the complexity of the maneuvers they are watching, onlookers do not dictate status. Unlike other traceurs, though, they are prone to being easily impressed with flashy tricks. As such, they serve as a selective looking glass for the traceurs to assess just how brave, graceful, and outrageous their performances are. To paraphrase Simmel, when stepping back out of the mist of uncertainty, strangers in the city serve to validate the traceurs' adventures. Through the shocked expression of the crowd and their eagerness to film the next stunt, traceurs affirm their position as men with power and control.

An Audience to the Adventure

In attempting to articulate what attracted him to parkour, Jaska stated, "[. . . T]here is [. . .] the element that a normal person could not do this." Alex said, "It's also the fact that you have that feeling that no else can really do this kind of stuff, and that's kind of cool. [. . .] You have this feeling [that] you're the only one in a way." Likewise, Sync told me, "I would have to say my favorite part of doing parkour is the ability to do the things the average person can't [. . .]." Steve's antics at the riverfront one afternoon illustrated this perspective perfectly. A passing group of teenagers on the bridge overhead called out, "Do something cool." Never one to turn down a chance to perform, Steve did a flip off a small wall, and the crowd above was pleased. Soon after, another group of onlookers requested more flips, and Steve complied again and again. At one point, he did a series of jumps culminating in a flip onto the sidewalk, but instead of stopping he kept running and vaulted over the railing separating the sidewalk from the river below—as if he was going to dive in. But, as he vaulted, he held onto the railing and twisted into a one-handed grab that left him dangling just a few feet above the water. This produced mad screams from the onlookers, thinking he had just plunged into the Chicago River. It was an almost vaudevillian act of risk and skill.

Steve's flamboyant stunts set him apart from the onlookers requesting the flips. They most certainly could not replicate what he had done. Steve also distinguished himself from the rest of the traceurs present that day because they lacked his remarkable ability. And, from the astounded looks and approving comments offered up by those standing on the bridge, Steve's gendered performances were given an unambiguously positive reception. Conversely, when I asked Sync to describe the worst part about doing parkour he, again, brought up non-traceurs. "I think the worst part of parkour is the mixed reactions you get from people. [...] You'll do a wall climb and they'll just walk by [...]. I think the negative reactions you get are [...] more common [... P]eople [...] ignore you because [they've seen you do parkour ...]." Nearly identically, Cody, told me:

> It's also nice training in parks because kids are around. It's when you do a flip and all the kids are like "Whoa!" [...] That's probably one of the best feelings from training, just doing something and hearing kids losing their mind. [... Alternatively,] I'll do a [complicated flip] and some kid will be like, "Ehh" and keep on playing. "Really? What is wrong with you? How did you not think that was awesome?" I also like crowds because it means people are fascinated with what you do. It means they like seeing what you're doing. What's the problem with wanting to be an entertainer? It's fun.

Sync and Cody's concerns about being ignored are particularly notable. They highlight just how important the structural resource of an audience of strangers was to the traceurs' training. As Jael said, "I like to see people's expressions. 'Whoa, how'd you do that?'" In other words, despite their occasional claims to the contrary, traceurs did not want to be left alone in the city, free to do as they chose. Most skilled practitioners wanted to perform for others. The adventure of parkour needs validation. Traceurs want these others to acknowledge their power and control within the urban environment. Just as the proverbial tree falling in a remote forest might not make a sound, a manhood act without a witness might not matter.

While the talent Steve displayed at the riverfront was exceptional, his showboating was commonplace. Likewise, the desire for attention from outsiders expressed by Sync, Cody, and Jael was by no means rare. However,

FIG. 19. A typical scene at the "Wall of Death" (Monroe Street and Columbus Drive).

such overt grandstanding was generally discussed by other traceurs in negative terms. Just as training is supposed to be serious, traceurs tended to claim training should only be for one's own personal development. Trying to impress others was derided as an unnecessary risk. Reflecting this general sentiment, Stephan exclaimed, "That is a fast way to get injured. 'I don't feel comfortable doing this. My body's telling me [not to do it], but there's people watching me, so I need to impress them.' Boom: injury. Some people [have] actually died from trying to impress people. [. . .] Stop trying to impress people!" However, as with much of parkour's ascetic philosophy, such views were frequently sidestepped in actual practice.

Ryan offered a perceptive explanation. "[P]eople won't admit this. People in parkour don't like admitting this at all, [but] a lot of it is an ego booster—as bad as that sounds. [. . .] People try to persuade themselves that they don't do it for anyone else, but I think everyone does at least a little bit." Similarly, during interviews, several traceurs expressed ambivalence about performing for others. As Jake explained, "I don't do insane stunts just to entertain people. That's not parkour [i.e., it goes against the philosophy of the discipline]. It's more within yourself, not to entertain other people. Although, people love to watch it, and I don't mind that at all, but that's not the reason that I do it. [. . .] It's a very blurred line, because it overlaps a lot."

My field notes reflect the overlap Jake described between training for oneself and entertaining others. Sometimes, as with Steve's flips at the riverfront, the overlaps were quite intentional. Steve was not only aware others were watching, he was explicitly performing for them. Occasionally, the overlaps were unintentional. During highly focused training, it is certainly conceivable that a traceur might not have realized that he had drawn in observers. Most commonly, though, the traceurs crafted performances that were meant to appear as if they were not performances at all. In other words, practitioners studiously worked to make their intentions of attracting a crowd *seem* unintentional. This allowed traceurs the opportunity to disavow showboating (as Stephan did) while still garnering the praise of outsiders—a necessary component to successful manhood acts.

As they trained in public places, skilled practitioners usually kept a subtle eye out for potential onlookers. These traceurs would then time their flashier moves to coincide with people walking by. The implicit goal was for the traceur to look as if he was just minding his own business and that it was merely a coincidence that a back flip happened right as the double-decker tour bus was stopped at a red light by the park. For example, in our formal interview, Wyld insisted, "I just do it for me. It's not like I'm doing [tricks] to show off. [Drawing an audience is] just a coincidence." Sometimes, though, a traceur's façade of indifference to others would show cracks. A practitioner seeking to impress outsiders might get in position too soon and then have to awkwardly wait for his unsuspecting audience to queue themselves in front of the impending action. Or, an overly eager traceur might actually blurt out what usually went unspoken by yelling across the park for someone to do a particular maneuver because a group was getting ready to walk by. In fact, my field notes are spotted with various incidents in which Wyld himself waited to do stunts or rushed to complete them in order to garner maximum attention from onlookers. The "coincidence" was manufactured.

Most notably, some traceurs would even leave their usual training spots with the stated intention of finding a bigger audience to perform for. In these instances, any pretext to serious training was totally foregone. The goal during these sessions was simply to attract crowds and elicit responses from them. For example, one practitioner explained that he preferred to train parkour, "but I do enjoy the attention tricking brings." That is, by incorporating flashy spins and twists into a routine (and not just focusing on "efficient" movements), traceurs attracted more onlookers. To this end, Scales once persuaded a group training in another part of the city to move to Millennium Park by telling them how popular the location was for wedding and prom photos. "There's like a billion proms there now. That means pictures." Unlike Sir Georg Solti Gardens, Chase Tower, and the other key downtown training spots, Millennium Park (even without proms) was always crowded on Saturday afternoons. Thanks to the park's many tourist attractions, a gawking audience with cameras at the ready was nearly guaranteed, and, occasionally, this is what the traceurs enjoyed about parkour. As Alex proudly told me, "I had people come up to me while I was doing a flip going, 'Oh my gosh, can I film you.' I've seen video of me on YouTube because of that."

Gendering the City

When traceurs say that they like parkour because other people cannot do it, and when practitioners like Alex, Cody, Steve, and Wyld pander to the crowd, they are all helping redefine life in the city. This redefinition is inherently creative, exciting, and transgressive. Michael Atkinson refers to parkour as a form of poïesis exactly for this reason.[35] But, in these same instances, the performance of parkour was also a way for these young men to assert their masculinity. Their appropriations were about power and control—over themselves and over their surroundings. Further, crowds were awestruck by the sight of the traceurs turning urban forms into dangerous obstacles. As a masculine social world that is produced and reproduced in public space, therefore, the traceurs' use of that space influences the meaning these places have for themselves and also for others. Through parkour, ostensibly safe environments are transformed into sites of masculine identity-making. That is, the public spaces used by traceurs—often reductive architecture[36]—are made meaningful as affordances for manhood acts. Thus, when Grant Park comes alive Saturday afternoons, its heart is beating to a rhythm pounded out by the cultural expectations of masculinity. In particular, traceurs and the people passing by come to see these parts of the city as an environment for men putting themselves at risk.

Of course, females can (and do) perform parkour. Regardless, parkour is a masculine social world. It is dominated by men doing activities culturally coded as manly. This became apparent when female traceurs in the group discussed their own training and contrasted it with the training of their male counterparts. Angela, for example, explained, "A lot of the stuff on YouTube and the media, a lot of it is hype. It's big stuff. It's pretty crazy what they do. For any girl, it's intimidating to get into something like that." She went to on say, "The women that I've seen, the very few that I've trained with, they usually focus on strength and conditioning, and smaller things. [. . .] A lot of the guys, it's big stuff. They don't really seem to care for things that seem easy to them, or something small. They're definitely [more into having] fun, and I think the girls take it more seriously than the guys do. [. . . The guys] are more explorative. They just mess around with stuff. They mainly focus on just having fun."

Angela's point about the guys wanting to have "fun" and being more "explorative" spoke to the specific ways in which male traceurs made use of public space. As Angela intimated, female traceurs I observed were more reserved and methodical in their training. Frequently, when more than one woman was present, they would team up and go off to train on their own— far out of sight of the men and the general public. For Angela this denoted that women took their training "seriously." Some of the men in this study might have interpreted this as a sign of timidity. At the same time, because it was the men inserting themselves into public view, it was their risky appropriations (and not those of the female traceurs) that redefined the cityscape. Often at the large jams I attended, female traceurs and the less skilled male traceurs took on the role of spectators themselves—watching the boldest and the bravest men vie for completing the most outlandish feats. Comparing the men she knew across her various sporting experiences, Miko stated, "This is what I noticed in boxing and Muay Thai, the difference between male and female practitioners, men seem to have this whole, 'Hoorah, I don't want to look weak in front of my friends.' They're more likely to do stupid moves, just so they don't look weak. The woman will [more likely say], 'I can't do this. I don't care what name you call me. I'm not jumping.'"

Parkour is by no means unique for being gendered; we all "do" gender in all sorts of ways.[37] While challenging traditional gender norms in many important aspects, most lifestyle sports continue to bolster perceptions of male athletic superiority. In fact, in a society that ostensibly promotes gender equality, such activities provide young men the opportunity to reassert the significance of masculine performances.[38] Moreover, the risky practices

FIG. 20. Traceurs train quadrupedal movements on the stairs near the former Daley Bicentennial Plaza (now Maggie Daly Park).

of such men tend to become the most highly valued within sports, and parkour is no different. By emphasizing the spatial aspects of gender, however, sociologists are better positioned to understand the complexity of this social process. In the case of parkour, we can see how the affordances of the physical world become embroiled in the social world.

Parkour represents one way of carving chance out of the urban environment. With acrobatic feats of skill and strength, traceurs appropriate the city in creative and dangerous ways—turning ledges, stairs, and walls into obstacles to jump, run, and vault over. If, as described in the introduction, postmodernity involves an increased emphasis on performance in the establishment of identity,[39] parkour is a manifestation of larger cultural changes. As taken-for-granted assumptions become problematized, all people seek out new ways to assert valued identities for themselves. Being a traceur is a particularly potent option for young males to project a desired image of the self. Through demonstrations of power and control, practitioners of the discipline show themselves in possession of the culturally valued attributes of manhood. The mist of uncertainty burns away to reveal men in control of themselves and their surroundings.

The next chapter will demonstrate that, despite the danger inherent in their actions, traceurs do not view themselves as wanton thrill seekers. For all of traceurs' adventure-seeking behavior, the social world of parkour is actually filled with rhetorical appeals to precaution. The analysis provided in this chapter, therefore, is not complete. To adequately grasp the meaning of parkour, it is essential to understand how traceurs situate their risk taking within rituals of symbolic safety. As we will see, it is through collectively enacted, communicative performances that parkour becomes more than a senseless death wish. Without the symbolism of safety, the manhood acts of parkour would produce men whom other traceurs did not respect.

4

Hedging Their Bets

•••••••••••••••••••••

The subway entrance outside of the Daley Center has a deep stairwell lined by a low wall on either side. One evening, I filmed Martin, a traceur visiting from Tennessee, precision jump the eight-foot gap between the walls (see figure 21). It was a straightforward maneuver. Martin even admitted that the mechanics of his feat required little in the way of specialized training. With a modicum of practice, most physically fit adults can jump that far. What made it a worthwhile exercise was the possibility of a twenty-foot fall should something go awry. In fact, Martin could have done the exact same jump toward the top of the staircase and been less than three feet off the ground. Instead, he calmly walked to the deepest part of the stairwell, counted to three, and leapt. When I asked him about it later, he explained that such a stunt takes "confidence" but then immediately corrected himself. 'It's not confidence, because if you feel confident about something you'll get hurt. It's about being *comfortable* with something.'

Dylan Baker is a well-known traceur from Denver. He has a sizable following on YouTube and was a contestant on *Jump City: Seattle*. During a training session many years ago, he attempted a kong vault into a cat leap (see figure 22). That is, Dylan's plan was to take off by doing a kong, fly over a gap, and then land, cat-like, by grabbing onto an opposing structure.

FIG. 21. Video still of Martin's precision jump at the subway entrance at the Daley Center.

The "kong to cat" is a popular (and impressive-looking) parkour maneuver. For a traceur as experienced as Dylan, there was little to worry about. He had executed similar stunts countless times, and the distance between the vault and his opposing grab was not too difficult. However, the location was the top of a multistory parking garage, and Dylan intended to land on a neighboring building. In other words, like Martin's jump at the Daley Center, Dylan's maneuver was notable not because of the physical prowess of the stunt, but because it would be done at a height such that a mistake

FIG. 22. Video still of Dylan clipping his foot on the takeoff of a high-risk vault. He flies through the air off balance and narrowly avoids what would have been a deadly fall. This image is from a YouTube video posted by American Parkour, https://www.youtube.com. Courtesy of American Parkour.

could easily result in death. In Dylan's case, a worst-case scenario was only narrowly avoided. During the kong vault, Dylan clipped his foot, slowing his forward momentum and setting him off-kilter. Fortunately, despite the botched takeoff, he was still able to reach his target with just enough control to maintain his grip—and prevent himself from plummeting to the ground below.

In downtown Chicago, I watched as several traceurs considered performing a kong to cat on the railings surrounding a stairwell to an underground parking garage near Millennium Park (see figure 23). While the stunt would not be quite as dramatic as Dylan's, if the traceurs failed to make the span, they would fall at least a story onto concrete steps. With only the slightest hint of reservation, Bill decided to execute the maneuver, and he did it flawlessly. The others continued to mill about, deliberating the possibility of doing it themselves. Shilo, a traceur of considerable girth for such an acrobatic feat, intently eyed the gap. He discussed the specifics of the takeoff and landing with Bill. After several minutes of hesitation, Shilo broke into a run. He adequately vaulted the first railing and managed to successfully grab hold of the other side. However, he lacked Bill's grace. His launch was a bit shaky and the conclusion a bit unsteady. We would soon learn that Shilo smashed his forearm into the railing. It was nothing

FIG. 23. Entrance to the underground Lakeside Garage. Shilo attempted to kong vault across the gap.

too serious, but he was cut and bruised. Unlike Martin, who appeared imperturbable through the build-up to the completion of his jump, Shilo never seemed all that comfortable with what he was planning to do. In fact, even months later, Shilo still seemed somewhat jarred by the event. As he told me, "I'd never done that before then. It was fucking terrifying. [. . .] There was no point to it, but I did it because I was training."

Wexin Yang, a traceur affiliated with American Parkour, attempted a kong to cat on the campus of the University of Illinois at Chicago. It was a maneuver very similar to the ones attempted by Dylan and Shilo, and, like Martin, Wexin chose the deepest part of a stairwell to try it. Regrettably, Wexin misjudged the landing and fell approximately ten feet onto hard concrete (see figure 24). As in the other three moments described, at least one person was filming and numerous people were watching. Wexin later posted the footage to YouTube himself. In the video, the viewer can see that in the split second following his contact with the opposite railing, Wexin bounces backwards, falling out of the camera's frame. There is a loud thud as his body slams onto the ground. The fear and urgency of those nearby

FIG. 24. Video still of Wexin lying hurt at the bottom of a UIC stairwell, having fallen during a failed kong to cat. YouTube video posted by the traceur, https://www.youtube.com. Courtesy of Wexin Yang.

can be felt in the video: before Wexin has even completed the fall, the person holding the camera starts moving toward the stairwell. Almost immediately, others rush into view—running down the stairs to offer aid. Wexin can be seen holding his head, appearing dazed. The video cuts off as soon as the onlookers reach him. Wexin's subsequent posts to social media describe a frustrating recovery from a seriously injured knee as a result of the fall.

Based on a reading of these four fateful moments, parkour might seem wildly dangerous. The physical risks of their activities are readily apparent: young men hurtling themselves across caverns of concrete and steel. Described out of context like this, parkour might seem utterly foolhardy. In these examples, the traceurs often selected the locations for their stunts precisely because they added peril to an already hazardous sport. As discussed in the previous chapter, such decisions were made in the service of carving out action. When Martin chose to walk to the deepest part of the stairwell, he showed he was "comfortable" in assuming such risk. Martin demonstrated for all in attendance that he could keep cool under pressure. However, as Dylan's stumble and Wexin's fall demonstrate, even extremely skilled traceurs make mistakes. Things can and do go wrong.

Not surprisingly, throughout the course of my fieldwork, I witnessed countless minor injuries at jams. As they trained, traceurs ended up bruised and scraped, sometimes nursing sprains of varying severity. These types of mishaps were utterly routine and of little consequence to those involved. In only the most extreme cases were practitioners forced to noticeably modify their typical activities. Injuries necessitating immediate medical attention were actually quite rare. Counsel tore his ACL. It was excruciating, and his recovery was slow.[1] No more pleasant was Sam's broken ankle. Slipping on mud while trying to flip off a tree, another traceur split open his scalp severely enough to require stitches. This injury, however, reportedly looked worse than it felt.

The brazen actions of some traceurs notwithstanding, it would be a mistake to assume parkour is inherently more dangerous than other sports. All physical activities involve the potential for injury. Putting the human body into motion means stepping into harm's way, and there is a great deal of public misperception about the hazards of lifestyle sports in relation to those of traditional sports. It is true that, in traditional sports, the risk of injury is often ancillary to the goals of the game. For example, in baseball, a batter wants to make a hit into the outfield without the opposing team catching it. The fear of getting beaned by a pitch—a very real concern—is probably not part of the sport's appeal. Conversely, the reason surfers drop into big waves and skaters ollie onto kinked handrails is hard to separate from the physical jeopardy involved in such acts.[2] At the same time, research shows that injuries may actually be less likely to occur in activities like surfing and skateboarding than they are in popular team sports like basketball, soccer, and softball.[3] While there is little reliable medical data on parkour specifically, there is also no reason to believe the discipline is especially risky.[4]

Risk refers to the probability of loss versus gain from an event. It involves exposure to peril and the effort to control an uncertain future in relation to that peril. Risk is often treated as if it is the product of hard science—something that can be objectively calculated. Perceptions of risk, though, actually derive from social processes.[5] That is, there are very real hazards in numerous aspects of life, but we view them through a cultural lens that shapes the meaning of potential danger. For example, in the United States, over five million motor vehicle crashes occur every year. About 30,000 people die, and another two million or so are injured in these accidents. However, despite these statistics, few Americans feel gripped by fear at the thought of driving. Likewise, operating a table saw is not generally considered a daredevil act, but tens of thousands of people a year require emergency medical treatment as a result of table-saw mishaps. Hot dogs account for over fifteen percent of food asphyxiations among children, but it is unlikely that parents would be castigated for serving such a "risky" meal to their children.[6] In short, the mortal coil can unravel in numerous ways. However, we make different assessments about how risk is woven into our lives depending on our social positions. To quote anthropologist Mary Douglas, "The question of acceptable standards of risk is part of the question of acceptable standards of living and acceptable standards of morality and decency, and there is no way of talking seriously about the risk aspect while evading the task of analyzing the cultural system in which the other standards are formed."[7]

My goal in this chapter is to analyze how traceurs give meaning to their risk taking—how what often seems wildly dangerous and foolhardy to outsiders becomes acceptable and meaningful to traceurs. As we will see, traceurs have a particular way of explaining their actions, both to themselves and to others. That is, they can account for their training in a manner that conveys a sense of profound purpose, at least to those also enmeshed in the sport. Within the social world of parkour, the discipline is not viewed as an extreme sport performed by daredevils. Far from boasting that they performed dangerous stunts, nearly all the traceurs in this study insisted that they studiously assessed the potential risks of their maneuvers beforehand. Instead of carelessly chasing an adrenaline rush, they contended that they simply managed the fears that would otherwise have stifled their potential. Ultimately, I propose that understanding parkour and its growing popularity means understanding how traceurs conceptualize risk and the symbolic practices they associate with it. This also requires connecting the discipline to the neoliberal rhetoric prevalent in postmodern culture—for this represents a major component of the social context of contemporary risk taking.

Parkour and Postmodernity

Following sociologist C. Wright Mills, taking part in parkour (or any social activity) involves a "vocabulary of motive." People understand and explain situations with particular types of accounts—or vocabularies—that can be used to justify their conduct. In other words, socially meaningful actions cannot be reduced to biological or psychological factors. Men and women do not simply respond to environmental stimuli; individuals always act with a sense of purpose. Further, vocabularies of motive are always embedded within their cultural and historical context. Overall, Mills's perspective on the study of social action "translates the question of 'why' into a 'how' that is answerable in terms of a situation and its typal vocabulary of motive, i.e., those which conventionally accompany that type of situation and function as cues and justifications for normative actions in it."[8]

Changing Accounts

Stephen Lyng and David Snow use Mills's vocabulary of motive to study the changing accounts within the skydiving subculture.[9] While skydiving always involves individuals jumping out of aircrafts with parachutes, the motivational orientation practitioners have for their actions can vary quite widely. In particular, Lyng and Snow explore three different phases of meaning, each characterized by successive waves of practitioners. First, the activity can be viewed as an individualistic, competitive sport focused on visceral pleasures. The primacy of this motivational orientation resonated most strongly with the older members of the subculture—individuals who also tended to have military connections to parachuting. Alternatively, skydiving can be conceptualized as a collective practice for achieving transcendental experiences. This motivational orientation grew out of the 1960s and 1970s counterculture: as older skydivers aged out of the sport, younger skydivers found meaning in the Zen-like qualities of the activity, increasingly choosing non-competitive group formations over individual jumps. Finally, during the 1980s, an entirely different motivational orientation to skydiving came about. This third phase of meaning gives priority to the activity's inherent dangers.

Lyng and Snow refer to the third motivational orientation of skydivers as edgework. In this ascending segment of the subculture, practitioners framed skydiving as a way to push themselves to the very precipice of death, only managing to survive through poise and skill. The edgeworkers' account of the sport, in other words, was less focused on either visceral pleasure or transcendence, and more focused on whether the skydiver had the right stuff to handle the anxiety and pressure of a life-threatening situation. Like Mihaly Csikszentmihalyi's concept of flow, edgework requires total immersion in an embodied practice; individuals lose themselves in the task at hand. In edgework, though, the stakes are raised. A lapse in concentration can be disastrous. Thus, if flow crosses the threshold between boredom and anxiety, Lyng positions edgework well inside the territory of anxiety.[10]

While it is useful to distinguish between the flow experienced in a challenging game of chess and that felt during activities in which a person is flirting with his own mortality, the difference is one of degree, not kind. Lyng is correct to draw attention to the fact that edgeworkers find release in activities that the uninitiated would find highly stressful, if not terrifying. This may seem to be far beyond the happy medium of flow, but it is really just a more intense version of the same experience. While Lyng's respondents use adjectives like "stressful" and "anxious" to describe their experiences, their ability both to survive and to desire repetition prove that edgeworkers are (as Csikszentmihalyi's theory implies) simply engrossed in tasks perfectly matched by their skills.[11]

For the analysis provided in this chapter, the most pertinent aspect of Lyng's elaboration on the concept of edgework is that he locates the phenomenon within a particular sociohistorical period. Specifically, Lyng posits edgework as a response to the sense of alienation common in contemporary life. As discussed in the previous chapter, recreational pursuits like mountain climbing allow individuals the opportunity to develop and use their own skills to ensure their survival. Such a sense of personal efficacy is often absent in the institutional spheres of society. "People find in some leisure pursuits a requirement for the types of skills that have been systematically purged from the labor process under capitalist ownership and experience what they cannot in work—an opportunity for action that is conscious, purposive, concentrated, physically and mentally flexible and skillful." Specifically, edgeworkers find purpose in the most extreme instances of such experiences. Further, Lyng argues that the motivational orientation of edgework only makes sense within a culture in which people often feel bereft of agency.[12]

In many respects, parkour can be understood in terms similar to the motivational orientation of edgework. As this chapter's opening four vignettes highlight, the discipline's practices can represent an existential threat. As Nathan told me, "Catastrophic injury: it's a risk. It's a risk we're deliberately courting. Part of the fun is the fact that you could really get hurt if you did it wrong." However, parkour is a sporting practice that matured in the new millennium. As such, the vocabulary of motive surrounding parkour has transitioned from the accounts of Lyng and Snow's skydivers in the 1980s. In particular, traceurs' emphasis on assessing risk and managing fear has an affinity with neoliberal rhetoric—the economic discourse of postmodernity.[13] This is to say, traceurs' vocabulary of motive has shifted away from risk for risk's sake, and toward the *costs and benefits* of such risk taking. Concurrently, traceurs emphasize the *responsibility* of individuals to demonstrate that they can successfully negotiate the risks they take.[14] These rhetorical moves are part of the neoliberal perspective that increasingly shapes everyday interactions.

At the outset, it is important to note that this is not a causal argument—that neoliberal ideologies and policies are the cause of parkour's emergence or its growing popularity. Such a claim would be quite difficult to support and would require more than the ethnographic and interview data contained in this study. Instead, this chapter offers an analytic framework for critically assessing the meanings traceurs give their discipline, and proposes that parkour's vocabulary of motive resonates *with* the neoliberal rhetoric of postmodern culture. The way traceurs discuss parkour makes sense within the terms of neoliberalism, and it is difficult to imagine traceurs' discourse independent of the neoliberal context.

Of course, young people (males in particular) have long climbed on things, and attempting dangerous and foolish stunts is certainly not a new phenomenon. However, in the discipline of parkour, these actions have a particular motivational orientation that I call hedgework. Traceurs are more interested in hedging bets than they are in pushing the edge of survival. To be clear: the hedging I am describing is *symbolic*. It is not focused on the actual physical hazards practitioners face. No daredevil who lives past his first few stunts truly disregards safety. However, the symbolic framing—the vocabulary of motive—used for action varies. And, parkour, a sporting practice that arose within postmodernity, is couched in the terms of neoliberalism. That is, instead of glorifying bravery in the face of death, in place of praising a willingness to endure pain, traceurs tout their adherence to regimes of precaution—less daringness and more due diligence. Anecdotally, it seems other lifestyle sports and leisure pursuits are incorporating neoliberal rhetoric into their practices as well. Traceurs are not alone in being hedgeworkers; nonetheless, parkour epitomizes this new motivational orientation.

Neoliberal Risks

In literary critic Fredric Jameson's conception, postmodernism is the cultural logic of late capitalism. According to David Harvey, the time-space compression enabled by advancements in communication and information technologies, combined with the global flow of capital, disrupts social relationships and produces a fragmented sense of self and ethics. Taken together, these define what he considers to be the conditions of postmodernity.[15] Grand narratives (be they religious, scientific, or political) are viewed with incredulousness; taken-for-granted roles and identities are disrupted; reality is superseded by images of reality (pseudo-events and simulacra). Subsequently, as modernity's utopian promises of democratic equality and technological advancement fail to materialize, the supposed preeminence of markets stands in for social solidarity. Ergo, Harvey contends that neoliberal ideology flourishes in a popular culture that is cynical toward ethics, knowledge, and collective power. In his words, "That there is some connection between the postmodernist burst and the image-making of Ronald Reagan, the attempt to deconstruct traditional institutions of working-class power [. . . and], the masking of the social effects of the economic politics of privilege, ought to be evident enough."[16]

Neoliberalism, like postmodernity, is a term used in diverse ways. It is best conceptualized as a political project for the upward distribution of wealth.[17] Ideologically, neoliberalism gives primacy to the power of free trade, and the market is understood as the ultimate arbiter of human affairs. In actual practice, neoliberal policies seek to dismantle the welfare state while entrenching new forms of state power. The result is economic insecurity and unemployment for many segments of the population.[18] For the present discussion, it is most pertinent to attend to the fact that neoliberal rhetoric has become hegemonic. Politicians, political pundits, and ordinary people increasingly describe the world in market-oriented terms. As Harvey writes, "[Neoliberalism] has pervasive effects on ways of thought to the point where it has become incorporated into the common-sense way many of us interpret, live in, and understand the world." Or, in Bourdieu's phrasing, it is a "strong discourse" that "has on its side all the forces of a world of relations of forces, a world that it contributes to making what it is."[19]

A defining feature of neoliberalism is the new social significance it ascribes to risk. In sociologist Ulrich Beck's famous description, we now live in a risk society.[20] Risk society, it should be noted, does not refer to increasing danger but to attempting to control future consequences.[21] Hence, risk is a particular perspective on danger involving the assessment of potential hazards and attempts to mitigate those problems. Additionally, risk is not always negative. Successfully negotiated risk is rewarded. From the neoliberal perspective, harm only befalls those who imperfectly assess risks or who fail to take the necessary precautions. The market metaphor of this perspective should be readily apparent. Additionally, neoliberalism places a strong emphasis on personal responsibility in risk taking.[22] Individuals must be held accountable for assessing risks, and, as such, they deserve the rewards they reap or the harm they suffer.

One of the major consequences of neoliberal policies has been the shifting of collective risk onto individuals.[23] No single person has control over the environmental fallout of toxic sludge seeping into groundwater or over the economic impact of trade deals that incentivize factory closings. However, individuals are increasingly expected to adequately manage these matters. Ideologically, and in terms of policy, the potential role of the state is being removed from the equation. Families threatened by pollution should take "responsibility" to move to a new location (regardless of whether that is financially or socially feasible). Likewise, in a restructuring economy, workers must take the "initiative" to obtain new job skills (primarily through borrowing money to enroll in college courses).

Neoliberalism, in and of itself, is not contingent on urbanization or urbanism, but its ideologies and policies become manifest in urban development decisions.[24] In fact, Harvey connects the rise of neoliberalism in Western politics with the austerity programs instituted in New York City during the financial crisis of the 1970s. Sociologist Loïc Wacquant links the re-entrenchment of racial stigmatization and segregation to neoliberal policies on both sides of the Atlantic.[25] Even for more advantaged and affluent members of society, everyday urban life has been permeated with the hegemony of neoliberalism. This can be seen, for example, in architectural historian Ocean Howell's analysis of public skateparks. Howell argues that after years of resisting such facilities, municipalities now attempt to use skateparks to foster the character traits glorified in neoliberal ideology: personal responsibility, self-sufficiency, and entrepreneurialism.[26] Correspondingly, in the neoliberal city we see the localization of these broader social and political trends—from atrophying state support for disadvantaged citizens and policies that benefit elites to efforts at instilling free-market ideologies at the individual level.

Unlike Howell's analysis of skateboarding, which emphasizes the ways politicians and urban planners might see pedagogical value in lifestyle sports, the discourse of risk in parkour originates from traceurs themselves.

The neoliberal city is the backdrop for their grassroots application of these terms and ideas. As such, my analysis underscores the hegemony of free-market ideology and rhetoric. In chapter three we saw how testing one's character is an integral part of the parkour adventure, and in this chapter we will see how these risky practices are given meaning. In place of edgework's anarchism and nihilism, the symbols of safety and responsibility abound.[27] In this sense, traceurs can be thought of as hedgeworkers. Instead of asserting themselves as bold and brash, traceurs insist they are highly trained and calculating.

By thinking about parkour symbolism in this way, we get a sense of how large-scale structural forces become integrated into everyday life. That is, the traceurs in this study were not politically conservative, and none of them expressed any interest in economic theories. Indirectly, though, their leisure-time pursuits reflected the abstract cultural values promoted by neoliberalism. Thus, even if, as Michael Atkinson claims, parkour is "a mode of bringing forth or revealing dimensions of the physical and spiritual self through a particular type of urban gymnastics [that] destabilizes and disrupts technocapitalist meanings," traceurs do so within the lexicon of a free-market vocabulary.[28] "Ideology doesn't just happen," as sociologist Jay Coakley insists. Instead, as "highly valued and visible cultural practices, sports are sites at which neoliberalism is reproduced or resisted at the same time that they are influenced by neoliberal ideas and beliefs."[29]

The analysis that follows considers parkour training as involving the related practices of what I call rites of risk and the rituals of symbolic safety. These are what form the discipline's vocabulary of motive. Rites of risk pertain to the urban adventure of parkour. As discussed in the previous chapter, they provide the tests of character that serve as manhood acts for traceurs. In these rites, traceurs show they can manage their fears. Rituals of symbolic safety, on the other hand, give the discipline its meaningful frame. Without these rituals, parkour would be senseless danger for traceurs, but with them the experience of fear is given purpose. Instead of threatening to obliterate the self through pointless stunts, the discipline is understood as affirming the self. Individuals willingly confront challenges, and through their skill and poise they show they can persevere through these risks. Specifically, these rituals emphasize the ways in which traceurs calculate and assess risk. Again, my point here is on the significance of these claims as symbolic. There is no reason to believe traceurs are—in any objective sense—more or less safe than other young men involved in other lifestyle sports.

Rites of Risk

As we have already seen, the uncertainty of parkour primarily hinges on the potential for physical harm. In most cases traceurs are not risking their lives, but they are certainly making wagers with their flesh. Even the most basic jump can easily, and frequently does, result in painful mishaps.

Fear and Commitment

Because of the ever-present potential for injury, a good deal of parkour talk revolves around sensations of fright. Which is to say, practitioners do not deny experiencing fear. In fact, traceurs frequently referred to themselves as cowards. Cody, for example, told me, "I'm quite a pussy when it comes to pushing my limits." However, despite this claim, I personally witnessed Cody do an array of stunts that would have made the uninitiated blanch. Likewise, disregarding a rather impressive résumé of risk taking, Scales stated, "A lot of stuff—I just flat-out pussy out, honestly." The gendered nature of these comments further supports the argument from the previous chapter: manhood acts are demonstrations of traceurs resisting the urge to "pussy out." They managed their fear and showed themselves capable of action (like "men").

Rites of risk, therefore, involve not letting fear hold the traceur back. As David explained:

> [People are] physically capable of doing a lot more than they think they are, but it's [fear] holding them back. [. . .] A lot of it is not about getting rid of that fear, because that fear really does help in a lot of cases. In some sense it's a very good thing to know, "I physically can't do this. I shouldn't do it." A lot of times that's just not true, and learning how to recognize when you should just let go [. . .] is probably one of the hardest [aspects of parkour]. [. . .] It's something you really have to find for yourself, and it's something that I really like.

To put this succinctly, traceurs acknowledge that fear is necessary; sometimes the peril really is too great. After all, even the most talented practitioner can only jump so far, or successfully land from a height of so high. Conversely, when not faced with the outer limits of biomechanical potential, "you should just let go."

David provided his explanation about fear in the context of recounting an incident I had witnessed a day earlier at a jam. Several experienced traceurs were helping beginners learn the proper techniques for cat leaps. The drill involved running and jumping across a stairwell in order to cat the wall on the opposite side. Even as a mere spectator, I found the scenario terrifying. When David jumped the first time he said, "Oh shit" just as he took off. He made the cat leap, but he looked anxious. The instructor admonished him, "When you jumped, I'm pretty sure you said 'Oh shit.' [. . .] Freak out there [pointing to the start of the runway] not there [pointing at the takeoff position]." David did the jump a second time without shouting an expletive, but he was warned again, "Stay focused."

The point here is that David was not embarrassed by his fear, or even his faltering because of it. Working within himself to better manage his fear was something he claimed to enjoy. In many ways, David's efforts at this jump were similar to Shilo's kong to cat. Like David, Shilo was nervous, but felt compelled to push past his reservations. To repeat Shilo's quote, "It was fucking terrifying. [. . .] There was no point to it, but I did it because I was training." Similarly, Sync explained, "Fear is [. . .] a factor. [. . .] I would say eighty percent of parkour is in your head. Typically, physically you are able to do something, but it is the mindset that 'What if this happens? What if that happens?' Then you get scared of it. That fear is what would limit you. When people say that parkour is sort of a philosophical thing where you can overcome the obstacles physically, as well as mentally, that mental part, a lot of it is getting over fear."

These remarks by Sync, David, and Shilo all underline the importance of what traceurs refer to as commitment. In the social world of parkour, it is perfectly acceptable to feel fear. In fact, fear is necessary; lacking fear is problematic.[30] This was Martin's point about being comfortable, not confident. Parkour training requires one to become comfortable with the uncertainty of an outcome, but not necessarily confident about what the outcome will be. To this point, Sam explained:

There's so many things that could go wrong. Your foot could slip. You could not get enough power. Anything could happen. [. . .] I found out throughout the years [. . .], if there's a trick you're going to do, it's better to just commit entirely than bail in midair. That's when the serious injuries come about. [. . .] Everyone's always afraid of getting hurt. No one wants that to happen. When you [get into a trick] midair [and think] "Oh no, I'm not going to make it. I'm going to get hurt." You do whatever you can to prevent [from getting hurt, but] often times [it makes matters worse].

For Sam, therefore, learning to commit was about learning to calm his mind. "I definitely know [now] how to stay calm and focused. If I think about something else right before or in midair, if I'm distracted, even a little bit, things are going to go south."

As Sam implied, commitment is the opposite of ambivalence. When traceurs commit, they show they are determined to complete the maneuver—despite the risks involved. Take a hypothetical example of jumping from a ledge three feet off the ground to a brick wall of equal height six feet away. It is easy to imagine not committing to the jump: if you only jumped halfway across the gap, it would be pretty easy to land without injury. Alternatively, if you committed to the jump—hitting it at full speed and preparing to land on the wall—but made a mistake—slipping on the takeoff or not quite reaching the other wall—injury would be far more likely. Your body would be prepared for one type of impact, but you would experience another. The wrong muscles would be tensed—hands, feet, and knees all cocked at the wrong angles. Your contact would be jarring and painful.

Further, unlike this hypothetical example, to hesitate during a jump like David's or a vault like Shilo's could be disastrous. Once the maneuver is started, often there is only one way to not get injured—and that is to complete it successfully. This is underscored by Dylan's and Wexin's vaults. Had Dylan not been able to grab the side of the building, it is almost certain he would have died. Wexin seriously injured his knee, and it is easy to imagine a much worse scenario had he hit his head harder. Jaska offered an insightful explanation on these points:

> To do certain things you have to be physically fit to do it. [...] You also have to be mentally good for it as well. [...] A lot of moves, let's say you have the leg power to do a [ten-foot] precision [...] but if you don't focus and you don't visualize and think it through [...] you won't be able to make it [...]. [...] Your brain will try to make you bail, which is deadly. [...] It's when it's on the line where you're pretty sure you can do it, but it still *looks* scary and you can't out think it, that's when you're going to be halfway through [and] your reptile brain is going to say, "bail," and then it's going to be bad.

It is worth noting that Dylan and Wexin's vaults were not botched because of a failure to commit. However, traceurs do not really have a vocabulary for these types of mishaps. No one could claim that Dylan and Wexin were untrained. They were capable of doing the stunts they attempted, and they had performed similar maneuvers countless times previously. However, in these specific instances, they made mistakes when there was very little margin for error. Dylan's own reflections on his near-death experience are surprising in his seeming denial of the possible peril involved. "At the time, when I first looked at it, I didn't think 'Oh, this is a death-defying stunt.' I didn't look at it as anything more than a kong to cat. [. . .] I never would have thought that doing something so 'risky,' I guess, that's where I would make a mistake. So, when it happened I was in shock. It gave me the realization that no matter how much you train, no matter how certain you are of something, there's always that chance that something can happen."[31]

Dylan is expressing a key component of parkour's rites of risk. These rites are about traceurs committing to their maneuvers. The inevitability of human error does not factor into the equation. Instead, the point is to manage the fear that might hold the traceur back. Fright is what must be kept at bay. Again, feeling such unsettling emotions is acceptable; it is even expected. Letting fear dictate behaviors, though, violates the mores of the community.[32] In fact, APK made a short documentary about Dylan's "near-death experience and how he then overcame his fear and went back to conquer this monster kong to cat between two buildings."[33] Speaking of his return to that fateful spot to once again try the maneuver, Dylan stated, "[My fear] made me go through each and every step that usually happens at a subconscious level, but I brought it to consciousness. I figured out why I wanted to do it, and, really, the last piece was just getting myself to do it. I got up, and I was like, 'I just really want to do this.' [. . .] I just ran at the wall, and I made myself do it. It wasn't the prettiest kong I've ever done or anything, but it felt like such a relief and accomplishment for me."[34]

APK turned Dylan's failed stunt into a morality tale of trying again—recommitting to a stunt he now feared—in order to demonstrate the need for commitment (to successfully manage fear) in parkour. At the cat leap workshop, David was chastised for his hesitation, for not fully committing to the maneuver. Counsel similarly admonished students at one of his instructional workshops, 'I'd rather you go all out than give eighty percent and then not commit to something. That's how I tore my ACL. I did not commit, and I got hurt.' In the jump that tore his ACL, Counsel was attempting a precision that he knew was going to be difficult. As he understood it, his failure was not in attempting something too challenging, but in allowing himself to hesitate. Like APK's retelling of Dylan's saga, Counsel used this story not as a cautionary tale about the dangers inherent in training parkour, but as a cautionary tale about the hazards of not committing to one's movements. Traceurs must adequately manage their fear so that their actions are not inhibited. That is, if one is going to take part in the rites of risk, he or she must do so wholeheartedly.

Because managing fear lies at the core of the discipline of parkour, beginners in this study were encouraged to commit despite their doubts. Fear was frequently discussed as a mental block—an imaginary barrier to be surmounted. Strafe, for example, frequently made this an issue when instructing others. In his words, a failure to commit 'will create a mental block that you will never get over.' Further, in committing to actions that one fears, individuals discover new joys. That is, they open a part of the world previously closed to them. This, of course, is the essence of adventure— uncertainty leading to discovery. In Strafe's case, he claimed he used to be afraid of speed vaults, but noted, 'I was so scared of them I set out to learn them, and now they are my favorite vault.' In a similar vein, Max commented (as quoted in chapter two), "I used to have a fear of high drops, and I love them now. It's like a night-and-day thing for me with parkour. It's just awesome." Or, as Counsel stated, pushing through one's fears (in spite of them) "are what make parkour fun."

Commitment and Character

In sociologists Lori Holyfield and Gary Fine's study of adventure, they describe a program in which juveniles found guilty of minor felonies and misdemeanors are mandated by the court to complete a fear-inducing ropes course. The exercises are scary and stressful, but through teamwork and trust, the teens prevail (or so the instructors hope). The assumption is that the rope course will build character and that the teens will become better people. "To engage in the building of character via adventure is to take an emotional journey *inward*, to *feel* sensations, and to learn how to express appropriate emotions."[35] As described in the previous chapter, traceurs are taking the same type of journey. To practice parkour is to experience fear. In committing to action, though, traceurs manage their fear. That is, to truly take part in the discipline, individuals must not be stifled by the risks they face. Further, while learning to commit involves inward sensations, parkour is a collective journey. As we have seen, the traceurs often worked together in the development of their individual characters.

What was often notable about the parkour training I studied was its conflation with risk taking. Improvements to coordination and strength—which are absolutely essential to the successful completion of parkour maneuvers—were commonly the mere byproducts of traceurs' repeatedly practicing stunts. To quote David again, "[People are] physically capable of doing a lot more than they think they are, but it's [fear] holding them back." This is also reflected in Angela's point from chapter three about male traceurs only wanting to do "big stuff" and to have "fun." While female traceurs focused more on strength and conditioning, men in the community frequently assumed they had the physical ability to do various maneuvers. The most pertinent matter for them was commitment. That is, could they adequately manage their fear to attempt a stunt without reservation? As Cody explained:

> You can jump from this line from that line [motions to the concrete slabs in the sidewalk]. [If you] put it [off the ground] two feet, still no problem. Put it up ten feet, [you're] kind of a little bit hesitant now, right? Put it up a hundred feet. If you've done that [maneuver] a hundred times on the ground, and never messed it up once, why would you mess it up the one time you go up to a hundred feet up in the air? Once it's actually a risk, your brain starts to kick in. "This is stupid!" When you're on the ground, that exact same movement isn't even worth questioning. That's the irrational fear part. While you do have the risk [when you're higher off the ground], why would you fall that one time? There's just little to no chance. [. . .] Having that irrational fear can really shut you down. [Parkour involves] just learning how to push through that [fear and] lets you really push your boundaries.

Further still, the collective nature of such risk taking was often explicitly acknowledged. As discussed in chapter two, the joy of jamming in parkour is having an opportunity to push and be pushed by other traceurs. To quote Ando again, "You can surprise yourself, 'Wow, I actually could do that' when the pressure's on [. . .]." Or, as Sync said, "Let's see if you can do it."

As a rite of risk, parkour involves traceurs working together to commit individually to fateful action. That is, the parkour community provides a social environment (through the affective appropriation of the physical environment) in which traceurs can push themselves into affirming and building their character. They show to themselves (and to others) that they can act cool when the pressure is on. In Jaska's terms, they resist the reptilian brain's directive to bail. As Cody told me:

> When you see someone facing a jump that [...] really pushes them—something that they know is within their limits, but they cannot get themselves to commit to it—you get to see them break down to their most fragile positions. [...] People handle it differently. People get angry. People get sad. [...] I've seen people walk away. [...] Seeing people overcome that challenge [...] gives you a connection with them that you normally wouldn't have. Just by training with somebody, you can see them for who they are [...]. It's really hard to be fake when you're training and pushing yourself down to who you really want to be.[36]

In many ways, this type of character building is what advocates have always claimed participation in sports accomplishes. Sports are said to mold boys into men.[37] From a sociological perspective, though, what is especially interesting about parkour (and several other lifestyle sports) is the emphasis placed on individual risk taking within the context of an urban adventure among like-minded peers. While there is no formal competition—traceurs cannot "win" at parkour—every day practitioners can commit to do something that appears (or is) dangerous. Moreover, these risks happen within an otherwise prosaic setting; traceurs are carving action out of the uneventful and showing their willingness to experience adventure.

This will to urban adventure (and the chances for injury that it entails) is a rite. It is what those faithful to the discipline complete. Without participation in these rites of risk, a person cannot claim to be a traceur. This is to say, there are any number of people who *watch* parkour on YouTube videos and films who will never take part in the embodied practices. These individuals—removed from real-world commitments—cannot make credible claims to being a traceur. Rites of risk, therefore, are acts of membership. Individuals can only be full members of the social world if they actually take part in such acts. Moreover, as Emile Durkheim insists, participation in rites precedes beliefs.[38] In other words, traceurs' understanding of parkour's risks (and their significance for one's sense of character) arises from their participation in these rites. At the same time, rites of risk cannot be adequately understood in isolation. As the next section will show, parkour is a meaningful adventure for traceurs—it is a worthwhile test of character—because of the rituals of symbolic safety that define parkour as something more than action for action's sake.

Rituals of Symbolic Safety

The hypothetical example of standing on a three-foot-high ledge and preparing to jump across a six-foot gap to an opposing wall is a clear instance of carving action out of a seemingly uneventful environment. It is hard to imagine any objective need that would justify attempting this jump. On the contrary, our built environments are designed specifically to make pedestrian travel easy, efficient, and safe. Traceurs, however, appropriate the urban form for other ends. As Micca told me, "I look at stairs and I look at rails and I instantly see opportunities. Everywhere you look, even if you're just sitting in an auditorium, you randomly will just be like, 'Hmmm, I wonder what I would do there?'" As explained in the previous chapter, by "opportunities" Micca meant the potential for of action. When Micca looked at stairs and railings, he saw the chance to commit to something that might result in the pain of injury or the elation of success.

Risk and Progression

While it is true that traceurs find opportunities for adventure where others only see walls and stairwells, it would be wrong to think of traceurs as pathologically attracted to uncertainty. Erving Goffman rather disparagingly refers to "puddles of people" on the outskirts of society willing to disregard the safety and security the rest of us take for granted to feel the thrill of action.[39] Alternatively, parkour is steeped in a rhetoric of responsible training, and those who act out of control, or even speak brashly about danger, are quickly upbraided. For example, when I asked a newer participant at jams if he ever pushed his limits, he replied, in a proud and cocky tone, "Every day." Upon hearing this, ZK, a more experienced traceur, disapprovingly chimed in, "Don't get hurt. [...] That could get you killed."

Instead of lauding unrestrained courage, traceurs continually spoke of "progression"—slowly building up to more complex and dangerous maneuvers. As Brandon explained, "If you actually take it step by step and figure out your limits first and then work from there—and if you don't just [not] know your limits and [...] try to do something—you're going to get injured a whole lot less. Unless you're just doing something completely outrageous, you're not going to get hurt if you know your limits and you stay within them." By taking it step by step, traceurs mitigate the uncertainty of their action. The principle of progression creates an order and logic to their behaviors.

Risk, it is assumed, is buffered by following a set of progressive steps. Thus, Ryan T., a traceur who routinely performed maneuvers other Chicago traceurs were unable (or unwilling) to replicate, explained his abilities by stating, "A lot of people aren't like this, but I get excited from little progressions." As such, when Ryan vaulted across an enormous gap, he could cognitively fit that single maneuver into a much longer timeline of ascending complexity and danger. As Ando explained, "You really need to do your research, and do it in a logical and smart way. [...] Taking your time, taking small steps. You don't want to take really big jumps or really big gaps when you first start. You want to start small, practice, and get comfortable with your own body and anything else around you."

Ando went on to state that it is obvious when people have not taken the time to properly progress, and that such individuals are subtly sanctioned:

> You can tell [someone's experience level] by their body language: if they're stomping on the ground, landing really hard, their arms are moving in a weird way, or [their] legs are hitting the ledges all the time, they are just blindly going into stuff, just trying whatever on impulse. [...] It worries kind of everyone if [...] someone [is] doing something out of the ordinary for them. They're going to be approached, "Hey, why don't you have a seat? Why don't you chill and think about this? Let's go do something smaller first. We don't quite think you're quite ready for something like this."

That is, Ando not only asserted his personal dedication to safety, he also stressed the parkour community as collectively dedicated to responsible training.

During my time in the field, I never witnessed someone being specifically told to stop doing something, but I observed a great deal of boundary work. People who landed hard or moved "in a weird way" were quickly approached and given advice on how to improve their technique. These people were also the focus of much discussion when they were not present. For example, after a young (and particularly flamboyant) traceur was injured doing a flip, several of the community's more senior members used the occasion to criticize the injured traceur's lack of skill. Similarly, during an interview with a more experienced member of Aero, he critiqued a young traceur. "When I was talking about the reckless thing, he kind of came to mind. [...] He throws a lot of really big tricks. I haven't seen him get seriously hurt, but if you see him and compare it to somebody who's been doing it for years, you'll see a form difference. [...] It seems like he's more about, 'Oh, I really want to learn this trick. It's a hard trick. I'm going to go for it.' Instead of, 'Okay, I'm going to clean up the tricks I have.' I feel like we're the opposite in that way."

In both cases, there is no doubt that the senior members were capitalizing on an opportunity to solidify their status in relation to these rising stars' ever-brightening light. But, it is still instructive that the means by which this was done was through an appeal to the importance of slowly developed technique. Injuries and bravado do not need to be framed negatively at all. Young men in other sports often discuss pluck, injury, and suffering with pride.[40] In parkour, however, an injury (or merely looking like you are headed for an injury) was often used as proof that one did not adhere to the principles of progression.

The Symbols of Progression

Most essential to the analysis in this chapter is the obvious contradiction between commitment and progression. Traceurs must commit because they are fearful, and they are fearful because they might fail to execute a maneuver properly and hurt themselves. In extreme cases, a mistake can even be deadly. Alternatively, if progression is truly seamless, the fear one feels when preparing to jump the gap between two buildings should be no more than the fear a non-traceur would feel jumping over cracks in the sidewalk. As Luke explained, "Everything is done from the ground up. You start with the lazy vault. You start with the little precision. [...] You're progressing. You're getting better. [...] As you progress and as you get better, you're able to see more. [...] When you see something new, it's exciting. [...] If you're seeing it, it's because you can do it." "Seeing something new" was a reference to PK vision, and he implied that traceurs only notice the affordance they are capable of successfully completing. If this was totally true, managing fear as one progressed would be simple. Commitment would not be an issue.

However, when pressed, traceurs acknowledged progression was rarely seamless. For example, in describing an impressive flip Luke and I witnessed at the 2014 Colossal Jam (see figure 12 in chapter two), Luke explained, "That situation would be the make-it-or-break-it mindset. There's definitely a time where it's make it or break it." Luke's point was that some maneuvers cannot be slowly progressed up to. "You get it or you don't and you're going to be hurting. [. . .W]hen I did my first kong-gainer [i.e., a kong vault into a backward flip while the body continues to move forward], that was not a calm kong-gainer. That's make it or break it. It's exhilarating, yet terrifying. It's learning to recognize when your brain—or whatever it is—when it's like, 'Okay, we're doing it.' [It is] in that moment when [you need] to go. [. . .] Most of the time you get it then. There's only been a few times when [I] didn't [successfully make the maneuver]." In other words, the discipline of parkour requires traceurs to negotiate a balance between the rites of risk—which are essential to character—and the principle of progression.

Mostly, progression is a way of *talking* about one's actions. Like all athletic talents, parkour skills improve with practice, but traceurs use the principle of progression as a rhetorical device for justifying and rationalizing the risks they take. To peel back the illusion promoted within parkour, the principle of progression is a symbol, and training in terms of progression is a ritual process in which the traceur affirms the importance of self against the destructive potential of his or her stunts. Lyng, for example, insists that skydivers (even those who seemingly relish danger) do not believe they are gambling with their lives.[41] On the contrary, they believe they have the necessary skills to survive the hazards they encounter. In parkour, talk of progression is mated with phrases including appropriate risk, calculated risk, risk assessment, and safety precautions. The traceurs who are progressing properly are not, as Ando put it, "just trying whatever on impulse." Instead, they believe they are responsibly developing their skills over time by calculating their risk taking and making appropriate decisions based on the necessary safety precautions.

Talk of progression, therefore, is a ritual of symbolic safety.[42] Whereas rites are acts of membership and faith, rituals are the prescribed modes for carrying out symbolic actions.[43] For example, among Christians, the Eucharist is a rite in which devotees consume bread and wine in remembrance of Christ's Last Supper. Rituals, by contrast, are composed of such rites, which is to say, the Eucharist is set within a series of formulaic behaviors that (explicitly and implicitly) denote the sanctity of the event. Receiving the bread and wine is not treated in the same manner that one might accept a light snack. Most importantly, rituals are communicative performances.[44] Rituals are public events, and they signal to those gathered that all involved belong to the same community of meaning. Thus, a lone Christian can perform the *rite* of the Eucharist, but it is only through its public enactment with others of the faith that it becomes a *ritual*. Further still, and following Durkheim, the meaning of the Eucharist emerges from its communal enactment.[45]

Returning to parkour and the ritualistic use of symbolic safety, talk of progression is a way for traceurs to frame events as positive or negative. What might appear as an incessant parade of foolish maneuvers to outsiders can be assessed by traceurs as worthwhile or worthless objectives, depending on how the traceurs performing them are able to appeal to the ideal of studious training. Even totally brazen stunts, like Dylan's kong from a multistory parking deck to an adjacent building, can fit into the symbolic framework of progression. After all, Dylan is a remarkably fit young man who has spent years training in the discipline. At the same time, while risk taking is praised in some instances, certain people are chastised for it. As Ando explained, if individuals appear to have not progressed properly, their actions are scrutinized. Those who successfully use the talk of progression make clear that they belong to the community of those that value the self. That is, they are individuals who take calculated risks, not reckless actions.

Symbolic Practices

While progression is a form of ritualized talk, stretches and warming-up exercises are forms of ritualized practice that symbolize safety for traceurs. Of course, warming up and stretching muscles and joints before strenuous exercise does reduce the risk of certain types of injuries and can improve athletic performance. The traceurs were keenly aware of this, and they discussed these activities with grave seriousness.[46] In fact, injuries were often attributed to not warming up. One traceur, for example, accounted for his sprained wrists by explaining that the incident happened 'the only time [he] didn't do joint stretches first.' In the same fashion, senior members of the community would often claim that the long-term, pervasive problems with their joints were the result of youthful ignorance about stretching when they first started training. Alternatively, some traceurs attributed their lack of injury to what they felt was their naturally imbued flexibility.

Stretching and warming up were used as an extension of the principle of progression. That is, the first step in responsible training was to prepare muscles and joints for the impacts and strains of parkour. This was part of assessing risk and taking safety precautions. Accordingly, one of the more surprising aspects of the jams I first attended—especially in light of the fact that the jams were organized by young men, some still in high school— was the practice of regimented calisthenics and stretching routines at the beginning of the events. In a format similar to a martial arts class, a few traceurs would lead the rest of the group through a series of movements. Some jams lacked specified conditioning and stretching periods, but other events actually made such activities a primary focus. Even when built into the day's proceedings, not everyone always wanted to participate. Some people wandered off during these rituals, only to return once more exciting activities were underway. Alternatively, when there was no specified time to warm up, many traceurs did so anyway. Whether prompted by others or not, some traceurs consistently warmed up before training. Most, though, were inconsistent. More importantly for the present discussion, however, was that even when people did decide to stretch or warm up, this often did not coincide with the start of their training for the day.

Stories of the injuries borne by those who failed to stretch and the preventative powers attributed to flexibility, along with the inconsistent timing for warming up, draw attention to these practices as symbolic. That is, traceurs' incorporation of stretching and warm-up routines cannot be explained on purely physiological grounds. A useful example comes from a gym training session I attended. Several people arrived at the gym early, and the session itself started a little late. In the interim, everyone, aside from myself, was engaged in some sort of parkour training. Several people, including one of the event organizers, were doing very complex flips and vaults. In order for them to get the height and distance required, these traceurs were fully exerting themselves. This high-intensity activity went on for at least ten minutes, but it was not until the gym session officially started that anyone did stretches. Further, even though everyone (aside from myself) was thoroughly warmed up, the usual warm-up protocol was followed. We did a mid-tempo jog around the gym to "activate the muscles," which was followed by stretches. This was the typical order of things at jams. People arrived early, trained hard, and then, once the jam officially started, they would perform the ritual. Some people warmed up and stretched on their own, but the majority of people (the majority of the time) performed the actions in an order that greatly reduced (if not totally nullified) the stated health benefits.

As a form of symbolic safety, however, the ritual of warming up and stretching was potent.[47] Like talk of progression, these practices were believed to mitigate the risks involved in parkour. Further, by participating in the ritual, traceurs demonstrated that they were not reckless fools, even though they were subjecting themselves to the rites of risk. They were serious about their safety. Ultimately, there was an important divide between those who successfully demonstrated a symbolic commitment to safety and those who did not. For example, one afternoon Strafe expressed his frustration with the attendees at a recent jam. During the warm-up exercises, Strafe said that many people 'just want to stand around and talk.' He then dismissed the sincerity of these individuals stating, 'It means there [are] less people I need to wrangle with, and it allows me to focus on the people that really want to learn.' Strafe saw the people who were not interested in warming up and stretching as insincere and thus undeserving of his knowledge as an instructor. For Strafe, being interested only in the risk taking of parkour was understood as meaningless. As Cody insisted, "There's going to be people that train wrong and stupid. That's always going to happen. I don't really consider them [as] doing the same thing [as me]. [. . .] It's just people that don't even think about their limits. [. . . They are] purely reckless. That's where the philosophy [of the discipline comes in]. It's training to make yourself stronger and pushing yourself to be better."

Over the course of my research, many members of Aero became less regimented about stretching and integrating conditioning exercises into their jams. Other practices, though, took their place. During the last year of my fieldwork, many traceurs began emphasizing the importance of healthy eating. As a case in point, during our interview, Zach listed various injuries he sustained. The most serious was a neck injury from playing on a trampoline. This injury happened before he was involved in the parkour community. When I asked how he was trying to prevent such injuries in the future, his immediate response was, "Eating better. Paying more for high-quality food." Likewise, Pasha discussed psyching himself up for a technical maneuver by telling himself, "We ate good food. [. . .] I can make it." For his part, Wolf told me that over the years he had learned a great deal about avoiding injuries. "I know better recovery methods, proper nutrition, so on and so forth. I know how to eat with the seasons. [. . .] Most definitely [these measures will help prevent injuries]. One thing I actually do to help build up all of my tendons and ligaments [. . .] is eat lots of bone broth."

Most notably, as gyms became a more ubiquitous aspect of training, these facilities were incorporated into rituals of symbolic safety. Specifically, traceurs began using indoor training to validate their outdoor risk taking. Alex provided a useful illustration:

> I always train in the gym. When I try a new move, I think of a way to set it up appropriately in the gym without injuring myself. The more I train, the more comfortable I am with my body—the less careful I have to be. [. . . Gyms are] how I become comfortable [with a maneuver]. [. . .] If I'm even messing up in between good landings, I will not bring it outside. That's when you start to get injured. If you do it once [or twice] in the gym and then you bring it outside—that's what I consider reckless. If it's slop, and you land like chicken legs—they like start shaking when you land—you shouldn't be doing it outside. That's reckless.

Likewise, Sam explained, "For me, what I like to do is just practice enough to do whatever [I'm] trying to do [to develop] muscle memory [in a gym]. [. . .] If I feel like I'm ready to try something outside, I'll go through the motions in the gym. I'll imagine myself doing it [outside the gym]." Nearly identically, Steven told me, "I like to train very safely. [. . .] I do things in a safe environment, and then transfer them to the real, concrete environment. [. . . You use] a gymnastic gym first. [You] try to train with squishy mats as much as possible first, then once you're ready, then you can train more on concrete stuff."

It is imperative to stress here that, just as stretching and warming up mitigates some forms of injury, learning high-velocity, technical maneuvers in a padded environment obviously reduces the risks involved. Slamming one's head onto the padded floor of a gym is less dangerous than doing so on the sidewalk. However, there are two sociologically interesting points here. First, no traceurs advocated limiting parkour training only to the gym. Over and over, practitioners insisted that "real parkour" takes place outside. As Stephan told me, "The definition of parkour is to traverse the urban environment. If you're in a gym, there's nothing really to traverse." It is for this reason that when I asked Sam why he did not confine his activities entirely to the gym he replied, "I don't know. That's a good question. For me, I just feel like I'm conquering a fear of mine. You can do anything in a gym. It's really easy. It's no problem. When you're out here, [. . .] you can't half-ass it and think you'll be fine. You have to fully commit yourself to it. That's also what appeals to me about parkour. You're shutting out that fear, or at least learning to work with it [and] work around it. You're doing these things that people think you're crazy for doing." Similarly, Miko also discounted the maneuvers that individuals can only perform within the safety of the gym:

> I think [training] outside is when you know whether or not you can throw something [i.e., complete a maneuver]. You have to commit a hundred percent of the time. In a gym you can bail halfway through it and you'll be okay. You can't bail outside. [. . .] In a gym I will do really long kongs, just dive into [them]. It won't be a problem. [. . .] I'm not scared. The floor's padded; the obstacle's padded. Outside, I can maybe do a kong that's half that size. Everything is concrete. If people ask me which [vaults] I can do, I will say the ones I can do outside. [. . .] My brain is still preventing me from doing really big [maneuvers outside]. The fear is still there.

Second, traceurs almost always emphasized gym training in relation to mitigating the risks of the discipline. As just explained, though, such safety precautions were always positioned as a pedagogical resource. They allowed one to learn a maneuver without the danger of serious injury; they also provided a strategy for *talking* about training. In this latter sense, the gym is a symbolic object. It is a way to demonstrate to others that the traceur knows how to "train very safely." Unlike the idiomatic rookie who is said to try "whatever on impulse," responsible traceurs methodically plot out their goals and slowly progress up to them. For example, ZK told me, "I drill it on the really easy things to get my form better. Right now I'm working on a [kong vault into] a ten-foot drop. [. . .] Now I'm just working on getting my kong distance right, getting my hand placement right, and then once I feel I've gotten that down, all it is is just the music in my head and the people watching." And, gyms became an important part of this symbolic progression—a way to assure others that the traceur cares about the self.

Meaningless Risks

The treatment of Arnold, the traceur from chapter three who flipped into the Chicago River, offers valuable insights into the importance of symbolic safety rituals. There is no doubt that Arnold relished taking part in rites of risk. He routinely refused to "pussy out." In addition to his river jump, there is a YouTube video of him jumping a petrifying gap between a five-level parking garage and a three-story building. This stunt was quite similar to Dylan's kong to cat, but it was less technically challenging. Regardless, Arnold propelled himself across a span of nearly thirteen feet as he descended over ten feet, risking a plummet of at least forty feet (see figure 25). It was most certainly a fateful moment. Arnold also bragged about intentionally falling onto thirty light bulbs and having the stunt aired on television. But, despite his commitment to such adventure, Arnold occupied a marginal position in the Chicago parkour community.

Arnold's low status among most other traceurs, while certainly not helped by his grating personality, stemmed from his failure to combine his risk taking with the appropriate respect for the symbols of safety. What Arnold communicated to others in the community was that he was cavalier about his physical well-being. His urban adventures tested his character, but the self that emerged from the trials was one the other traceurs did not respect. Unlike most traceurs, Arnold did not highlight his efforts at training safely. By most people's account, he did not seem to be hedging his bets at all. Instead, he cultivated the image of going into stunts half-cocked. In response, others in the community felt he had not adhered to the principles of progression. Arnold's efforts to portray a daredevil persona were openly displayed when he talked with newcomers at jams. In contrast to the usual script of stressing calculated and properly assessed risks, he would eagerly spout off a list of outlandish stunts he had performed to anyone who would listen.[48] Further, around other traceurs Arnold expressed little interest in conditioning and stretching—again distinguishing himself from those "that really want to learn."

At the opposite extreme was Ryan, who studiously adhered to the principles of progression. I watched Ryan do countless dangerous things, but he performed them in a manner that seemed more akin to the artistry of

FIG. 25. Arnold jumped from the top of this five-level parking garage (right) to the roof of the neighboring three-story building (left).

Baryshnikov than the antics of Evil Knievel. It is hard to imagine Ryan wanting to jump into a polluted river or onto a pile of light bulbs, but, methodical approaches aside, Ryan also took great risks in his training. The difference was in his presentation—and in his reception. To provide just one example among many, I watched Ryan perform a massive jump between two low-lying walls near the Van Buren Street Metra station (see figure 26). While far less dramatic than Arnold's leap from the roof, the speed and distance required for Ryan's jump also left little room for error.

FIG. 26. Video still of Ryan T.'s massive jump near the Van Buren Street Metra Station.

Over- or undershooting the landing could have easily resulted in serious bodily harm. Of course, as was almost always the case, Ryan executed the maneuver flawlessly. Both Ryan and Arnold were engaged in the same types of adventure. They wanted to carve action out of an otherwise uneventful urban environment. Conversely, their different orientations to the rituals of symbolic safety resulted in very different tests of character.

Ryan preached regimentation, and his demeanor was staid. In every aspect, he embodied the principle of progression. In chapter three, he is quoted praising the virtues of repetition and adherence to arduous training regimes. In many ways, though, he was the exception that proved the rule. Few traceurs consistently demonstrated Ryan's ascetic approach to the discipline. Instead, most reflected Arnold's more whimsical version of training. But, it was traceurs like Ryan to whom all practitioners claimed allegiance. Even Arnold, shenanigans aside, would occasionally insist on his adherence to responsible training, but he did so inconsistently and in a manner others found unconvincing.[49] By contrast, most traceurs (even those who spent a lot of time goofing off) successfully buttressed their risk taking in parkour with rituals of symbolic safety. This allowed them to view their actions as meaningful, and it allowed others in the parkour community to share this perception.

Traceurs as Hedgeworkers

In closing this chapter, I want to again stress that while traceurs occasionally suffer serious injuries or near-fatal incidents, the day-to-day risks they face are generally quite mundane—mostly scrapes and sprains. When compared with other threats to our mortality (automobile travel being one of the most common, nuclear disaster being one of the more horrifying), the potential hazards posed by training in parkour are almost trivial. What is not trivial, though, is gaining a better understanding of the methods people use to symbolically mitigate risks when they intentionally place themselves in harm's way. By studying parkour we develop sharper theoretical insights into the rites and rituals that allow fateful moments to become tests of character. We also see glimpses of how young people adapt to life in the neoliberal city. Abstract ideologies and political initiatives are given interpersonal meaning. To quote Coakley one more time, "Ideology doesn't just happen." Instead, sporting practices become one of the ways cultural values are given shape.

Ultimately, for those inclined to find it, fateful action is always easy to come by, but having such moments become individually and collectively meaningful requires an involved social process. Insulting a stranger, jumping a subway turnstile, booking an airline ticket and leaving town with no notice to friends and family: the opportunity to take a potentially life-altering action lurks around every corner—should a person choose to look. For most people, most of the time, such actions are so nonsensical they do not even register as options. Some risky actions, however, do make sense to some people, at least some of the time. This requires a vocabulary of motive to align practices within a given community of meaning.

As we have seen, in parkour this process begins with rites of risk. These actions induce fright, but traceurs work to manage their fears. The corporeal self is put on the line, and the individual commits to the challenge at hand. Such rites show faith and membership in the discipline of parkour. Despite the danger inherent in their actions, traceurs do not view themselves as wanton thrill seekers. While rites of risk require working the edge, traceurs emphasize the ways in which they hedge their bets. To this end, the social world of parkour is filled with rhetorical appeals to safety and overt displays of precaution. To adequately grasp the urban adventure of parkour, therefore, it is essential to understand how traceurs situate their rites of risk within rituals of symbolic safety.

It is through collectively enacted, communicative performances that parkour becomes more than a senseless death wish. Talk of progression, stretching and warm-up exercises, claims of good nutrition, and gym training all help assert the sacredness of the self. And, it is only when the self has been demonstrated as something valuable for the traceur that the rites of risks in parkour can have meaning. As David Le Breton writes of extreme sports, "Going right on to the end of the self-imposed task gives a legitimacy to life and provides a symbolic plank on which they can rely."[50] Concurrently, in parkour, at least, the symbolic plank is actually generated in ritualistic adherence to the ideals of safety. Such safety may be illusory (in a scientifically objective sense), but for traceurs it turns personally dangerous moments into socially significant events.

While there is nothing historically unique about young men doing hazardous and outlandish stunts, parkour's vocabulary of motive resonates with the neoliberal rhetoric of postmodern culture. Specifically, in parkour, edgework becomes hedgework. The self is shown as sacred precisely because of the willingness to face risk in a calculated, responsible manner. In a world in which individuals are increasingly expected to assume personal responsibility for navigating socially produced risks, the rites and rituals of parkour provide one way for young people to assert their preparedness for the uncertainties that will inevitably define their adult lives. Thus, if as anthropologist Clifford Geertz suggests, cockfights teach the Balinese what it looks like for a man in a status-driven society to symbolically lose everything,[51] maybe parkour provides young men and women with metaphorical displays of the caution and courage required to succeed in the neoliberal city.

Conclusion

• • • • • • • • • • • • • • • • • • • •

Appropriating the City

When Georges Hérbert promoted his *méthode naturelle,* he was react-
ing against perceptions of modern indolence. Science, technology, and an
ever-expanding array of consumer goods promised to make life easier, but
Hérbert worried these conveniences made people weak in mind, body, and
spirit. By training in the rigors of the parcours, though, Hérbert insisted men
and women could develop a moral sense of self. They could "be strong to be
useful." The legacy of Raymond Belle exemplifies this vision of the parcours.
From French Indochina to Paris, it is said that the elder Belle combined his
corporeal talents with outright bravery in the service of others. Inspired by
the mythic tales of his father, David Belle took up the challenge of training
the parcours. However, the younger Belle did not just train the parcours. He
and his friends adapted it to fit into their teenage lives and their youthful
fantasies. This is to say, they were not training for civil or military service.
These young men were running and jumping through the banlieues because
it could be fun. They challenged themselves with arduous, daring feats, and
they honed their athletic skills. As Sébastien Foucan recalled, "It became
our game. [. . .] We would play at being ninja, superheroes. [. . .] It was all in
our imagination. [. . .] So, the years passed, and our game carried on, and we
progressed until we were able to face [more significant] heights and jumps."[1]

A Quintessential Postmodern Sport

When thinking about the genesis of parkour, it is paramount to appreciate that Belle, Foucan, Yann Hnautra, and the rest of that original group incorporated parcours into the built environment of the French suburbs. They did not merely train parcours *in* the banlieues; the Brutalist architecture of the postwar years *became* the parcours itself. These "dull and isolated places" were reimagined.[2] Utilitarian features of the cityscape—rooftops, stairwells, and walls—became sites of playful risk taking. These degree-zero spaces were infused with new forms of significance through the group's flow-inducing games. Of course, climbing, jumping, and running are ubiquitous in childhood. What set the founders of parkour apart was their codification of such play. Their activity became something more akin to a discipline. It was something to be trained. There were specific movements, and these movements were highly refined. The goal was not merely to provide kinetic efficiency; the goal was to have style—aesthetic flair. Speaking of his younger brother, Jeff Belle explained, "Instead of stopping at a reasonable point, [David] just kept going."[3]

Eventually, and with Jeff's help, the group's nascent discipline drew interest from the media. Advertisers and filmmakers saw potential for marketing a new lifestyle sport—a Z-Boys for the new millennium.[4] It is unclear if the promises of money frayed the bonds of friendship or if fame merely came along too late, but the original group splintered soon after their initial television coverage. Belle and Foucan emerged as the most prominent figures of the new sport. They made flashy commercials and starred in movies. And, following along with this mainstream attention came a growing stream of young people—mostly teenage boys—who wanted to learn the discipline for themselves. With the documentary *Jump London*, what had been an obscure activity from France became accessible to English-language audiences. In turn, Urban Freeflow's website served as the central hub for English-speaking traceurs throughout the world.

The original business model in parkour—to the extent that there was a model at all—was based around a handful of prominent practitioners landing roles in commercials and movies. Urban Freeflow helped usher in the second generation of parkour profit-making based around sportization. UF developed relationships with companies, sponsored athletes, promoted competitions, and sold parkour merchandise. Running in tandem with UF were American Parkour (APK; which was started by a former affiliate of UF) and the World Freerunning and Parkour Federation (WFPF). These second-generation organizations still maintained performance teams that did commercial work, but the emphasis was on increasing participation in the activity and marketing the sport—all of which was buttressed by establishing a brand and selling clothing emblazoned with it. Today, over a decade after *Jump London* aired, the contemporary parkour business model still involves merchandising and performing, but the sportization of the discipline has moved away from the large-scale competitions promoted by UF (Red Bull's Art of Motion being the notable exception) and toward offering paid instruction for beginners (especially young children). Along with this training came the formal certification of instructors and purpose-built gyms. This new business model is exemplified by Parkour Generations (PKGen). Several parkour organizations, large and small, have also begun to expand and professionalize their merchandising. Companies have moved beyond just screen-printing logos on t-shirts to actually designing sneakers and more technical clothing, which they advertise in online catalogues rivaling those of any major corporate retailer.

Affectively Appropriating Urban Space

The defining features of parkour are encapsulated in what I call the affective appropriation of space. The discipline involves stylized athletic movements that are realized by traceurs reimagining the built environment. When journalists and academics have written about parkour—or even when traceurs themselves describe their activities—appropriation of the material world is a common focus. This is the essence of the discipline's appeal. Without reimagining the urban form, parkour would just be gymnastics. To quote Pasha again, "Your imagination creates ways [for] how you would go through these roofs by using parkour. People who don't know what parkour is, they would just look at these roofs, and their imagination wouldn't do anything with that. People who do parkour, they have [a] completely different [...] imagination."

The spatial appropriations of the discipline are important because, as Henri Lefebvre argues, the material world has obdurate qualities, and this reifies the social relations that produced it.[5] This is to say that, once built, the concrete, glass, and steel of a downtown business district can seem immutable. A universe of contingencies is narrowed down by profits and politics, with the matter-of-fact yet undeniably imposing facades of corporate centers demonstrating whose special interests have won. At the same time, such abstract spaces can also be utilized for other means. Official conceptions of space and everyday perceptions of them can be overturned by creative spatial practices. A built environment that had heretofore seemed only to afford one set of activities explodes with new possibilities. A structure designed to allow pedestrians or motorists safe egress now becomes a ladder for reaching what had been an inaccessible nook.

This spatial potential is why so many youths are enamored with graffiti and skateboarding, too. Such activities allow participants to lay claim to their physical surroundings in unauthorized and exciting ways. The anonymity of the metropolis is erased by turning subway cars into personal billboards. The monotony of the shopping mall is disrupted by grinding its curbs. This is also why graffiti artists' and skaters' relatively minor transgressions—paint and scuff marks—can evoke such strong reactions from those who seek to maintain the existing social order.[6] If spatial appropriations threaten to overturn taken-for-granted assumptions, then from the perspective of those in power, there are good reasons to police those practices.

Writing about skateboarding, Iain Borden discusses the intersection of body, board, and terrain.[7] Skaters interface with the space through which they travel. Following sociologist Anthony Giddens, in this sense, structures—typically seen as constraints to action in social theory—have to be appreciated as equally enabling of those actions.[8] In other words, the seemingly agentic practices of graffiti writers, skateboarders, and traceurs are made possible by the very structures they appropriate. Their transgressions do not happen in spite of such structures; they happen through them. We have seen this throughout the book as practitioners reimagine the affordance of the built environment. For all of traceurs' creativity, parkour cannot simply occur in any given space; the material world is inseparable from the process.

Because spatial appropriations require an engagement with the material world, the discipline is also an embodied practice. To be in the world is to be engaged with one's corporeal self. While much of everyday life can be alienating, there are moments in which all people become highly attuned to what they are doing. Mihaly Csikszentmihalyi refers to this as flow, and he considers such engrossment in the task at hand as an optimal experience.[9] The flow experience is actively sought out and deeply enjoyed. Csikszentmihalyi adopted the term "flow" because the individuals he studied frequently used it themselves. Likewise, traceurs refer to a long series of maneuvers as a "flow run" or practicing the transitions between maneuvers as "flow work." And, it is no coincidence that Paul "EZ" Corkery named his organization Urban Free*flow*.

The experience of flow is at the heart of both play and rituals. When either is successful, the activities take on a quality of unquestionable reality. Clifford Geertz describes this as the "really real."[10] This is to say, flow states feel subjectively profound, and when experienced collectively, these subjective feelings take on an objective quality. To quote Eric again, "It's a very, I'm going to say, spiritual [experience]—not in a religious context, but in a context that has to do with understanding the self in a manner that creates [...] great joy and relaxation. [...] I don't want to call it nirvana, because that's not technically correct. I'm going to use the term 'moksha'—awareness of the universe." Individually or collectively, the flow of parkour happens in and through the built environment. It is the affective appropriation of space, and it is a dialectical process. Which is to say, it is in seeking out flow that traceurs reimagine the material world, and it is in this reimagining that practitioners become engrossed in their embodied practices.

The concept of affective spatial appropriation is integral to the argument laid out in this book. Chapter two considered the global ethnoscape of parkour. In that chapter we saw how traceurs' use of new media intertwines with their reimagining of the city. Perceptions and experiences of urban life are altered as virtual worlds and the real world continually feed back into each other. Chapter three looked at how traceurs' affective appropriations of space constitute urban adventures. In particular, young men are attracted to these types of activities because they have the potential to affirm culturally valued attributes of masculinity. Chapter four built on these previous two chapters to offer an analysis of risk and safety as critical to the meaning traceurs give to their affective appropriations of the city.

Dialectic of the Virtual and the Real

Arjun Appadurai discusses the ideas and images circulating through new media as global ethnoscapes that allow individuals to rethink what is possible at the local level.[11] As we have seen, parkour exemplifies this concept. Most would-be traceurs first learn about the activity from spending time on the Internet. By and large, it is YouTube videos that reveal new prisms of the possible for these individuals. As ZK recalled, "Oh, wow. They're running, jumping, flipping. I enjoy watching this. I could probably do this if I put in the time." Even after someone becomes a seasoned practitioner, the Internet continues to be an integral aspect of their participation in the community. Showreels, tutorials, and posts to social media inspire traceurs and help shape their training. In short, life on screen is a ubiquitous part of experiencing parkour.

The discipline's portrayal through new media is not truly analogous to the activity as it exists in the real world. In this sense, like so much of postmodern culture, parkour can be considered as simulacra—edited and framed to highlight the spectacular. Photographs and videos are never more than approximations of the events they purport to represent. The planning and practice that go into stunts are removed, as are the false starts and aborted attempts.[12] What remains is a procession of disjointed actions fused together in a form that can only be experienced virtually. In other words, the on-screen depictions of parkour are a montage of movements collected across time and space, stitched together into a cohesive whole and usually set to music. Most notably, traceurs own participation in the discipline often becomes subservient to the requirements of producing what Daniel Boorstin calls pseudo-events.[13] When the camera is rolling (and it frequently is), visceral moments get evaluated less in terms of immediate experience and more in terms of how they will appear when spliced together for consumption on the screen.

At the same time, for all its mediated aspects, parkour is also an embodied practice. Without bodies in motion—and the attendant somatic sensations—there could be neither flow nor spatial appropriation. Traceurs become engrossed in their activities because, not only are the tasks challenging, there are also real consequences to what they are doing. Those too flippant about their physically situated selves will not last long as traceurs. As such, while parkour may be inseparable from the interplay of signs circulating within the virtual world, it cannot be reduced to simulacra. Instead, as traceurs train, the global ethnoscape of parkour becomes instantiated through traceurs' off-screen activities. The on-screen is impossible without the off-screen, and vice versa.

PK vision and the dialectic of the virtual and the real are highlighted in chapter two by Tommy's efforts to find a spot to perform a double kong vault. Tommy learned about the maneuver watching videos of traceurs from Europe, but he had to scour suburban Chicago to find just the right obstacles to attempt the movement himself. As Appadurai emphasizes, mediated ideas and images alter the imagined possibilities of individuals throughout the world. To be realized, though, these new prisms of the possible must be interfaced with the traceur's body and his local environment. Practitioners must venture out into the real world and put their bodies into motion, and this requires reimagining the types of movements afforded in one's physical surroundings.

Urban Adventures and Manhood Acts

In pursuing the optimal experience of flow, traceurs make use of the city in risky ways. Practitioners carve action out of otherwise prosaic environments. Sometimes their urban adventures are social in nature—for example, passive-aggressively taunting security guards or hitting on women. Usually, though, traceurs are interested in reimagining the affordances of physical space. Walls become structures to climb; stairwells become cavernous pits to jump across. To seek out these risks and tempt fate involves demonstrating one's power and control. These vagaries of the environment must be bested, and to do this one must be in command of his body and stay cool under pressure. Thus, these adventurous actions align with contemporary Western notions of masculinity, and participating in them tests one's masculine character. From this analytic vantage point, parkour involves manhood acts, to use Michael Schwalbe's term.[14] Through training, a traceur can positively affirm his identity as a "man." Or, to put this somewhat differently, the manhood acts of parkour help distinguish those who successfully adhere to the cultural attributes of masculinity and those who do not.

As we saw in chapter three, the city provides a series of structural resources for traceurs' gendered performances. First, the physical form of the city affords certain movements—and not others. For example, construction scaffolding allows for lachés, and mulch makes for a softer landing after a long drop. The PK vision inspired through the global ethnoscape of the discipline helps transform the built environment into obstacles that constrain and enable action. To quote Jaska again, "Whenever there's one of those little scaffold things I can't help but under-bar through it and then go back to walking like I'm a normal person." By appropriating space, and putting their bodies on the line in the process, traceurs align their discipline with manhood acts.

Second, the crowds of strangers who fill the city provide another structural resource that traceurs make use of in their gendered performances.

Practitioners' power and control over themselves and the environment must be validated for their performances to have any significance. Therefore, it is onlookers who consummate the traceurs' bravery in the face of peril. The applause and shocked expressions of their ad hoc audiences give traceurs claim to culturally valued attributes of masculinity. As Cody said, "It's when you do a flip and all the kids are like 'Whoa!' [. . .] That's probably one of the best feelings from training, just doing something and hearing kids losing their mind. [. . .] I also like crowds because it means people are fascinated with what you do. It means they like seeing what you're doing."

When researchers study male-dominated social worlds like parkour, it is common to question why more women do not participate in them. A frequent answer is that women are intentionally and unintentionally marginalized by male participants. Alternatively, Nancy Macdonald reverses the question to inquire, not why more women do not take part, but why so many men do.[15] What is it that men get out of their own participation? With parkour, we see that despite the many ways traceurs challenge the traditional masculine norms of sport subcultures, training still serves as a manhood act. Women, of course, can and do train, and many train far more rigorously than the men. However, in many respects, female traceurs are defying cultural stereotypes about women. Male traceurs, on the other hand, are living up to the cultural ideals of manhood. And, for this reason, more young men are attracted to the discipline than women. Risk taking affirms their identities in ways that it does not for young women.

Edgework and Hedgework

At first blush, the fact that traceurs so willingly embrace risk aligns with Stephen Lyng's concept of edgework—the state of flow created when individuals push the very edges of survival.[16] The prototypical edgeworker, however, lauds risk for risk's sake. The vocabulary of motive found in parkour, on the other hand, is very different. Vocabularies of motive are always situated within a given sociohistorical context, and they offer justifications for normative actions. They allow members of a social world or subculture to account for their practices. Edgework, a motivational orientation that rose to prominence in the 1980s, was, according to Lyng, one kind of anarchistic and nihilistic response to the alienation of contemporary life. By contrast, traceurs roundly disavow the notion of wanton thrill seeking.

Instead, they emphasize the ways in which their practices are safe and responsible. Like edgeworkers, traceurs intentionally submit themselves to fear-inducing situations. This fear, though, is almost always described as something to be managed through the slow progression of skills. Risks exist, but traceurs emphasize the reasoned manner in which they have assessed them and prepared themselves to surmount them. The point I am making here is not that traceurs are actually more safety-minded than prototypical edgeworkers. Rather, the accounts practitioners give for their actions (irrespective of what those actions are) are different: are dangerous situations highlighted or downplayed? Is facing uncontrollable hazards viewed as a positive or negative for one's sense of identity?

The motivational orientation of traceurs resonates with the neoliberal rhetoric pervasive in postmodern culture. I refer to this as hedgework. Practitioners focus far more on the ways they are mitigating risks than on the ways they are seeking out these risks. Putting the nihilism of edgework in stark relief, as hedgeworkers, traceurs continually affirm their dedication to protecting the self. The daredevil—irresponsible and chasing a rush—is the straw man practitioners repeatedly knock down in their incessant talk of precaution. And, in a society that increasingly shifts myriad collective risks onto the individual, it is, perhaps, only to be expected that young people would adopt these cultural tropes in exaggerated and symbolic form.

The hedgework of parkour involves rites of risk and rituals of symbolic safety. Rites of risks are the urban adventures of the discipline. They come from spatial appropriation, and they are the source of flow. They are also the manhood acts of traceurs. When a practitioner stands on a ledge and steels himself for a jump, he is practicing a rite of risk. He knows he might be injured, and he acknowledges that he feels scared of the possibility. However, to fully participate in the rite, he must manage this fear and act in spite of it. This is the test of character Erving Goffman discusses as fateful action.[17] At the same time, a stunt's riskiness does not automatically make it meaningful—quite the opposite. Traceurs generally deny that they tempt fate at all. Instead, the rites of risk found in the discipline are only meaningful when properly couched in the rituals of symbolic safety. Thus, talk of progression, stretching and warming up, using gyms, and having a healthy diet are posited as counterbalances to the destructive potential of their stunts. Ultimately, by emphasizing the precautions that have been taken leading up to a given maneuver, practitioners affirm the sacredness of the self.

Reimagining the Neoliberal City

The final day of the 2014 Colossal Jam, a three-day annual event sponsored by Aero, took place at Cummings Square in River Forest, Illinois. River Forest is a wealthy village just outside Chicago, with sprawling homes on tree-lined streets. It sits just west of Oak Park, another affluent town that butts up against the big city. They are both streetcar suburbs—just far enough from the supposed ills of urbanization, but still conveniently connected by public transportation. Ernest Hemmingway was born in Oak Park. Frank Lloyd Wright built his studio there, and the neighborhoods are dotted with his stunning architecture. Cummings Square is one block from the west end of Oak Park's bustling downtown shopping district and directly across the street from River Forest's Whole Foods Market. Regretfully, it is the kind of park that exemplifies urbanist William H. Whyte's critique of public spaces.[18] Despite its prime location, Cummings Square is almost always empty. Its most common occupants are vagrants waiting for the bus. The design of the area cuts it off from the surrounding pedestrian traffic. It has a wide grassy lawn and attractive features, but still feels confining. Thus, even on a beautiful summer afternoon, hardly any residents or tourists venture inside. In fact, aside from the traceurs, the only other notable visitors that day were a church group who gave out food and held a sermon for the homeless.

Cummings Square is interesting because it is not reductive architecture; it is forgotten architecture. It is a place that was maybe once a vibrant part of the social fabric, but now lies mostly unused. If occasionally traceurs train in spots solely to attract the attention of onlookers, the selection of Cummings Square for the final day of Colossal was driven by the opposite impulse. There are ample features to train on, but barely any passersby to serve as an audience. It is quiet and secluded—a place traceurs can technically be out in public, but, for all intents and purposes, also be on their own. Barren and forgotten as it might have been, Cummings Square took on a whole new feeling as the traceurs occupied its spaces that day. A few randomly placed picnic tables were moved around to use as platforms, landing pads, and barriers (see figure 4 in the introduction and figure 15 in chapter two). The park's grand stone stage, with its ornate walls and ledges, offered all sort of opportunities for vaults and jumps (see figure 27). I spent the afternoon walking from one pocket of activity to the next. Some traceurs were doing flips of almost unbelievable height, plummeting to the

FIG. 27. ZK in mid-rotation at Cummings Square in River Forest, Illinois.

grass below into perfect PK rolls that absorbed their impact. Others were working on more nuanced and technical aspects of the discipline. Some were just goofing around: adding odd variations to vaults, playing with the bokken Eric brought with him,[19] or kicking around a soccer ball another traceur supplied.

Around the same time as the 2014 Colossal, plans to renovate Cummings Square were getting underway.[20] The backers of these changes, no doubt, hoped it would be a boon for businesses in River Forest and

Oak Park. Shoppers from across the street could buy food and then have lunch in the park. With the proposed new stage lighting, park events could encourage attendees to patronize local restaurants afterwards. A revived Cummings Square really could improve the quality of public space in the community. Traceurs, though, show us how spaces can be renovated without the bulldozer and hammer. While business interests guide the sportization of the discipline, at the individual level, parkour is an example of what philosopher Michele de Certeau calls "tactics"—a way for the weak to make use of the strong.[21] Places are reinvented in terms of spatial affordances. As Sophie Fuggle, a scholar on French culture, argues, "Parkour is also a form of writing, constructing a new city from the one presented to us by architects and town planners. It is a form of writing which is both collective and individual."[22] Meaning is reinfused by traceurs through embodied practices unaligned with typical consumer routines. Joyous risk taking and the honing of corporeal skills transform places like Cummings Square through the affective appropriation of space.

In this book we have seen the ways new media is integrated with traceurs' training. We have looked at how the risk taking so prevalent in the discipline serves as gendered performances. We have also discussed the rituals of symbolic safety that give purpose to what might otherwise be interpreted as self-destructive acts. There is something quintessentially postmodern about parkour. The embodied practices of the discipline cannot be completely disentangled from its pseudo-events on the screen. The activity itself is highly performative. It is life imitating art, imitating life—inspired by superheroes and comic books. Unlike parcours, parkour is not a utilitarian activity; it is stylistic. Performative aspects of the self have an increasing significance in postmodernity, and as taken-for-granted roles become suspect, performances give veracity to identity claims. Parkour is one such performance type—allowing individuals to show they are men. Most importantly, the vocabulary of motive used by traceurs resonates with the neoliberal rhetoric of postmodern culture. Parkour teaches traceurs how to hedge their bets. This is to say, it shows they are a particular type of person—someone willing to take risks, not because he is reckless, but because he has studiously prepared himself for it.

If we live in a risk society, parkour is a sport that reflects this new ethos for affirming personal responsibility in navigating the hazards of contemporary life.[23] It is a way for young people—especially young men—to give meaning to the confluence of factors (many contradictory and many totally out of their control) that are shaping their lives. As discussed in chapter four, just as the cockfight transposes the status insecurities of Balinese men onto roosters,[24] parkour takes the all too real (but intangible) obstacles of living life in advanced capitalism and projects them onto symbolic (but tangible) challenges that the brave and the talented can overcome. Of particular importance, whereas several researchers have considered lifestyle sports as a form of soft diplomacy for the neoliberal agenda, with parkour we see how this free-market hegemony can also work its way from the bottom up.[25]

Throughout the preceding pages, I have attempted to offer a more complete exploration of the discipline—to appreciate the complex sociological landscape that contours the environment (socially and physically) in which traceurs actually operate. Traceurs, like all of us, live in a globalized, postmodern culture. The study of parkour—or any aspect of life—must acknowledge this context. In turn, understanding the discipline and what traceurs get out of it also opens our eyes to new modes of living within the neoliberal city and finding meaning in postmodernity. Ultimately, traceurs show us tactics—however small—for moving and thinking in new ways for new purposes. Traceurs' affective appropriations of Cummings Square that Sunday afternoon were not blueprints from a revolution. Parkour is a lifestyle sport, after all, not a social movement. Still, the traceurs' actions were far from mundane. In their jumps and vaults there were flickers of a much brighter light—of living creatively, of challenging what others take for granted.

Appendix A
Brief Note on Data
and Method

As explained in the introduction, the data for this book derive from several years of participant observation among traceurs in Chicago and the surrounding suburbs. My first jam was in March of 2010, and my last parkour event was the opening half of a two-day training course in July of 2014. In the interim, I attended thirty-four other jams and six parkour classes. Sometimes I was an active participant in training; other times I was a more passive observer. In all cases, I used social gatherings as an occasion to talk with traceurs about their activities. By learning the basic parkour maneuvers and training with participants, I developed an appreciation for the discipline. Like the traceurs in this study, I came to see new "opportunities" in my environment. I began to think about how it would be possible to climb over a structure in front of me, jump down from it, or swing across it. I also developed an understanding of progressing from awkward first attempts to successful completion of maneuvers. I experienced the fear of trying a new action and the excitement that can come from mastering it.[1]

My direct fieldwork was augmented by semi-structured interviews with forty participants from the Chicago area. I used the interview setting to encourage traceurs to discuss their personal experiences training. I also used the interview setting to question participants about their impressions of specific episodes I had previously observed them taking part in.

Combining fieldwork with interviews was particularly useful because I could compare and contrast actual behaviors with stated ideals.[2] Not surprisingly, there was often a rather wide gap between how traceurs described the discipline in the abstract and how they enacted parkour in real life. In particular, the discipline is steeped in an ascetic philosophy for training the body. But, as we have seen throughout the book, parkour practices—like all other lifestyle sports—were primarily a means for having fun while socializing with friends.

Training in parkour frequently overlaps with open engagement with new media, and most traceurs described in this book could be considered public figures in the local parkour community. Some even had national or international reputations. These traceurs regularly posted photos and videos of themselves online or had themselves tagged in images posted by others. Further, while some traceurs may disagree with various parts of my analysis, little of this research is of a sensitive nature to the people in it. For this reason, I have not followed the usual sociological conventions of confidentiality for informants. Instead, I asked my respondents to decide whether they preferred me to use their given names or a pseudonym. Many traceurs were already known by nicknames, and in most cases I use these nicknames. For traceurs who did not use nicknames, real first names are generally used. In cases where I could not get in touch with former respondents, or in the rare instances when I discuss something that may be embarrassing to a traceur, I err on the side of caution and use pseudonyms. Following urban ethnographer Mitchell Duneier, though, I believe (in this limited regard) that the practices of journalists are actually a more honest and open method for conducting certain (but certainly not all) sociological research projects.

Because much of the data from this study is derived from interactions in the field (usually without the aid of a recording device), many of the quotations cannot be replicated verbatim. Following Anselm Strauss and his co-researchers, I use standard quotation marks for passages that are verbatim.[3] I use single quotation marks for passages that are nearly verbatim. I use no quotation marks when the writing in my field notes was only able to capture the general gist of what I heard. All block quotations are verbatim. I use brackets to indicate instances in which I have made minor alterations to aid in the clarity of a quotation.

Complementing my primary data is an array of secondary sources. There are a handful of instructional books on parkour that I have consulted. Most notable is Dan Edwardes's book *The Parkour and Freerunning Handbook*. I also watched numerous documentaries on the topic. Beyond the foundational *Jump* series (discussed in chapter one), Michael Alosi's *Point B* and Kaspar Schröder's *My Playground* deserve special recognition in helping shape my views on the discipline.[4] I also read a smattering of *Jump Magazine* issues, produced by the now-defunct Urban Freeflow (also discussed in chapter one). To this list can be added an array of websites, blog posts, Facebook pages, and the like. Perhaps most importantly, I read nearly every English-language news article about parkour available from the LexisNexis database up to 2012.[5] My total sample (some of which come from sources other than LexisNexis) is comprised of over 400 newspaper and magazine articles. While journalists rarely demonstrate much depth or originality in their knowledge of the discipline, these articles were invaluable in helping to piece together the history of parkour. They detail the mainstreaming of the activity and the influence of corporations and financial interests. Finally, documentary filmmaker Julie Angel's interviews with the French originators of the discipline and her chronology of parkour's ascending popularity in England during the mid-2000s were also extremely helpful.[6]

Some Words on My Own Participation and Perspective

At no point in this project would I have self-identified as traceur. Those who trained with me would probably find such a notion quite laughable. I was always marked as an outsider, and, as a thirty-three-year-old when this project started, I was older than any traceur I personally met. There were a few other participants in their early thirties, however, and some were reasonably skilled, too. Truthfully, it was less my age and more my lack of gusto that distinguished me from the others. While I enjoy physical activities (especially endurance sports), the head-on approach to confronting fear that is an explicit aspect of parkour was—frankly—much too frightening for me. Thus, like many traceurs, I learned the basic parkour maneuvers in the padded environment of a gymnasiums, but unlike a true devotee to the discipline, my actions outside the gym remained extremely reserved.

For the first several months of this project, I performed conditioning and warm-up exercises with the traceurs at all the jams and training sessions I attended. I also worked on rolls, small jumps and vaults, and low-level wall runs during the events. Following basic ethnographic conventions, my goal was to fit in.[7] However, because of my general lack of athletic ability and obvious reservations in trying anything I felt was too scary, I never fit in all that well. At the same time, though, I was also always forthright about my interest in eventually writing a book about parkour. Through my continued presence in the community, I became something of a fixture. As the project went on, I stopped bothering trying to look and act the part of a traceur, and took on the role of a sympathetic and interested outsider. While my original active participation helped me better understand parkour as an embodied practice, my later adoption of a more passive observer role actually helped me establish better rapport with the traceurs. Namely, it eliminated confusion on the part of others about my presence. Instead of viewing me as the timid old guy who really sucked at training, it prompted traceurs to view me as the professor writing a book about the discipline— which for most practitioners seemed to be a more legitimate excuse for me sticking around and asking a lot of questions.[8]

Appendix B
On the Parkour Terminology
Used in This Book

Aero: *See* community.

APK: American Parkour (see chapter one).

l'art du déplacement: *See* parkour.

art of movement/displacement: *See* parkour.

cat leap: Landing from a jump or vault by grabbing the top of an opposing wall or railing with the rest of the body positioned below the top of the structure. While the traceur ends the maneuver by holding on with his hands, his feet and legs actually make contact with the structure first and absorb most of the impact. To the uninitiated, a cat leap might appear to be a jump in which the traceur falls short of his intended target and is left hanging off the structure. Once stabilized, the traceur then uses his arms and legs to propel himself onto the top of the wall or over the railing.

community: The term traceurs use to refer to the social world of parkour. It can be used to refer to the local (the Chicago parkour community) and the global (the global parkour community). Throughout the book, I follow the emic usage of this term. I occasionally use the term Aero, which is the local name for the Chicago parkour community (see chapter one). I also frequently refer to parkour as a social world.[1] While I often compare traceurs to members of various subcultures, I do not use the term subculture to describe the parkour community. To the extent that subculture is a useful sociological concept, it denotes a much higher level of boundary work between insiders and outsiders than what I found among traceurs. Therefore, I believe the concept of a social world is more fitting in this regard.[2]

cork: *See* flips.

discipline: *See* parkour.

freerunning/free running: Parkour training that has "expressive" movements (e.g., flips and other complex aerial maneuvers) incorporated into it. Many traceurs claim that the distinction between parkour and freerunning is very important. In practice, however, these supposedly different types of movement tend to blur together.

flips: Jumps that rotate the body upside down and back to vertical. Flips include basic forward and backward rotations as well as off-axis spins, twists, and counter-rotations (see figure 12 in chapter 2 and figure 27 in the conclusion). Complex aerial maneuvers have become an increasingly ubiquitous part of parkour practice. However, they are usually designated as part of freerunning, not of parkour. For simplicity, I will rarely belabor the nuanced differences in these stunts. I most commonly just note that a traceur is engaged in a complex or difficult flipping maneuver without labeling or defining the trick.

flow run: Using parkour skills to fluidly move through a long string of obstacles.

gainer: *See* flips.

jams: Parkour-themed social gatherings. Jams vary (sometimes intentionally, sometimes unintentionally) in the degree to which they involve serious training or lackadaisical socializing (see figures 7 in chapter one, figures 12 and 14 in chapter two, and figure 19 in chapter three).

jumps: Propelling the body off the ground and into the air. Two key jumps are the tic-tac and the precision. The tic-tac (also known as a tic) involves jumping toward one vertical object (e.g., a wall or a tree) and then kicking off it to propel oneself in another direction, usually while gaining height as well (see figure 15 in chapter two). The precision jump refers to landing simultaneously with both feet and not moving, usually because the landing surface is small (see figure 21 in chapter four).

kong: *See* vaults.

lachés: *See* swinging maneuvers.

parkour: The performance of stylized athletic movements for traversing the built environment in ways unintended by urban designers. In contrast to this etic definition, traceurs nearly universally define their discipline as finding the quickest, most efficient way to get from point A to point B, using only the human body. However, traceurs have virtually no interest in efficiency (understood as the conservation of energy in human motion) and little interest in charting out routes based solely on limiting their time in motion. Contrary to finding the path of least resistance, practitioners generally want to challenge themselves to successfully complete a difficult route. This added difficulty usually (but not always) corresponds with added risk. Parkour movements themselves are comprised of stylized actions, such as specialized jumps and vaults. Further, while parkour can be practiced anywhere, in its contemporary form it is an urban and suburban phenomenon. Other terms for parkour include: art of movement, art of displacement (l'art du déplacement), and freerunning. The majority of traceurs in this research project preferred the term parkour to freerunning, regardless of whether their training did or did not incorporate flips and other acrobatic movements. Following its emic usage in the community, I use the term parkour to describe a wide variety of stylized movements. Parkour is often abbreviated in the community as PK (e.g., PK roll or PK vision). Most traceurs prefer the term discipline to the term sport. Throughout the book I use a variety of words to denote parkour: activity, discipline, parkour, and sport (I generally reserve the latter to indicate more institutionalized and regulated versions of parkour).

PK: *See* parkour.

PKGen: Parkour Generations (see chapter one).

PK roll: Learning how to absorb the impact of a jump (or fall) by rolling. The PK roll is often described as the most basic movement in parkour. Instead of simply stomping down on one's feet, a controlled roll allows the traceur to distribute her energy across a longer span of time and wider span of space.

PK vision: Perceiving affordances conducive to parkour in the environment (see chapter two).

precision: *See* jumps.

samplers, showreels: Video montages, often featuring footage produced over the previous one-year period (e.g., "Damien Walters 2011 Official Showreel"). Watching and demonstrating knowledge of prominent traceurs' samplers and showreels is an important part of parkour socialization. Producing one's own sampler or showreel can be a milestone in a traceur's personal progression in the discipline.

swinging maneuvers: There are numerous variations for swinging under and around bars and branches. Swinging maneuvers are often referred to as lachés. Swinging under a bar (often to fit into a narrow space) is called an under-bar.

tic-tac: *See* jumps.

traceur: Practitioner of parkour. Within the community, this term is universally known but not universally used. While nearly all practitioners in this study preferred the term parkour to describe their activities, a few (rather counterintuitively) preferred the term freerunner to describe themselves. I use the term traceur to cover *all* individuals who train in parkour (broadly defined). Because the boundary between parkour and freerunning is fluid, and individual views on the topic changed throughout the project, the uniform application of the term is the most practical. Some practitioners use traceur for males and traceuse for females, but I apply the term gender-neutrally.

training: Engaging in parkour activities is called training. Traceurs do not *play* parkour, nor do they participate in parkour*ing*. Claiming to *do* parkour is acceptable, but the preferred terminology is to say one *trains* parkour (or trains in parkour).

tricking: Complex aerial rotations performed on flat ground. Tricking evolved out of martial arts and is a distinct social world from parkour. In recent years, traceurs have begun incorporating tricking-inspired techniques into their training (*see* flips et al.).

under-bar: *See* swinging maneuvers.

UF: Urban Freeflow (see chapter one).

vaults: Jumping toward an obstacle and then pivoting off it with one's hands. Vaults are the single-most identifiable type of maneuver in parkour. As with jumps and flips, there is a wide variety of vaults (and new variations are continually being developed). During this research, the three most popular vaults were the speed, dash, and kong vaults. In the speed vault the traceur jumps forward while simultaneously swinging his legs and body out to the side (high enough to the clear the obstacle). As he passes over the obstacle, he uses one hand to push off the obstacle and redirect the body and legs back down, landing in a run. In a dash vault, the traceur jumps forward while simultaneously bringing both legs forward (see figure 2 in the introduction). As she passes over the obstacle—in a seated position in mid-air—both hands are used to push off the obstacle, allowing for greater distance. In a kong vault the traceur dives head first towards the obstacle (see figure 4 in the introduction). Both arms are extended onto the object, helping the traceur to gain distance and enough height to bring his feet through his arms and land feet first on the other side. A double kong vault is a variation in which the traceur first uses her arms to pop herself off the obstacle (propelling herself forward) and then (with her second contact) pivots her feet through her arms for the landing.

wall flip: Kicking off a vertical structure to propel oneself upward and backward into a back flip (see figure 13 in chapter 2).

wall run: Kicking off a vertical structure to propel oneself upward in order to summit an object (see figure 19 in chapter 3).

WFPF: World Freerunning and Parkour Federation (see chapter one).

Notes

Introduction

1 Alice O'Grady provides an insightful analysis on the way traceurs collaboratively share in the discipline and learn from each other. Alice O'Grady, "Tracing the City—Parkour Training, Play, and the Practice of Collaborative Learning," *Theatre, Dance & Performance Training* 3 (2012).

2 On this point see Becky Beal, "Disqualifying the Official: An Exploration of Social Resistance through the Subculture of Skateboarding," *Sociology of Sport Journal* 12 (1995). Likewise, Olympic snowboarder Todd Richards reflects back on the changing expectation of being an elite athlete in his sport by stating, "Ugh, really? I don't train. I skateboard in the summertime. I snowboard every single day in the wintertime. That's my training." Orland von Einsiedel and John Drever, *We Ride: The Story of Snowboarding* [film] (Grain Media, 2013), accessed May 28, 2015, https://vimeo.com/60571386.

3 There are, of course, exceptions. Various individuals and organizations promote an extremely ascetic version of the discipline—one that is often at great odds with the description provided in this book. These things said, the ascetic version of parkour is quite frequently an idealized image of the discipline—disconnected from the actual practices of individuals who self-identify as traceurs and freerunners. This book is about parkour *as it was actually practiced* at my field site. Readers interested in the more ascetic philosophy of parkour can consult the work of Julie Angel, *Ciné Parkour* (self-published, 2011).

4 Discussing the increasing popularity of the sport, Sam Sanders reports that parkour may become an Olympic sport. "Parkour May Run, Flip, Dive and Slide Its Way into Olympics," *All Things Considered,* National Public Radio, September 11, 2014.

5 Erving Goffman, "Where the Action Is," in *Interaction Rituals: Essays on Face-to-Face Behavior* (New York: Anchor Books, 1967).

6 Kyle Kusz, for example, describes the mainstream appeal of antinomian styles among extreme sports participants. "In 'Live Fast Die,' [a BMX video] countless images show white male BMX youth participating in rebellious activities by consuming large amounts of alcohol, smashing beer bottles on their heads, setting hair on fire, blowing up aerosol cans, and obstructing traffic by riding couches and shopping carts down the middle of busy city streets. The absence of an adult presence, the frequent use of images of BMX riding at night, the Generation X 'grunge' sartorial style worn by BMXers, and the loud, disruptive skate-punk musical score operate to legitimate the marginal identity of these youth and of BMX culture." Kyle Kusz, "BMX, Extreme Sports, and the White Male Backlash," in *To the Extreme: Alternative Sports Inside and Out*, eds. Robert E. Rinehart and Synthia Sydnor (Albany, NY: State University of New York Press, 2003), 164. Also see David J. Leonard, "To the White Extreme in the Mainstream: Manhood and White Youth Culture in a Virtual Sports World," in *Youth Culture and Sport: Identity, Power, and Politics*, eds. Michael D. Giardina and Michele K. Donnelly (New York: Routledge, 2008).

7 Belinda Wheaton, "Introduction: Mapping the Lifestyle Sport-Scape," in *Understanding Lifestyle Sports: Consumption, Identity and Difference*, ed. Belinda Wheaton (New York: Routledge, 2004).

8 A good example is the open disdain many snowboarders feel toward Shaun White—the most prolific (as well as the richest) winner of half-pipe competitions in the history of the sport. For those who identify with the snowboarding subculture, White is often characterized as too focused on competitions, and his dedication to winning (e.g., building a private half pipe to work on tricks in seclusion) is viewed as a perversion. See von Einsiedel and Drever, *We Ride*. Ugo Corte describes similar tensions within the professional BMX community as top riders began to prioritize training to win over hanging out with their friends. Ugo Corte, "A Refinement of Collaborative Circles Theory: Resource Mobilization and Innovation in an Emerging Sport," *Social Psychology Quarterly* 76 (2013).

9 Researchers have used a variety of names to characterize individualistic, non-traditional, non-competitive physical activities: adventure sports, alternative sports, post-sports, and whiz sports. See (respectively) Gunnar Breivik, "Trends in Adventure Sports in a Post-Modern Society," *Sport in Society* (2010); Robert E. Rinehart, "Emerging Arriving Sport: Alternatives to Formal Sports" in *Handbook of Sports Studies*, eds. Jay Coakley and Eric Dunning (Thousand Oaks, CA: Sage Publications, 2000); Brian Pronger, "Post-Sport: Transgressing Boundaries in Physical Culture" in *Sports and Postmodern Times*, ed. Geneviève Rail (Albany, NY: State University of New York Press); Nancy Midol and Gérard Broyer, "Toward an Anthropological Analysis of New Sport Cultures: The Case of Whiz Sports in France," *Sociology of Sport Journal* 12 (1995). There are important distinctions between some of these labels and the demographic characteristics of the people participating in them (e.g., mountaineers and skydivers are very different from BMX riders and inline skaters). Regardless, these activities are generally understood (or, at least, in their early years had the potential) to represent some sort of challenge to the mainstream sporting establishment. That is to say, they are not sports that can be easily reconciled with the high school, collegiate, and professional models of coaching and team-based competition.

10   Michael Atkinson and Kevin Young discuss the changing analytic orientation of
lifestyle sport studies. Michael Atkinson and Kevin Young, *Deviance and Social
Control in Sport* (Champaign, IL: Human Kinetics, 2008). The competitive aspects
of football are detailed by the following, among many others: Michael Messner,
"When Bodies are Weapons: Masculinity and Violence in Sport," *International
Review for the Sociology of Sport* 24 (1990) and Donald F. Sabo, "Best Years of My
Life" in *Jock: Sports and Male Identity*, eds. Donald F. Sabo and Ross Runfola
(Englewood Cliffs, NJ: Prentice-Hall, 1980). Conversely, Beal famously studied the
anticompetitive views of skateboarders. Beal, "Disqualifying the Official." Duncan
Humphrey makes a similar point about snowboarders. Duncan Humphrey, "Selling
Out Snowboarding" in *To the Extreme: Alternative Sports Inside and Out*, eds.
Robert E. Rinehart and Synthia Sydnor (Albany, NY: State University of New York
Press, 2003).

11   Wheaton describes the demographic characteristics of lifestyle sports participants.
Belinda Wheaton, *The Cultural Politics of Lifestyle Sports* (New York: Routledge,
2013). Numerous researchers have looked into the ways that aspects of lifestyle
sports reinforce gender norms. For example, Mathew Atencio, Becky Beal, and
Charlene Wilson, "The Distinction of Risk: Urban Skateboarding, Street Habitus,
and the Construction of Hierarchical Gender Relations," *Qualitative Research
in Sports & Exercise* 1 (2009); Becky Beal and Charlene Wilson, "'Chicks Dig
Scars': Commercialisation and the Transformation of Skateboard Identities" in
Understanding Lifestyle Sports: Consumption, Identity and Difference, ed. Belinda
Wheaton (New York: Routledge, 2004); Holly Thorpe, *Snowboarding Bodies in
Theory and Practice* (New York: Palgrave Macmillan, 2011); Gordon Waitt, "'Killing
Waves': Surfing, Space, and Gender," *Social & Cultural Geography* 9 (2008).

12   Examples of the corporate influence and profit motive in lifestyle sports can be
seen in Douglas Booth's historical look into surfing, David Browne's writing on
the use of extreme sports in marketing, and Thorpe and Wheaton's analysis of
how such sports have (among other things) changed the Olympics. See Douglas
Booth, "Paradoxes of Material Culture: The Political Economy of Surfing," in
The Political Economy of Sport, eds. John Nauright and Kimberly S. Schimmel
(New York: Palgrave Macmillan, 2005); David Browne, *Amped: How Big Air, Big
Dollars, and a New Generation Took Sports to the Extreme* (New York: Bloomsbury,
2004); Holly Thorpe and Belinda Wheaton, "'Generation X Games,' Action
Sports, and the Olympic Movement: Understanding the Cultural Politics of
Incorporation," *Sociology* 45 (2011). Robert Rinehart has been especially critical of
the way alternative sports have become co-opted by the mainstream. See Robert
Rinehart, "Inside of the Outside: Pecking Orders within Alternative Sports at
ESPN's 1995 'the Extreme Games,'" *Journal of Sport & Social Issues* 22 (1998);
"Dropping into Sight: Commodification and Co-Option of In-Line Skating,"
in *To the Extreme: Alternative Sports Inside and Out*, eds. Robert E. Rinehart
and Synthia Sydnor (Albany, NY: State University of New York Press, 2003);
"Exploiting a New Generation: Corporate Branding and the Co-Option of
Action Sports," in *Youth, Culture, and Sport: Identity, Power, and Politics*, eds.
Michael D. Giardina and Michele K. Donnelly (New York: Routledge, 2008); also
see Rebecca Heino, "What's So Punk About Snowboarding," *Journal of Sport &
Social Issues* 24 (2000). Counterpoints to the co-option perspective can be found
in Thorpe, *Snowboarding Bodies in Theory and Practice*; Belinda Wheaton, "Just Do

It': Consumption, Commitment, and Identity in the Windsurfing Subculture,"
Sociology of Sport Journal 17 (2000); Belinda Wheaton and Becky Beal, "'Keeping It
Real': Subcultural Media and the Discourse of Authenticity in Alternative Sports,"
International Review for the Sociology of Sport 38 (2003).

13 Henri Lefebvre, *The Production of Space*, trans. Donald Nicholson-Smith
(Cambridge, MA: Blackwell 1974 [1991]). The more abstracted space becomes,
the more often perceptions of that space are unable to move beyond capitalist
rationality. "Within this space, and on the subject of this space, everything is openly
declared: everything is said or written. Save for the fact that there is very little to
be said—and even less to be 'lived,' for lived experience is crushed, vanquished by
what is 'conceived of.'" (51). Through its seeming transparency, the abstract space
of capitalism is not only self-evident, but seemingly inevitable. Individuals act
according to pre-established conceptions (regardless of how such action may work
against their own self-interests) because the physical, mental, and social structures
of space render alternatives impossible.

14 Lefebvre, *The Production of Space*, 362.

15 Maria Daskalaki, Alexandra Stara, and Miguel Imas, "The 'Parkour Organization':
Inhabitation of Corporate Spaces," *Culture & Organization* 14 (2008): 62; Paula
Geyh, "Urban Free Flow: A Poetics of Parkour," *M/C Journal* 9 (2006), accessed
December 31, 2011, http://journal.medi-culture.org.au/0607/06-geyh.php;
Michael Atkinson, "Parkour, Anarcho-Environmentalism, and Poïesis," *Journal of
Sport & Social Issues* 32 (2009): 169; also see Lieven Ameel and Sirpa Tani, "Parkour
and the Production of Loose Spaces?," *Geografiska Annaler: Series B: Human
Geography* 94 (2012); Broerick D.V. Chow, "Parkour and the Critique of Ideology:
Turn Vaulting the Fortresses of the City," *Journal of Dance & Somatic Practices* 2
(2012); Sophie Fuggle, "Discourses of Subversion: The Ethics and Aesthetics of
Capoeira and Parkour," *Dance Research* 26 (2008); Matthew D. Lamb, "Misuses
of the Monument: The Art of Parkour and the Discursive Limits of a Disciplinary
Architecture," *Journal of Urban Cultural Studies* 1 (2014); Peter Mörtenböck, "Free
Running and the Hugged City," *Thresholds* 30 (2005); Oli Mould, "Parkour, the
City, the Event," *Environment and Planning D: Society & Space* 27 (2009); Jimena
Ortuzar, "Parkour or L'Art du Déplacement: A Kinetic Urban Utopia," *The Drama
Review* 53 (2009); David Thompson, "Jump City: Parkour and the Traces," *South
Atlantic Quarterly* 107 (2008).

16 Lefebvre, *The Production of Space*, 142.

17 Iain Borden, *Skateboarding, Space, and the City: Architecture and the Body* (New
York: Berg, 2001), 101, 96 (respectively). On the matter of space enabling and
constraining action, also see Allan Pred, *Place, Practice, and Structure: Social and
Spatial Transformation in Southern Sweden 1750–1850* (Totowa, NJ: Barnes &
Noble, 1986).

18 There are, of course, notable exceptions to this claim. As David Harvey has noted,
space is a keyword in the social sciences. David Harvey, "Space as a Keyword," in
David Harvey: A Critical Reader, eds. Noel Castree and Derek Gregory. Over
the last several decades an increasing number of sociologists have helped initiate
a spatial turn in the discipline. To take just one prominent example, there is
Robert J. Sampson, *Great American City: Chicago and the Enduring Neighborhood
Effect* (University of Chicago Press, 2012). However, on the whole, sociologists (even
when using the term "space") are generally not interested in the abstract geometry of

the material world—a point underscored in Thomas F. Gieryn, "A Space for Place in Sociology," *Annual Review of Sociology* 26 (2000). As Herbert Gans explains, "Bad design can interfere with what goes on inside a building, of course, and good design can aid it, but design *per se* does not significantly shape human behavior." Herbert J. Gans, "Planning for People not Buildings," *Environment & Planning* 1 (1969): 37–38.

19   Thomas Gieryn distinguishes space and place in sociological studies. Gieryn, "A Space for Place in Sociology"; also see Tim Cresswell, *Place: A Short Introduction* (Malden, MA: Blackwell, 2004). On Fenway Park see Michael Iain Borer, "The Importance of Place and Their Public Faces," *Journal of Popular Culture* 39 (2006). On poor people's interpretations of spaces culturally coded as middle class, see Mario Small, *Villa Victoria: The Transformation of Social Capital in a Boston Barrio* (Chicago: University of Chicago Press, 2004).

20   James Gibson, *The Ecological Approach to Visual Perception* (Boston: Houghton Mifflin Company, 1979). As Nathaniel Bavinton writes, "Traceurs need the fences, walls, and hand-railings designed to regulate the movements of people in order to transform these constraints into resources for resistance." Nathaniel Bavinton, "From Obstacle to Opportunity: Parkour, Leisure, and the Reinterpretation of Constraint," *Annuals of Leisure Research* 10 (2007): 407.

21   Ameel and Tani discuss this point in their analysis of parkour in Finland. "[Parkour has the] power to make people see the surrounding world in a different way [. . . and] also opens possibilities for emotional attachment to often unexpected everyday places." Lieven Ameel and Sirpa Tani, "Everyday Aesthetics in Action: Parkour Eyes and the Beauty of Concrete Walls," *Emotions, Space, & Society* 5 (2012): 171.

22   See especially Anthony Giddens, *The Constitution of Society: Outline to the Theory of Structuration* (Berkeley: University of California Press, 1984); also see Derek Gregory, *Geographical Imagination* (Cambridge, MA: Blackwell, 1994); Edward W. Soja, "The Socio-Spatial Dialectic," in *Postmodern Geographies: The Reassertion of Space in Critical Social Theory* (New York: Verso, 1989).

23   Loïc Wacquant, *Body and Soul: Notebooks of an Apprentice Boxer* (New York: Oxford University Press, 2004).

24   Mihaly Csikszentmihalyi, *Beyond Boredom and Anxiety* (San Francisco: Jossey-Bass Publishers, 1975); also see Richard G. Mitchell, *Mountain Experience: The Psychology and Sociology of Adventure* (Chicago: University of Chicago Press, 1983).

25   John Stephen Saville, "Playing with Fear: Parkour and the Mobility of Emotion," *Social & Cultural Geography* 9 (2008): 903.

26   See Jeffrey L. Kidder, *Urban Flow: Bike Messengers and the City* (Ithaca, NY: Cornell University Press, 2011).

27   Norbert Elias, "Introduction," in *The Quest for Excitement: Sport and Leisure in the Civilizing Process*, eds. Norbert Elias and Eric Dunning (New York: Basil Blackwell, 1986), 26; also see Norbert Elias, *What is Sociology?*, trans. Stephen Mennell and Grace Morrissey (New York: Columbia University Press, 1978); Giddens, *The Constitution of Society*.

28   David Harvey, *The Conditions of Postmodernity: An Inquiry into the Origins of Cultural Change* (Cambridge, MA: Blackwell, 1990).

29   On meta-narratives see Jean-François Lyotard, *The Postmodern Condition: A Report on Knowledge*, trans. Geoff Bennington and Brian Massumi (Minneapolis: University of Minnesota Press, 1984). On mediated images see Jean Baudrillard, *Symbolic Exchange and Death*, trans. Iain Hamilton Grant (Thousand Oaks, CA:

Sage Publications, 1993). On identities see Kenneth J. Gergen, *The Saturated Self: Dilemmas of Identity in Contemporary Times* (New York: Basic Books, 1991). On neoliberal discourse see Harvey, *A Brief History of Neoliberalism* (New York: Oxford University Press, 2005)

30 Ulrich Beck is quite critical of the notion of postmodernity. See especially Ulrich Beck, Wolfgang Bonss, and Christoph Lau, "The Theory of Reflexive Modernization: Problematic, Hypotheses, and Research Programme," *Theory, Culture & Society* 20 (2003); also see Anthony Giddens, *The Consequences of Modernity* (Stanford, CA: Stanford University Press, 1990).

31 See Jean Baudrillard, *Simulacra and Simulation*, trans. Shelia Faria Glaser (Ann Arbor: University of Michigan Press, 1994). Additionally, Sherry Turkle has written extensively on the consequences of technology and mediated forms of socialization. Sherry Turkle, *Life on the Screen: Identity in the Age of the Internet* (New York: Simon & Schuster, 1995); *Alone Together: Why We Expect More from Technology and Less from Each Other* (New York: Basic Books, 2011).

32 Arjun Appadurai, "Global Ethnoscapes: Notes and Queries for a Transnational Anthropology," in *Modernity at Large: Cultural Dimensions of Globalization* (Minneapolis: University of Minnesota Press, 1996).

33 Judith Butler, *Gender Trouble: Feminism and the Subversion of Identity* (New York: Routledge, 1990), 136. Jim Dowd discusses the performative aspects of postmodern identity more generally. James J. Dowd, "An Act Made Perfect in Habit: The Self in the Postmodern Age," *Current Perspectives in Social Theory* 16 (1996). According to Giddens, individuals are now responsible for undertaking reflexive projects of the self. As such, neither the physical body or the person's mind and spirit are by birthright. They must be continually worked at; constructing a suitable self is a lifelong project for the individual. Anthony Giddens, *Modernity and Self-Identity: Self and Society in the Late Modern Age* (Stanford, CA: Stanford University Press, 1991).

34 Michael Schwalbe, "Identity Stakes, Manhood Acts, and the Dynamics of Accountability," *Studies in Symbolic Interaction* 28 (2005).

35 Pierre Bourdieu, "Utopia as Endless Exploitation," *Le Monde Diplomatique* (English Edition), accessed May 28, 2015, http://mondediplo.com/1998/12/08bourdieu; Earl Gammon, "The Psycho- and Sociogenesis of Neoliberalism," *Critical Sociology* 39 (2012): 522.

36 Stephen Lyng, "Edgework: A Social Psychological Analysis of Voluntary Risk Taking," *American Journal of Sociology* 95 (1990): 851–886.

37 Numerous scholars have emphasized the ways neoliberalism relates to the shifting of risk onto individuals. See especially Ulrich Beck, *The Brave New World of Work* (Malden, MA: Polity Press, 2000); Jacob S. Hacker, *The Great Risk Shift: The Assault on American Jobs, Families, Health Care, and Retirement, and How You Can Fight Back* (New York: Oxford University Press, 2006); Susan S. Silbey, "Taming Prometheus: Talk About Safety and Culture," *Annual Review of Sociology* 35 (2009).

Chapter 1 Developing the Discipline and Creating a Sport

1 See Julie Angel, *Ciné Parkour* (self-published, 2011).

2 Alec Wilkinson, "No Obstacles: Navigating the World by Leaps and Bounds," *The New Yorker*, April 16, 2007.

3 See Michael Atkinson, "Parkour, Anarcho-Environmentalism, and Poïesis," *Journal of Sport & Social Issues* 32 (2009); Bill Marshall, "Running across the Rooves of Empire: Parkour and the Postcolonial City," *Modern & Contemporary France* 18 (2010); on the late nineteenth-century and early twentieth-century crisis of masculinity, see Michael S. Kimmel, "Consuming Manhood: The Feminization of American Culture and the Recreation of the Male Body, 1820–1920," in *The History of Men: Essays in the History of American and British Masculinities* (New York: State University of New York Press, 2005).

4 Wilkinson, "No Obstacles." Also see Michael Alosi, *Point B* [film] (2009), accessed December 15, 2011, http://www.pointbmovie.com/Watch.html.

5 David Belle discusses this himself in an interview. "You know, I was brought up not by my father, but by my grandfather, and my grandfather depicted my father as a sort of hero. He said, 'Your father was a fireman who saved lives,' and, naturally, you know, when you're a kid, you want to resemble your father, and so when I met him, when I found him, I had a lot of questions." Quoted in "AnnMay and Dave from Geek World Interview David Belle," Geek World (2010), accessed April 7, 2015, http://www .geekworldradio.com/DavidBelleIntv.html. Also see Wilkinson, "No Obstacles."

6 On this point, Belle has spoken of his affection for Spiderman comics and said, "That it was a childhood dream, to be in a Spider-Man costume." Wilkinson, "No Obstacles." Also see Belle, "Annamay & Dave from Geek World Interview David Belle." Additionally, Foucan has claimed that in developing parkour, "We would play at being ninja, superheroes." Quoted in Mike Christie, *Jump London* [film] (London: Channel 4, 2003). This film can be watched on YouTube, accessed March 1, 2011, https://www.youtube.com/watch?v=l8fSXGP9wvQ. Further, Angel, who conducted in-depth interviews with numerous member of the original parcours group, writes, "[They were] largely inspired and gained motivation from the superheroes they followed in the Japanese anime and manga series [...] as well as the comic and graphic novel characters [...]. The energy of the characters as well as the actions and the classic tales of bravery and endeavour of great achievements, fed into their conscious." Angel, *Ciné Parkour*, 30.

7 Play is most famously analyzed by Johan Huizinga, *Homo Ludens: A Study of the Play-Element in Culture*, trans. R.F.C. Hull (Boston: Routledge & Kegan Paul, 1949).

8 On the matter of style in lifestyle sports, see Robert E. Rinehart, *Players All: Performances in Contemporary Sport* (Bloomington, IN: Indiana University Press, 1998); also see Belinda Wheaton, *The Cultural Politics of Lifestyle Sports* (New York: Routledge, 2013).

9 Iain Borden discusses the subcultural mystique of skateboarding. Iain Borden, *Skateboarding, Space, and the City* (New York: Berg, 2001). Nancy Macdonald does the same with the graffiti subculture. Nancy Macdonald, *Graffiti Subculture: Youth, Masculinity, and Identity in London and New York* (New York: Palgrave Macmillan, 2001). Both note that young men are attracted to antinomian aspects of the activities and that eventually mainstream institutions (e.g., advertisers and the media) also attempt to capitalize on this imagery.

10 These points are developed in detail by numerous scholars. See especially Maxim Silverman, *Deconstructing the Nation: Immigration, Racism, and Citizenship in Modern France* (New York: Routledge, 1992) and Paul A. Silverstein and Chantal Tetreault, "Postcolonial Urban Apartheid," Riots in France (2006), accessed February 16, 2015, http://riotsfrance.ssrc.org/Silverstein_Tetreault/).

11 Étienne Balibar, "Uprising in the Banlieues," *Constellations* 14 (2007): 48; also see Mustafa Dikeç, *Badlands of the Republic* (Malden, MA: Blackwell, 2007) and Silverman, *Deconstructing the Nation*.

12 Susan S. Fainstein, "The Changing World Economy and Urban Restructuring," in *Leadership and Urban Regeneration*, eds. Dennis Judd and Michael Parkinson (Thousand Oaks, CA: Sage Publications, 1990).

13 Poverty and racial segregation in the United States have famously been analyzed by William Julius Wilson, *The Truly Disadvantaged: The Inner City, the Underclass, and Public Policy* (Chicago: University of Chicago Press, 1987). In particular, Wilson writes of the disconnection between the structural causes of inequality and the political policies and popular understandings about them. Loïc Wacquant compares and contrasts the American and French context behind what he calls advanced marginality. Loïc Wacquant, *Urban Outcasts: A Comparative Sociology of Advanced Marginality* (Malden, MA: Polity Press, 2008).

14 Graham Murray, "France: The Riots and the Republic," *Race & Class* 47 (2006): 31, 29 (respectively).

15 Information on the original parcours group comes from Angel, *Ciné Parkour*; Hnautra is quoted on page 16.

16 News reports on Sacrelles include Dan Bilefsky, "A Militant Jewish Group Confronts Pro-Palestinian Protesters in France," *New York Times*, August 6, 2014; Lauren Frayer, "In a Paris Suburb, Jews and Muslims Live in a Fragile Harmony," *Morning Edition,* National Public Radio, January 15, 2015. Descriptions of Lisses can be found in Amelia Gentleman, "One False Jump Can be Fatal," *The Guardian*, August 21, 2003; Wilkinson, "No Obstacles."

17 Jane Jacobs, *The Death and Life of Great American Cities* (New York: Random House, 1961); Lefebvre quoted in Andy Merrifield, *Henri Lefebvre: A Critical Introduction* (New York: Routledge, 2006), 60.

18 Michael Kaplan, "Social Climbers," *New York Times*, March 9, 2003.

19 Borden, *Skateboarding, Space, and the City*, 195; on degree zero, see Roland Barthes, *Elements of Semiology*, trans. Annette Lavers and Colin Smith (New York: Hill & Wang, 1967).

20 Michel de Certeau, *The Practices of Everyday Life*, trans. Steven Rendall (Berkeley: University of California Press, 1984).

21 Nathan Guss, "Parkour and the Multitude: Politics of a Dangerous Art," *French Cultural Studies* 22 (2011): 75.

22 Wilkinson, "No Obstacles."

23 Marshall, "Running Across the Rooves of Empire"; Hnautra quoted in Mark Daniels, *Generation Yamakasi* [film] (France2 TV, 2005). This film (with subtitles) can be watched on YouTube, accessed March 17, 2016, https://www.youtube.com/watch?v=fOYpHLHg6io.

24 Angel, *Ciné Parkour*.

25 Angel, *Ciné Parkour*.

26 Scott Stapleton and Susan Terrio provide an analysis of *Yamakasi: Les Samouraïs des Temps Modernes* (and other mainstream representations of the discipline) as it relates to the development of the parkour community. Scott Stapleton and Susan Terrio, "Le Parkour: Urban Street Culture and the Commoditization of Male Youth Expression," *International Migration* 50 (2010). Further, Neil Archer argues that films like *Yamakasi* actually have transgressive potential for the audience. "[T]he

representation itself, and the experience of viewing, themselves contain elements of the spatial and perceptual transformations experienced by the traceur." Neil Archer, "Virtual Poaching and Altered Space: Reading Parkour in French Visual Culture," *Modern & Contemporary France* 18 (2010): 103.

27 Lisa Nesselson, "Yamakasi," *Variety*, April 30, 2001.

28 Respectively: Alex Benady, "No Ropes of Safety Net for BBC's Spiderman," *Evening Standard*, April 18, 2002; Fiona McCade, "Le Parkour Becomes de Rigueur, and the City My New Gymnasium," *The Scotsman*, April 30, 2002.

29 Mike Christie discusses the impetus behind the *Jump* series in the interview "The Godfather Speaks," *Jump Magazine*, February, 2010.

30 In recent years, sociologists of sport have become increasingly interested in transnationalism—the micro-level, embodied aspects of globalization. See especially Thomas F. Carter, *In Foreign Fields: The Politics and Experiences of Transnational Sport Migration* (New York: Pluto, 2011); also see Holly Thorpe, *Snowboarding Bodies in Theory and Practice* (New York: Palgrave Macmillan, 2011). The importance of *Jump London* for the popularity of parkour is specifically discussed by Paul Gilchrist and Belinda Wheaton, "New Media Technologies in Lifestyle Sport" in *Digital Media Sport: Technology, Power, and Culture in the Network Society*, eds. Brett Hutchinson and David Rowe (New York: Routledge, 2013).

31 Christie, "The Godfather Speaks."

32 Christie, "The Godfather Speaks."

33 This article was Kaplan's "Social Climbers."

34 For example, see Anna Bahney, "New Way for Teenagers to See if They Bounce," *New York Times*, March 28, 2004; Kate Brumback, "Parkour: The Extreme Obstacle Course with Air," *Philadelphia Inquirer*, May 7, 2006.

35 Christie, "The Godfather Speaks."

36 Thomas Carter, for example, discusses the changing meaning of sports as they cross borders. "The dialectical notion of transculturation makes it possible to trace these relationships across borders as these relationships alter and change local conditions while simultaneously being changed by transnational sports migration. [. . .] Mobility informs not just how social entities move; it also incorporates the means by which mobility is produced as well as the degree and rate to which the entity can move and, through that movement, change." Carter, *In Foreign Fields*, 44.

37 Respectively, Foucan's quotes are from Alex Dominguez, "'Matrix' in the Park: Parkour, a Sport of Fluid Movement, Converts Items in the Landscape to Obstacles," *Telegraph Herald*, January 10, 2005; and Marina Takahashi, "It's Called Free Running," *Akron Beacon Journal*, September 9, 2005. Belle's quotes are from Mel Hunter, "Spider Gang," *The Sun*, June 1, 2002; and Belle, "A Warrior's Journey," Parkourpedia (2009), accessed February 15, 2015, http://parkourpedia.com/about/ interviews-and-articles-of-interest/a-warriors-journey.

38 Ewart quoted in Nigel Reynolds, "'Spiderman' Trailer Thrills Viewers," *Daily Telegraph*, April 19, 2002. Foucan quoted in Bahney, "New Way for Teenagers to See if They Bounce."

39 Also see Wheaton, *The Cultural Politics of Lifestyle Sports*.

40 Daniels, *Generation Yamakasi*.

41 For example, ESPN chronicled famous American traceur Ryan Ford's trip to France to train with the French originators. This trip included a training session at the

Dame du Lac. Lisa Salter, "E:60: Parkour" [TV show], ESPN, November 6, 2007. This segment is viewable on YouTube, accessed June 25, 2015, http://youtu .be/5R7VL5ludOg. Also see Lieven Ameel and Sirpa Tani, "Everyday Aesthetics in Action: Parkour Eyes and the Beauty of Concrete Walls," *Emotions, Space, & Society* 5 (2012): 167–168. Similarly, Gregory Snyder discusses professional skateboarding as it relates to the urban environment. In particular, he describes how photographs and videos of tricks disseminated through the subculture make certain locations meaningful for members (e.g., Love Park in Philadelphia). Gregory J. Snyder, "The City and the Subculture Career: Professional Street Skateboarding in LA," *Ethnography* 13 (2012).

42 Interestingly, neither the sequel, *District 13: Ultimatum* (2009), nor the American remake (set in Detroit), *Brick Mansions* (2014), generated much interest among practitioners in Chicago. This is despite the fact that Belle starred in both and was still held in very high regard by local traceurs.

43 Numerous commentators on lifestyle sports have addressed the difficulty professionals face in courting mainstream popularity while maintaining authenticity within the sport itself. For example, see Becky Beal and Charlene Wilson, "'Chicks Dig Scars': Commercialisation and the Transformation of Skateboard Identities," in *Understanding Lifestyle Sports: Consumption, Identity, and Difference*, ed. Belinda Wheaton (New York: Routledge, 2004); David Browne, *Amped: How Big Air, Big Dollars, and a New Generation Took Sports to the Extreme* (New York: Bloomsbury, 2004). Both Atkinson and Wheaton discuss Foucan's tarnished image within the parkour community. Atkinson, "Parkour, Anarcho-Environmentalism, and Poïesis"; Wheaton, *The Cultural Politics of Lifestyle Sports*.

44 Bob Edwards and Ugo Corte, "Commercialization and Lifestyle Sport: Lessons from 20 Years of Freestyle BMX in 'Pro-Town, USA,'" *Sport in Society* 13 (2010).

45 Kate Burt, "One Giant Leap for Mankind," *The Independent*, August 25, 2004.

46 See Dominguez, "'Matrix' in the Park"; Kerry Folan, "For Parkour Fans, All the World's a Gym," *Washington Post*, August 31, 2007. Mark Toorock is quoted by Collin Bane, "Jump First, Ask Questions Later," *Washington Post*, January 13, 2008.

47 Bane, "Jump First, Ask Questions Later."

48 On consumption in lifestyle sports see especially Douglas Booth, "The Paradoxes of Material Culture," in *The Political Economy of Sport*, eds. John Nauright and Kimberly S. Schimmel (New York, Palgrave Macmillan, 2005); Belinda Wheaton, "'Just Do It': Consumption, Commitment, and Identity in the Windsurfing Subculture," *Sociology of Sport Journal* 17 (2000).

49 Adidas's relationship with the Krew is discussed in Valentine Low, "The East End High Life: French Free-Running Sport 'Parkour' Gets Off to a Flying Start in London," *Evening Standard*, July 4, 2006. Photos of the Krew modeling the Hyperride can be found on an archived APK message board, accessed March 31, 2015, http://www.americanparkour.com/smf/index.php?topic=1888.0. K Swiss's release of the Airake is mentioned in "K Swiss Signs up Youth Fashion Specialist," *PR Week*, July 13, 2007.

50 Edwards and Corte, "Commercialization and Lifestyle Sport."

51 Belinda Wheaton, "Selling Out?: The Commercialisation and Globalisation of Lifestyle Sport," in *The Global Politics of Sport: The Role of Global Institutions in Sport*, ed. Lincoln Allison (New York: Routledge, 2005).

52 See Robert E. Rinehart, "Exploiting a New Generation: Corporate Branding and the Co-Option of Action Sports," in *Youth Culture and Sport: Identity, Power, and Politics*, eds. Michael D. Giardina and Michele K. Donnelly (New York: Routledge, 2008). While by no means unique to parkour, such marketing is also a key component of the conditions of postmodernity. That is, images and signs become paramount to the performance of identity. See Zygmunt Bauman, *Intimations of Postmodernity* (New York: Routledge, 1992). Of course, training in parkour is a visceral, embodied experience, but it becomes intertwined with its representation through articles of clothing. Similarly, for all its anti-consumerist ideology and live-for-the-moment rhetoric, authenticity in the punk subculture is also mediated through consumption styles—namely, purchasing records, wearing band t-shirts, and being able to negotiate the fluid norms and expectations for displaying these symbols. See Ryan William Force, "Consumption Styles and the Fluid Complexity of Punk Authenticity," *Symbolic Interaction* 32 (2009).

53 See Norbert Elias, "Introduction," in *The Quest for Excitement: Sport and Leisure in the Civilizing Process*, eds. Norbert Elias and Eric Dunning (New York: Basil Blackwell, 1986); also see Eric Dunning, "The Dynamics of Modern Sport: Notes on Achievement-Striving and the Social Significance of Sport," *The Quest for Excitement: Sport and Leisure in the Civilizing Process*, eds. Norbert Elias and Eric Dunning (New York: Basil Blackwell, 1986).

54 Rebecca Heino, "What's So Punk About Snowboarding," *Journal of Sport & Social Issues* 24 (2000); Holly Thorpe and Belinda Wheaton, "'Generation X Games,' Action Sports, and the Olympic Movement: Understanding the Cultural Politics of Incorporation," *Sociology* 45 (2011).

55 Both Angel and Wheaton discuss the contentious aspects of UF. See Angel, *Ciné Parkour* and Wheaton, *The Cultural Politics of Lifestyle Sports*. In *Jump Magazine*, of which Corkery was the main contributor, there were off-handed homophobic jokes and sexual innuendoes. For example, Corkery made allusions to hiring strippers to entertain the Krew on trips and publicly professed his interest in taking naked photographs of a female traceur interviewed in the magazine. While Corkery's macho persona might not have raised eyebrows in more traditional sporting worlds, his viewpoints and actions were antithetical to how many traceurs envisioned the discipline. There is an ironic corollary to Urban Freeflow's strategy of incorporation. Lifestyle sports are also premised on an assertion of authenticity, and companies and organizations that court mainstream attention risk alienating core participants. See Wheaton and Beal, "Keeping It Real" and Browne, *Amped*. For all of its early success, there was a backlash against UF driven by newer organizations deemed more authentic by traceurs. Unlike Foucan, who, criticisms aside, is still respected, UF totally imploded under the weight of its prominence within the community. Recently, the name and logo of Urban Freeflow were acquired by four entrepreneurial traceurs from Germany. The new organization, they claim, is unaffiliated with Corkery. While hoping to transcend the stigma many in the parkour community associate with the original UF, the new UF is also hoping to reestablish the brand as a moneymaking entity.

56 Esther Addley and Camden Roundhouse, "One Giant Leap: Freerunning Joins Sport Establishment," *The Guardian*, September 4, 2008.

57 In fact, Red Bull has been astoundingly successful in underwriting numerous obscure sporting events and marketing them to mainstream audiences. See Rob

Walker, *Buying In: The Secret Dialogue between What We Buy and Who We Are* (New York: Random House, 2008).

58 Much of this information can be found on WFPF's website, accessed February 12, 2015, http://www.wfpf.com/history-wfpf/.

59 Robert E. Rinehart, "The Inside of the Outside: Pecking Orders within Alternative Sports at ESPN's 1995 'the Extreme Games,'" *Journal of Sport & Social Issues* 22 (1998).

60 Booth, "The Paradoxes of Material Culture"; also see Beal and Wilson, "'Chicks Dig Scars'"; Robert E. Rinehart, "Dropping into Sight: Commodification and Co-Optation of In-Line Skating," in *To the Extreme: Alternative Sports, Inside and Out*, eds. Robert E. Rinehart and Synthia Sydnor (Albany, NY: State University of New York Press, 2003).

61 Wheaton, *The Cultural Politics of Lifestyle Sports.*

62 Angel, *Ciné Parkour.* Examples of PKGen's critiques of Red Bull include Dan Edwardes, "A Question of Principle (or How to Resist the Red-Bullion)," danedwardes.com (2013), accessed April 7, 2015, http://danedwardes.com/2013/08/15a-question-of-principles-or-how-to-resist-thered-bullion; the history page on Parkour Way's website, accessed April 7, 2015, http://www.parkourways .com/history.

63 See Angel, *Ciné Parkour*; Paul Gilchrist and Belinda Wheaton, "Lifestyle Sport, Public Policy, and Youth Engagement: Examining the Emergence of Parkour," *International Journal of Sport Policy & Politics* 3 (2011); also see Parkour UK's website, accessed February 20, 2015, http://www.parkouruk.org/about/the-board/.

64 Information about the certifications can be found on the respective websites. WFPF, accessed February 12, 2015, http://www.wfpf.com/history-wfpf/; APK, accessed April 7, 2015, http://americanparkour.com/academy/parkour-instructor-certification/; also see Wheaton, *The Cultural Politics of Lifestyle Sports.*

65 Gym information can be found on the following respective websites: APK, accessed February 20, 2015, http://americanparkour.com/academy/; Apex, accessed February 20, 2015, http://www.apexmovement.com/about/; Apex, accessed April 7, 2015, http://www.apexmovement.com/coaching-certification/; Tempest, accessed February 20, 2015 https://www.facebook.com/events/120879504654239/. Information on Equinox is discussed in Christian Red, "By Leaps and Bounds: Parkour is Taking Off with International Following," *Daily News*, July 26, 2009. This is not intended as a complete list of parkour gyms in America. In recent years there has been a massive increase in the number of gyms catering to traceurs.

Chapter 2 New Prisms of the Possible

1 Sherry Turkle, *Life On the Screen: Identity in the Age of the Internet (New York: Simon & Schuster, 1995); Manuel Castells, The Rise of Network Society (Malden, MA Blackwell Publishers, 1996). In particular,* Barry Wellman emphasizes the ways in which virtual worlds and the real world are interconnected. See Barry Wellman, "The Three Ages of Internet Studies: Ten, Five, and Zero Years Ago," *New Media & Society* 6 (2004); also see Manuel Castells, *Communication Power* (New York: Oxford University Press, 2009). For example, instead of conceptualizing an inverse relationship between time on screen and time offscreen, studies show that participation in virtual communities can actually facilitate participation

in face-to-face interactions. See especially Keith Hampton and Barry Wellman, "Neighboring in Netville: How the Internet Supports Community and Social Capital in a Wired Suburb," *City & Community* 2 (2003). Alternatively, Norman Nie points out that time is finite and that online activities have the potential to limit, not enhance, real-world socializing. Norman H. Nie, "Sociability, Interpersonal Relations, and the Internet: Reconciling Conflicting Findings," *American Behavioral Scientists 45 (2001).*

2 The more radical versions of this view are summed up in Frances Cairncross, *The Death of Distance: How the Communication Revolution is Changing Our Lives, Second Edition* (Boston: Harvard Business School Press, 2001); also see Howard Rheingold, *The Virtual Community: Homesteading on the Electronic Frontier* (Reading, MA: Addison-Wesley Publishing, 1993). Alternatively, others are far less sanguine. Communication and information technologies cannot obliterate biological limits and structural inequalities. See Kevin Robins, "Cyberspace and the World We Live In," *Body & Society* 1 (1995).

3 Arjun Appadurai, "Global Ethnoscapes: Notes and Queries for a Transnational Anthropology," in *Modernity at Large: Cultural Dimensions of Globalization* (Minneapolis: University of Minnesota Press, 1993 [1996]), 55.

4 During the 1970s, for example, surf magazines and films helped spread the Australian style of "shredding" waves across the globe. See Douglas Booth, "Expression Sessions: Surfing, Style, and Prestige," in *To the Extreme: Alternative Sports Inside and Out,* eds. Robert E. Rinehart and Synthia Sydnor (Albany, NY: State University of New York Press, 2003). During the 1980s VHS tapes became a key aspect to the evolution of street skateboarding. See Iain Borden, *Skateboarding, Space, and the City: Architecture and the Body* (New York: Berg, 2001); also see Gregory J. Snyder, "The City and the Subculture Career: Professional Street Skateboarding in LA," *Ethnography* 13 (2012).

5 Appadurai, "Global Ethnoscapes," 53–54.

6 Paul Gilchrist and Belinda Wheaton also stress the significance of new media for parkour community. Paul Gilchrist and Belinda Wheaton, "New Media Technologies in Lifestyle Sport" in *Digital Media Sport: Technology, Power, and Culture in the Network Society,* eds. Brett Hutchinson and David Rowe (New York: Routledge, 2013).

7 Scott Stapleton and Susan Terrio also discuss global ethnoscapes in their analysis of parkour. Scott Stapleton and Susan Terrio, "Le Parkour: Urban Street Culture and the Commoditization of Male Youth Expression," *International Migration* 50 (2010).

8 Mizuko Ito and her co-researchers provide a thorough exploration of how youth use and interact with new media. Mizuko Ito et al., *Hanging Out, Messing Around, and Geeking Out: Kids Living and Learning with New Media* (Cambridge, MA: MIT Press, 2010).

9 danah boyd, *It's Complicated: The Social Lives of Networked Teens* (New Haven: Yale University Press, 2014); also see Ito et al., *Hanging Out, Messing Around, and Geeking Out.*

10 Daniel J. Boorstin, *The Image: A Guide to Pseudo-Events in America* (New York: Harper & Row, 1961); Guy Debord, *The Society of the Spectacle,* trans. Donald Nicholson-Smith (New York: Zone Books, 1994), 5; Jean Baudrillard, *Simulacra and Simulation,* trans. Shelia Faria Glaser (Ann Arbor: University of Michigan Press, 1981 [1994]).

11 To quote Susan Sontag, "Whatever the moral claims on behalf of photography, its main effect is to convert the world into a department store or museum-without-walls in which every subject is depreciated into an article of consumption, promoted into an item for aesthetic appreciation. Through the camera people become customers or tourists of reality." Susan Sontag, *On Photography* (New York: Farrar, Straus & Giroux, 1977), 85.

12 Scott Bass, "How to Start Filming Parkour," Ampisound.com (2011), accessed May 12, 2015, http://www.ampisound.com/featured/starting-howto-film-parkour/. Likewise, *Jump Magazine* advised traceurs: "In each scene you shoot, it's always good to let the person enter and leave the frame after the action. If the traceur runs out of one shot and into the next it helps the continuity of the video and make it seem like they're travelling from one place to the next, rather than just a collection of single tricks." Ben Milner, "Plan Your Work and Work Your Plan," *Jump Magazine,* March, 2010, 10. Again, in reality, the traceur being filmed is not traveling someplace and is merely performing a collection of single tricks.

13 Respectively: Robert E. Rinehart, "Exploiting a New Generation: Corporate Branding and the Co-Option of Action Sports," in *Youth Culture and Sport: Identity, Power, and Politics,* eds. Michael D. Giardina and Michele K. Donnelly (New York: Routledge, 2008), 80; Robert E. Rinehart, "Dropping Into Sight: Commodification and Co-Optation of In-Line Skating," in *To the Extreme: Alternative Sports Inside and Out,* eds. Robert E. Rinehart and Synthia Sydnor (Albany, NY: State University of New York Press, 2003), 44. In the case of skateboarding, Iain Borden traces many of the contemporary filming techniques back to motor-drive cameras in skateparks in the 1970s and video technologies in the 1980s. Borden, *Skateboarding, Space, and the City.*

14 Sontag, *On Photography, 67.*

15 Mihaly Csikszentmihalyi, *Beyond Boredom and Anxiety* (San Francisco: Jossey-Bass Publishers, 1975). Of course, to the extent that training and jamming are defined by reflexive concerns about how performances will be presented in mediated form, flow can be disrupted. Alternatively, the process of filming allows for its own generation of flow. Many traceurs enjoy filming themselves and others, and the tasks can be engrossing in their own right. On this point, see Rodney H. Jones, "Sport and Re/creation" What Skateboarding Can Teach Us about Learning," *Sport, Education & Society 16 (2011).* Regardless, the more one is attuned to the conditions required to produce visually appealing footage, the less one can be attuned to the enjoyment of the immediate moment. The fact that this distinction seems to be blurring for individuals only strengths the postmodern argument—reality can only be experienced through the representation of reality. See Jean Baudrillard, *Symbolic Exchange and Death,* trans. Iain Hamilton Grant (Thousand Oaks: Sage Publications, 1976 [1993]).

16 Stephen Lyng, "Edgework: A Social Psychological Analysis of Voluntary Risk Taking," *American Journal of Sociology* 95 (1990): 881.

17 Randall Collins offers a detailed theory of rituals and what he calls emotional energy. Randall Collins, *Interaction Ritual Chains* (Princeton, NJ: Princeton University Press, 2004). Jeffrey Alexander discusses rituals and the generation of flow. Jeffrey C. Alexander, "Cultural Pragmatics: Social Performance between Ritual and Strategy," *Sociological Theory* 22 (2004). Elsewhere, I apply these

concepts in the analysis of the bike messenger subculture. See Jeffrey L. Kidder, *Urban Flow: Bike Messengers and the City* (Ithaca, NY: Cornell University Press, 2011); also see Kenneth Allan, *The Meaning of Culture: Moving the Postmodern Critique Forward* (Westport, CT: Praeger, 1998).

18 Emile Durkheim, *The Elementary Forms of Religious Life,* trans. Karen Fields (New York: Free Press, 1912 [1995]). It is only in connecting with the collective that an individual can feel purpose in action and belief. As Durkheim states, "A society is to its members what god is to its faithful" (208). Further, rituals call forth the social self because, during the ritual, individuals act in unison. By acting in unison, the desires of the ego are subsumed by the group. "It is by shouting the same cry, saying the same words, and performing the same action in regard to the same object that they arrive at and experience agreement" (232). In experiencing agreement, the social state of the self becomes privileged. The individual internalizes an "active presence of religious force" (223). This religious force is not felt as coercion, but as individual nature—the heart, the soul. "Because social pressure makes itself felt through mental channels, it was bound to give man the idea that outside him there are one or several powers, moral yet mighty to which he is subject" (211).

19 James J. Gibson, *The Ecological Approach to Visual Perception* (Boston: Houghton Mifflin Company, 1979).

20 Numerous male-dominated subcultures and social worlds could be described thusly. Writing about windsurfers, Belinda Wheaton notes that status is based on "being willing to attempt hard and dangerous maneuvers [. . .] even if they fail, and being prepared/able to go out in all conditions, particularly the windiest days, and the most dangerous sea conditions [. . .]." Belinda Wheaton, "'Just Do It': Consumption, Commitment, and Identity in the Windsurfing Subculture," *Sociology of Sport Journal* 17 (2000): 259. Similarly, Nancy Macdonald equally stresses that status garnered in the graffiti subculture comes through bravery in the face of physical danger and police enforcement. "Writers do not risk their life and liberty for the sole sake of a written name. They take these risks because they know this will gain them other writers' respect." Nancy Macdonald, *Graffiti Subculture: Youth, Masculinity, and Identity* (New York: Palgrave Macmillan, 2001), 104.

21 As the phenomenological argument of Maurice Merleau-Ponty shows, all perceptions of the world are dialectically connected to the lived experience of the body. "It is, therefore, quite true that any perception of a thing, shape or a size as real, any perceptual constancy refers back to the positioning of a world and a system of experience in which my body is inescapably linked with phenomena. But the system of experience is not arrayed before me as if I were God, it is lived by me from a certain point of view; I am not a spectator, I am involved, and it is my involvement in a point of view which makes possible both the finiteness of my perception and its opening out upon the complete world as a horizon of every perception." Maurice Merleau-Ponty, *Phenomenology of Perception,* trans. Colin Smith (New York: Routledge, 1945 [2002]), 353–354.

22 It is worth mentioning here that the public nature of most parkour training can produce a great deal of social discomfort for those learning the discipline—especially older practitioners. While children are expected to climb and jump onto things, that behavior can be seen as quite bizarre when performed by adults. Counsel, for example, started training in his late twenties. He said of his initial involvement with the community, "I had to hide from all my friends and family what I was doing

because it sounded ridiculous." Oli Mould expands on these points in his analysis of parkour as an activity that necessitates individuals embrace a "childlike agency." This is to say, parkour vision involves the very un-adult practice of creatively using the built environment. Oli Mould, "Parkour Activism, and Young People," in *Space, Place, and Environment,* eds. Karen Nairn, Peter Kraftl, and Tracey Skelton (Singapore: Springer Singapore, 2015). As an illustration of this, a common retort when someone asks, "When did you start doing parkour?" is for a traceur to respond, "When did you stop?" Their point is that children engage in the basics of parkour on a routine basis. Adults, having become self-conscious about climbing, exploring, and running in public places not designated for such activities, have thus stopped practicing parkour.

23 Similarly, Lieven Ameel and Sirpa Tani offer an insightful analysis on how parkour training can produce new meanings for places through the traceurs' "parkour eyes." Lieven Ameel and Sirpa Tani, "Everyday Aesthetics in Action: Parkour Eyes and the Beauty of Concrete Walls," *Emotions, Space, & Society* 5 (2012).

24 Holly Thorpe and Nida Ahmad develop this point in their study of parkour in Gaza. Holly Thorpe and Nida Ahmad, "Youth, Action Sports, and Political Agency in the Middle East: Lessons from a Grassroots Parkour Group in Gaza," *International Review for the Sociology of Sport* 50 (2015).

25 See Michel de Certeau, *The Practices of Everyday Life,* trans. Steven Rendall (Berkeley: University of California Press, 1984); Henri Lefebvre, *The Production of Space,* trans. Donald Nicholson-Smith (Cambridge, MA: Blackwell, 1974 [1991]).

26 Sherry Turkle, *Alone Together: Why We Expect More from Technology and Less from Each Other* (New York: Basic Books, 2011).

27 Pokémon Go, a videogame for smartphones, represents a fascinating twist to these points. With Pokémon Go (and its precursor, Ingress) people use their phones to "augment" the real world with aspects of the virtual world. The game involves players physically going to various destinations (e.g., a particular street corner or a section of a park) in order to "capture" (via GPS tracking and cameras on their smartphones) characters from the game. Specifically, when a Pokémon Go player approaches an area populated with characters, they are able to look at the screen of their phone (as if they were shooting video) and see an augmented reality in which (in addition to the tangible world everyone can see) they find virtual monsters—a hyperreality indeed. See Nick Wingfield and Mike Isaac, "Pokémon Go Bring Augmented Reality to a Mass Audience," *New York Times,* July 11, 2016.

Chapter 3 Young Men in the City

1 Georg Simmel, "The Adventurer," in *On Individuality and Social Forms: Selected Writing,* ed. and trans. Donald N. Levine (Chicago: University of Chicago Press, 1911 [1971]); also see Jules J. Wanderer, "Simmel's Forms of Experiencing: The Adventure as Symbolic Work," *Symbolic Interaction* 10 (1987).

2 Gunnar Breivik, "Trends in Adventure Sports in Post-Modern Society," *Sport in Society* 13 (2010). Likewise, David Le Breton writes, "Constantly being called up to prove themselves in a society where reference points are both countless and contradictory and where values are in crisis, people are seeking, through radical one-to-one contest, to test their strength of character, their courage and their personal resources." David Le Breton, "Playing Symbolically with Death in Extreme Sports," *Body & Society* 6 (2000): 1.

3 Numerous researchers have contrasted the dangers faced and skills honed in mountaineering with the mundane aspects of contemporary life. For example, Peter Donnelly and Trevor Williams, "Subcultural Production, Reproduction, and Transformation in Climbing," *International Review for the Sociology of Sport* 20 (1985); Ian Heywood, "Urgent Dreams: Climbing, Rationalization, and Ambivalence," *Leisure Studies* 13 (1994); Jackie Kiewa, "Traditional Climbing: Metaphor of Resistance or Metanarrative of Oppression?" *Leisure Studies* 21 (2002); Neil Lewis, "The Climbing Body, Nature, and the Experience of Modernity," *Body & Society* 6 (2000); Richard G. Mitchell, *Mountain Experience: The Psychology and Sociology of Adventure* (Chicago: University of Chicago Press, 1983); Victoria Robinson, *Everyday Masculinities and Extreme Sports: The Male Identity and Rock Climbing* (New York: Berg, 2008). There are countless other lifestyle sports that could be mentioned here as well, for instance, adventure racing, fell running, and whitewater rafting. See (respectively) Joanne Kay and Suzanne Laberge, "Mapping the Field of 'AR': Adventure Racing and Bourdieu's Concept of Field," *Sociology of Sport Journal* 19 (2002); Michael Atkinson, "Fell Running and Voluptuous Panic: On Caillois and Post-Sport Physical Culture," *American Journal of Play* 4 (2011); Lori Holyfield, "Manufacturing Adventure: The Buying and Selling of Emotions," *Journal of Contemporary Ethnography* 28 (1999). On adventure more generally see Heinz-Günter Vester, "Adventure as a Form of Leisure," *Leisure Studies* 6 (1987).

4 Walter Benjamin, *The Arcades Project*, trans. Howard Eiland and Kevin McLaughlin (Cambridge, MA: Belknap Press, 1982 [1999]). Michel de Certeau famously describes walking in the city as a sort of poetry written by everyday practices. Michel de Certeau, *The Practice of Everyday Life*, trans. Steven Rendall (Berkeley: University of California Press, 1984); also see Henri Lefebvre, "Seen from the Window," in *Writings on Cities*, eds. and trans. Eleonore Kofman and Elizabeth Lebas (Cambridge, MA Blackwell Publishers, 1996); Lyn H. Lofland, *The Public Realm: Exploring the City's Quintessential Social Territory* (Hawthorne, NY: Aldine de Gruyter, 1998). Richard Sennett exalts the virtues of diverse social interaction fostered in the city, and decries the homogeneity of the suburbs. Richard Sennett, *The Uses of Disorder: Personal Identity and City Life* (New York: Knopf, 1970). In terms of urban planning, Jane Jacobs and William Whyte both champion designs that promote increasing the hustle and bustle of the metropolis. See Jane Jacobs, *The Death and Life of Great American Cities* (New York: Random House, 1961); William H. Whyte, *City: Rediscovering the Center* (New York: Doubleday, 1988). Such suggestions might seem commonplace today, but they ran counter to the political and cultural wisdom of the postwar years. See Andrés Duany, Elizabeth Plater-Zyberk, and Jeff Speck, *Suburban Nation: The Rise of Sprawl and the Decline of the American Dream* (New York: North Point Press, 2000). On urban exploring see Bradley L. Garrett, "Cracking the Paris Carriers: Corporal Terror and Illicit Encounter Under the City of Light," *ACME* 10 (2011). On bicycling see Phil Jones, "Performing the City: A Body and a Bicycle Take on Birmingham, UK," *Social & Cultural Geography* 6 (2005).

5 Stanford M. Lyman and Marvin B. Scott, *A Sociology of the Absurd* (New York: Appleton-Century-Crofts, 1970); Erving Goffman "Where the Action Is," in *Interaction Ritual: Essays on Face-to-Face Behavior* (New York: Anchor Books, 1967), 238.

6 Goffman, "Where the Action Is," 200.

7 Thomas J. Scheff, *Goffman Unbound! A New Paradigm for Social Science* (Boulder, CO: Paradigm Publishers, 2006).

8 Janice Kaplan, *Women and Sports* (New York: Viking Press, 1979). Sexism and male privilege have been at the forefront of studies attempting to understand the experiences of female lifestyle sport participants. Holly Thorpe, for example, shows that despite a fluidity of gender boundaries within the snowboarding subculture, the everyday practices on the slopes tend to marginalize women (as well as many men) who fail to perform challenging and dangerous maneuvers. Holly Thorpe, *Snowboarding Bodies in Theory and Practice* (New York: Palgrave Macmillan, 2011). Combining their research on skydiving and snowboarding, Jason Laurendeau and Nancy Sharara detail the difficulties faced by women in these sports and the differing tactics available for asserting their competencies in them. While highlighting the dynamic nature of gender relations (and the potential for structural change), Laurendeau and Sharara's analysis emphasizes the feelings of otherness often experienced by women in these sports. Jason Laurendeau and Nancy Sharara, "'Women Could Be Every Bit as Good as Guys': Reproductive and Resistant Agency in Two 'Action' Sports," *Journal of Sport & Social Issues* 32 (2008). As such, even when women participate in lifestyle sports, the accompanying social worlds still tend to be defined by the male participants.

9 Michael Schwalbe, "Identity Stakes, Manhood Acts, and the Dynamics of Accountability," *Studies in Symbolic Interaction* 28 (2005).

10 Judith Butler, *Gender Trouble: Feminism and the Subversion of Identity* (New York: Routledge, 1990); Raine Dozier, "Beards, Breasts, and Bodies: Doing Sex in a Gendered World," *Gender & Society* 19 (2005); C.J. Pascoe, *Dude, You're a Fag: Masculinity and Sexuality in High School* (Berkeley: University of California Press, 2007); Eva Kosopsky Sedgwick, "Gosh Boy George, You Must Be Awfully Secure in Your Masculinity!" in *Constructing Masculinity*, eds. Maurice Berger, Brian Wallis, and Simon Watson (New York: Routledge, 1995).

11 As Jim Dowd notes, "Important identity themes such as gender are indeed usually so well-rehearsed as to require no conscious effort to enact; this fact, however, should not blind us to the truth that gender roles, as with other social identities, do require practice and that individuals may choose to improvise upon these roles or to, in other ways, 'individualize' their social identities. The postmodern twist to the interactionist idea of role making is that we all have become much more aware not only of the dramaturgical requirements faced by others but also those that we as well must take into account. We reflexively analyze all social and personal identities, even those aspects like our gender identity that, in past eras, would not normally receive such careful scrutiny and reflexive analysis." James J. Dowd, "An Act Made Perfect in Habit: The Self in the Postmodern Age," *Current Perspectives in Social Theory* 16 (1996): 248–249.

12 In particular, masculine performances denote control and power over one's self and one's environment. For example, see Raewyn Connell, *The Men and the Boys* (Berkeley: University of California Press, 2000); Allan G. Johnson, *The Gender Knot: Unraveling Our Patriarchal Legacy, Revised and Updated* (Philadelphia: Temple University Press, 2005); Michael S. Kimmel, "The Cult of Masculinity: American Social Characteristics and the Legacy of the Cowboy," in *The History of Men: Essays in the History of American and British Masculinity* (New York: State

University of New York Press, 1987 [2005]). Exerting control and power allows one to persevere through the mist of uncertainty, and I am interested in how parkour can become part of this gendering process.

13 Connell, *The Men and the Boys.*

14 See Tim Carrigan, Raewyn Connell, and John Lee, "Toward a New Sociology of Masculinity," *Theory & Society* 14 (1985).

15 Douglas Schrock and Michael Schwalbe, "Men, Masculinity, and Manhood Acts," *Annual Review of Sociology* 35 (2009).

16 On sexist talk in lifestyle sports, see Douglas Booth, "Surfing: From One (Cultural) Extreme to Another," in *Understanding Lifestyle Sports: Consumption, Identity, and Difference*, ed. Belinda Wheaton (New York: Routledge, 2004); Deirdre M. Kelly, Shauna Pomerantz, and Dawn H. Currie, "'You Can Break So Many More Rules': The Identity Work and Play of Becoming Skater Girls," in *Youth Culture and Sport: Identity, Power, and Politics*, ed. Michael D. Giardina and Michele K. Donnelly (New York: Routledge, 2008); Laurendeau and Sharara, "'Women Could Be Every Bit as Good as Guys.'" On mainstream sports see Michael A. Messner, "Riding with the Spur Posse," in *Sex, Violence, and Power in Sport: Rethinking Masculinity*, eds. Michael A. Messner and Donald F. Sabo (Freedom, CA: The Crossing Press, 1994). On teenage boys see Pascoe, *Dude, You're a Fag.*

17 Nancy Macdonald criticizes the subcultural studies of the 1970s and '80s for asking why women were not present in male-dominated scenes such as punk and heavy metal. Alternatively, Macdonald poses that the question be asked in reverse: why are men attracted to these subcultures? In other words, what do they offer to men in terms of constructing and affirming masculine identities? Nancy Macdonald, *The Graffiti Subculture: Youth, Masculinity, and Identity in London and New York* (New York: Palgrave Macmillan, 2001).

18 Maria Daskalaki and Oli Mould, for example, propose that creative, transgressive urban activities—from flash mobs to graffiti—be considered fluid processes. Individuals and the practices they engage in are constantly fluctuating—opening up previously unimagined possibilities for new forms of action. Maria Daskalaki and Oli Mould, "Beyond Urban Subcultures: Urban Subversions as Rhizomatic Social Formations," *International Journal of Urban and Regional Research* 37 (2013).

19 Michael Hawthorne, "Chicago River Still Teems with Fecal Bacteria, Tests Show," *Chicago Tribune*, August 28, 2015. In this specific case, the outcome (once it was known) was ambivalent. The local media mentioned the stunt, which most traceurs seemed to take a certain degree of pride in. Conversely, the traceur's attraction of police attention angered many within the parkour community (even those who seemed impressed by the news coverage). Several weeks after the event, Arnold was covered in a full body rash, which he attributed to his exposure to the water. For his part, he attempted to situate his skin malady as proof that he was the sort of person willing to do bold and outlandish things. Alternatively, many Chicago traceurs took his persistent rash to indicate Arnold's unchecked recklessness (see chapter four).

20 Lieven Ameel and Sirpa Tani make a similar point about Finnish traceurs' interactions with the police. Lieven Ameel and Sirpa Tani, "Parkour: Creating Loose Spaces?" *Geografiska Annaler: Series B, Human Geography* 94 (2012).

21 Iain Borden, *Skateboarding, Space, and the City: Architecture and the Body* (New York: Berg, 2001); Francisco Vivoni, "Waxing Ledges: Built Environments,

Alternative Sustainability, and the Chicago Skateboarding Scene," *Local Environment* 18 (2013).

22 For example, see M. P. Baumgartner, *The Moral Order of a Suburb* (New York: Oxford University Press, 1988).

23 See especially Mary E. Pattillo, *Black on the Block: The Politics of Race and Class in the City* (Chicago: University of Chicago Press, 2007); Robert J. Sampson, *Great American City: Chicago and the Enduring Neighborhood Effect* (Chicago: University of Chicago Press, 2012); William Julius Wilson, *When Work Disappears: The World of the New Urban Poor* (New York: Knopf, 1996).

24 See Elijah Anderson, "The Iconic Ghetto," *Annals of the American Academy of Political and Social Science* 642 (2012).

25 Over the years, I watched teens from the white suburbs and teens from the city's segregated black and Latino neighborhoods become friends—friendships that occasionally extended outside of their training. In other words, the social ties facilitated by parkour sometimes spurred opportunities for these young men to visit different parts of town and meet new people. One black traceur, for example, described the pervasive threat of violent crime and gang activity in his neighborhood growing up. Through his friendships in the parkour community, however, he moved to the city's North Side (in a vibrant college area) to room with a white traceur. Conversely, I saw little evidence that white traceurs were willing to venture out to places populated primarily by non-whites. Again, this speaks to the white privilege permeating the discipline (and nearly all aspects of white Americans' lives). That is, while members of the parkour community embraced difference, they did so primarily within spaces cultural coded as white (and, thus, "safe").

26 Matthew Lamb also discusses traceurs' general compliance with authority over requests to leave areas and the high value placed on maintaining a positive public image of the discipline. Matthew D. Lamb, "Misuses of the Monument: The Art of Parkour and the Discursive Limits of Disciplinary Architecture," *Journal of Urban Cultural Studies* 1 (2014); also see Jennifer L. Clegg and Ted M. Butryn, "An Existential Phenomenological Examination of Parkour and Freerunning," *Qualitative Research in Sport, Exercise & Health* 4 (2012).

27 See J. Patrick Williams, *Subcultural Theory: Traditions and Concepts* (Malden, MA: Polity Press, 2011). Discussing the masculinity of the graffiti subculture, Macdonald writes, "By writing his name on a train or in an illegal area, the [graffiti] writer effectively says, 'I was there and it was my courage and resilience which got me there.' The nature of this challenge and the masculine qualities which enabled its completion are [. . .] authorized by [his painting]." Macdonald, *The Graffiti Subculture*, 103–104.

28 Le Breton, "Playing Symbolically with Death in Extreme Sports"; Steven Lyng, "Edgework, Risk, and Uncertainty," in *Social Theories of Risk and Uncertainty: An Introduction*, ed. Jens O. Zinn (Malden, MA: Blackwell Publishers, 2008); Jonathan Simon, "Taking Risks: Extreme Sports and the Embrace of Risk in Advanced Liberal Societies," in *Embracing Risk: The Changing Culture of Insurance and Responsibility*, eds. Tom Baker and Jonathan Simon (Chicago: University of Chicago Press, 2002). Alternatively, other researchers have questioned the importance of risk in alternative sports. For example, Mark Stranger, *Surfing Life: Surface, Substructure, and the Commodification of the Sublime* (Farnham, UK: Ashgate, 2011); Amanda West and Linda Allin, "Chancing Your Arm: The Meaning of Risk in Rock Climbing," *Sport in Society* 13 (2010). At the discursive

level, traceurs were ambivalent about risk. To outsiders, they were eager to downplay the dangers involved. Also see Paul Gilchrist and Belinda Wheaton, "Lifestyle Sport, Public Policy, and Youth Engagement: Examining the Emergence of Parkour," *International Journal of Sport Policy & Politics* 3 (2011). But, among themselves, "risk" was a ubiquitous topic for discussion. More importantly, the decisions traceurs made about what urban obstacles they wished to surmount and how they would surmount them left little doubt that a desire for risk taking was essential. In the examples of Scales (introduction) or Voigt (this chapter), had their interest simply been in performing the distance of the jump, they could have stayed at ground level. They moved higher up precisely because it increased the risk involved. Peter Donnelly and Trevor Williams make this same point in reference to mountaineering: "Jeopardy is a constitutive element of climbing. [. . .] Indeed, jeopardy is so important that to remove it from climbing would be to make the activity something else [. . .]." Peter Donnelly and Trevor Williams, "Subcultural Production, Reproduction, and the Transformation in Climbing," *International Review for the Sociology of Sport* 20 (1985): 4. Risk, and perceptions of it, will be explored in detail in chapter four.

29 Atencio et al., "The Distinction of Risk"; Borden, *Skateboarding, Space, and the City*.

30 It is important for the reader to note that I am not claiming such risks are inherently male. Obviously, many females take part in "masculine" sports. Further, I am not claiming that dangerous or painful endeavors are inherently masculine. Childbirth, for example, is characterized by both of these attributes while being quintessentially female. In modern Western culture, gymnastics is also considered a "feminine" activity for young girls, but it involves many risks similar to those of parkour. The difference, and this is essential, comes from how these risks are enacted and understood, individually and collectively.

31 As mentioned above, on this point see Atencio et al.'s discussion "The Distinction of Risk"; also see Clifton Evers, "Men Who Surf," *Cultural Studies* 10 (2004), Kyle Kusz, "BMX, Extreme Sports, and the White Male Backlash," in *To the Extreme: Alternative Sports Inside and Out*, eds. Robert E. Rinehart and Synthia Sydnor (Albany, NY: State University of New York Press, 2003); Jason Laurendeau, "'Gendered Risk Regimes': A Theoretical Consideration of Edgework and Gender," *Sociology of Sport Journal* 25 (2008); Michael A. Messner, "When Bodies are Weapons: Masculinity and Violence in Sport," *International Review for the Sociology of Sport* 25 (1990); Thorpe, *Snowboarding Bodies in Theory and Practice*; Christian A. Vaccaro, Douglas Schrock, and Janice M. McCade, "Managing Emotional Manhood: Fighting and Fostering Fear in Mixed Martial Arts," *Social Psychology Quarterly* 74 (2011); Gordon Waitt and Andrew Warren, "'Talking Shit Over a Brew After a Good Session with Your Mates': Surfing, Space, and Masculinity," *Australian Geographer* 39 (2008); Belinda Wheaton, "'Just Do It': Consumption, Commitment, and Identity in the Windsurfing Subculture," *Sociology of Sport Journal* 17 (2000).

32 The point here is *also* not that running and bicycling do not pose risks; they do. It is that parkour—like most lifestyle sports—posits the thrill to be had from engaging in those risks as an organizing principle of the activity—action for action's sake (see chapter four).

33 This is similar to the gendering that takes place in other lifestyle sports. For example, while more women have taken up skateboarding in recent years, street skating (as

opposed to riding in skateparks) is still an almost exclusively male terrain. Atencio et al., "The Distinction of Risk." The same is true when comparing snow sport participation at resorts to backcountry snowboarding and skiing. See (respectively) Thorpe, *Snowboarding Bodies in Theory and Practice*; Mark C. Stoddart, "Constructing Masculinized Sportscapes: Skiing, Gender, and Nature in British Columbia, Canada," *International Review for the Sociology of Sport* 46 (2010).

34 Peter Donnelly and Kevin Young, "The Construction and Confirmation of Identities in Sports Subcultures," *Sociology of Sport Journal* 5 (1988); also see Sheldon Stryker, "Identity Salience and Role Performance: The Relevance of Symbolic Interaction Theory for Family Research," *Journal of Marriage & the Family* 30 (1968).

35 Michael Atkinson, "Parkour, Anarcho-Environmentalism, and Poïesis," *Journal of Sport & Social Issues* 32 (2009).

36 Borden, *Skateboarding, Space, and the City*.

37 Candace West and Don H. Zimmerman, "Doing Gender," *Gender & Society* 1 (1987).

38 Kyle Kusz, "Extreme America: The Cultural Politics of Extreme Sports in 1990s America," in *Understanding Lifestyle Sports: Consumption, Identity, and Difference* (New York: Routledge, 2004).

39 Butler, *Gender Trouble*; Dowd, "An Act Made Perfect in Habit."

Chapter 4 Hedging Their Bets

1 The anterior cruciate ligament (ACL), which helps stabilize the knee, is commonly put under strain in a variety of sports. Depending on the severity of the injury, surgery may be required to reconstruct the joint.

2 See (respectively) Mark Stranger, *Surfing Life: Surface, Substance, and the Commodification of the Sublime* (Farnham, UK: Ashgate, 2011); Matthew Atencio, Becky Beal, Charlene Wilson, "The Distinction of Risk: Urban Skateboarding. Street Habitus, and the Construction of Hierarchical Gender Relations," *Qualitative Research in Sport & Exercise* 1 (2009).

3 Maria Clemmitt, "Extreme Sports: Are They Too Dangerous?" *CQ Researcher* 19 (2009). Conversely, Elizabeth Pike emphasizes the potential for injury in extreme sports and notes that the individual nature of these sports limits the reliability of reporting data. Elizabeth C.J. Pike, "Injury," in *Encyclopedia of Extreme Sports*, eds. Douglas Booth and Holly Thorpe (Great Barrington, MA: Berkshire Publishing Group, 2007).

4 In one of the few medical studies that exist on the topic, Jaime Da Rocha and his co-researchers consider parkour "a sport of high risk for injuries." However, they also note that the discipline's injury rate is actually comparable to other non-extreme sports. "Thus, it is possible to observe that the rate of injury in parkour is equivalent to rates observed in other sports considered less harmful." Jaime Da Rocha et al., "Prevalence and Risk Factors of Musculoskeletal Injuries in Parkour," *Archives of Budo Science of Martial Arts and Extreme Sports* 10 (2014): 41. Likewise, PubMed, maintained by the National Center for Biotechnology Information, summarizes the work of a German research team by noting, "Other than expected, parkour is an urban movement style with most of the injuries being neither severe nor common despite the lack of precautionary measures." "Parkour: 'Art of

Movement' and Its Injury Risk," PubMed (2013), accessed August 16, 2015, http://www.ncbi.nlm.nih.gov/pubmed/23860830.

5   Mary Douglas and Aaron B. Wildavsky, *Risk and Culture: An Essay on the Selection of Technological and Environmental Dangers* (Berkeley: University of California Press, 1982).

6   Respectively: "Traffic Safety Facts 2013," National Traffic Safety Administration (2014), accessed August 16, 2015, http://www-nrd.nhtsa.dot.gov/Pubs/812139.pdf; Sadeq R. Chowdhury and Caroleene Paul, "Survey of Injuries Involving Stationary Saws: Table and Bench Saws, 2007–2008," U.S. Consumer Product and Safety Commission (2011), accessed August 16, 2015, https://www.cpsc.gov//PageFiles/118311/statsaws.pdf; Gary A. Smith et al., "Policy Statement: Prevention of Choking among Children," *Pediatrics* 125 (2010), accessed August 16, 2015, http://pediatrics.aappublications.org/content/pediatrics/early/2010/02/22/peds.2009-2862.full.pdf.

7   Mary Douglas, *Risk Acceptability According to the Social Sciences* (New York: Russell Sage Foundation, 1985), 82.

8   C. Wright Mills, "Situated Actions and Vocabularies of Motive," *American Sociological Review* 5 (1940): 906.

9   Stephen Lyng and David A. Snow, "Vocabularies of Motive and High-Risk Behavior: The Case of Skydiving," *Advances in Group Processing* 3 (1986).

10   Stephen Lyng, "Edgework: A Social Psychological Analysis of Voluntary Risk Taking," *American Journal of Sociology* 95 (1990).

11   Stephen Lyng himself acknowledges this. "An examination of the similarities and differences between edgework and these other concepts [i.e., flow and action] suggests that they may each refer to different dimensions of the same general phenomenon. It appears that edgework activities represent a subset of those activities that Goffman has classified as action. At both levels, people seem to experience elements of the flow phenomenon [. . .]." Lyng, "Edgework," 863.

12   Lyng, "Edgework," 871. Commenting on survivalists, for example, Richard Mitchell writes, "Survivalists don't want liberation from oppressive yokes or demystification of grand confusions. They want a place between a rock and hard spot. A place of resistance. A firm, gritty, antithesis [to modernity's overt rationalizations] to test their talents, measure their mettle, and gauge their gumption." Richard G. Mitchell, *Dancing at Armageddon: Survivalism and Chaos in Modern Times* (Chicago: University of Chicago Press, 2002), 200.

13   David Harvey, *The Conditions of Postmodernity: An Enquiry into the Origins of Cultural Change* (Cambridge, MA: Blackwell); David Harvey, *A Brief History of Neoliberalism* (New York: Oxford University Press).

14   Similarly, Jennifer Clegg and Ted Butryn's study of San Francisco traceurs emphasizes both the inherent dangers of parkour and the ways traceurs situate themselves as responsible managers of these risks. Jennifer L. Clegg and Ted M. Butryn, "An Existential Phenomenological Examination of Parkour and Freerunning," *Qualitative Research in Sport, Exercise & Health* 4 (2012).

15   Fredric Jameson, "Postmodernism, or the Cultural Logic of Late Capitalism," *New Left Review* 146 (1984); Harvey, *The Conditions of Postmodernity*.

16   Harvey, *The Conditions of Postmodernity*, 336. Donald Trump's 2016 presidential campaign, the continued retrenchment of unions, and increasing economic disparities further underscores the evident connections.

17 Manuel B. Aalbers, "Neoliberalism is Dead . . . Long Live Neoliberalism!," *International Journal of Urban & Regional Research* 37 (2013); Miguel A. Centeno and Joseph N. Cohen, "The Arc of Neoliberalism," *Annual Review of Sociology* 38 (2012); Harvey, *A Brief History of Neoliberalism*.

18 Ulrich Beck, *The Brave New World of Work* (Malden, MA: Polity Press, 2000); Henry A. Giroux, "Neoliberalism and the Death of the Social State: Remembering Walter Benjamin's Angel of History," *Social Identities* 17 (2011); Arne L. Kalleberg, *Good Jobs, Bad Jobs: The Rise of Polarized and Precarious Employment Systems in the United States, 1970s to 2000s* (New York: Russell Sage Foundation, 2011).

19 Harvey, *A Brief History of Neoliberalism*; Pierre Bourdieu, "Utopia as Endless Exploitation," *Le Monde Diplomatique* (English Edition), accessed May 28, 2015, http://mondediplo.com/1998/12/08bourdieu.

20 Ulrich Beck, *World Risk Society* (Malden, MA: Polity Press, 1999). To reiterate my point from the introduction: I use "postmodern" to describe a collection of cultural changes, not as a definitive claim about whether Western societies have actually transitioned to something beyond modernity.

21 Also see Anthony Giddens, "Risk and Responsibility," *Modern Law Review* 62 (1999).

22 Ronen Shamir, "The Age of Responsibilization: On Market-Embedded Morality," *Economy & Society* 37 (2008).

23 Beck, *The Brave New World of Work*; Jacob S. Hacker, *The Great Risk Shift: The Assault on American Jobs, Families, Health Care, and Retirement and How You Can Fight Back* (New York: Oxford University Press, 2006); Susan S. Silbey, "Taming Prometheus: Talk About Safety and Culture," *Annual Review of Sociology* 35 (2009).

24 Jason R. Hackworth, *The Neoliberal City: Governance, Ideology, and Development in American Urbanism* (Ithaca, NY: Cornell University Press, 2007).

25 Harvey, *A Brief History of Neoliberalism*; Loïc Wacquant, "Marginality, Ethnicity, and Penality in the Neo-Liberal City: An Analytic Cartography," *Ethnic & Racial Studies* 37 (2014).

26 Ocean Howell, "Skatepark as Neoliberal Playground: Urban Governance, Recreation Space, and the Cultivation of Personal Responsibility," *Space & Culture* 11 (2008); also see Leslie Heywood, "Producing Girls: Empire, Sport, and the Neoliberal Body" in *Physical Culture, Power, and the Body*, eds. Jennifer Hargreaves and Patricia Vertinsky (New York: Routledge, 2007). Beyond Howell and Heywood, numerous other researchers have made connections between the hegemony of neoliberalism and contemporary athletic practices. For example, Joshua Newman contends that NASCAR is a "carnival of capital" reinforcing neoliberal ideology. Joshua I. Newman "A Detour through 'NASCAR Nation': Ethnographic Articulations of Neoliberal Sporting Spectacle," *International Review for the Sociology of Sport* 42 (2007): 293. To wit, NASCAR fans feel free to choose their pastime and their favorite racers all while losing tangible freedoms. Also see Joshua I. Newman and Michael D. Giardina, "Neoliberalism's Last Lap? NASCAR Nation and the Cultural Politics of Sport," *American Behavioral Scientist* 53 (2010). Likewise, Belinda Wheaton notes that lifestyle sports are increasingly seen as promoting neoliberal values. Belinda Wheaton, *The Cultural Politics of Lifestyle Sports* (New York, Routledge, 2013); also see Michael Atkinson and Kevin Young, *Deviance and Social Control in Sport* (Champaign, IL: Human Kinetics, 2008); Bruce Erickson, "Recreational Activism: Politics, Nature, and the Rise of Neoliberalism," *Leisure Studies* 30 (2011).

27 "The shift away from the counterculture orientation toward the more *anarchistic*, edgework orientation [in skydiving] corresponds to a basic transition that has occurred within American popular culture as a whole: the transition away from the countercultural orientation of the late 1960s and the early 1970s to the more *nihilistic* orientation of the late 1970s and early 1980s." Lyng and Snow, "Vocabularies of Motive and High-Risk Behavior," 169 (emphasis added).

28 Michael Atkinson, "Parkour, Anarcho-Environmentalism, and Poïesis," *Journal of Sport & Social Issues* 32 (2009).

29 Jay Coakley, "Ideology Doesn't Just Happen: Sports and Neoliberalism," *ALESDE Revista* 1 (2011): 74.

30 A similar claim is made by Jennifer Hunt about deep-sea divers. Fearlessness is viewed as a liability among divers because it can lead to excessive risk taking. Jennifer C. Hunt, "Divers' Accounts of Normal Risk," *Symbolic Interaction* 18 (1995).

31 Quoted in Michael "Frosti" Zernow, "Dylan Baker: The Story Behind Manhood" [film], American Parkour (2011), accessed August 13, 2015, https://www.youtube.com/watch?v=HoKBfx1lmek.

32 Likewise, Christian Vaccaro and his co-researchers discuss the pervasiveness of fear in mixed martial arts. Fighters are often fearful, and they openly discuss their fears (at least among trusted peers). "[. . . F]eeling fear itself was not the problem as long as they kept it under control." Christian Vaccaro, Douglas Schrock, and Janice M. McCabe, "Managing Emotional Manhood: Fighting and Fostering Fear in Mixed Martial Arts," *Social Psychology Quarterly* 74 (2011): 421. Fighting, therefore, involves emotional work that can transform fear into confidence.

33 Zernow, "Dylan Baker."

34 Quoted in Zernow, "Dylan Baker."

35 Lori Holyfield and Gary Alan Fine, "Adventure as Character Work: The Collective Taming of Fear," *Symbolic Interaction* 20 (1997): 358.

36 Cody acknowledged Blane, a famous English traceur and coach for Parkour Generation, for influencing his views on this topic. "Watching other people facing jumps that are close to their potential is an incredible experience. You can only appreciate it fully when the person and the jump are equally matched [. . .]. At that exact moment you are looking at a person stripped of all of their pretension and all of their ego. They can no longer hide behind their words or false claims . . . it is a time for action." Chris "Blane" Rowat, "50 Ways to Be and to Last in Parkour, Part 2: Training the Mind," Power is Nothing Without Control (2013), accessed September 18, 2015, http:/blane-parkour.blogsport.com.

37 For example, Arnold R. Beisser, *The Madness in Sport: Psychosocial Observation on Sport* (New York: Appleton-Century-Croft, 1967); Marc Feigen Fasteau, *The Male Machine* (New York: McGraw-Hill, 1974); Michael A. Messner, "When Bodies are Weapons," *International Review for the Sociology of Sport* 25 (1990); Michael A. Messner, *Taking the Field: Women, Men, and Sports* (Minneapolis: University of Minnesota, 2002); Donald F. Sabo, "Best Years of My Life," in *Jock: Sports and Male Identity*, eds. Donald F. Sabo and Ross Runfola (Englewood Cliffs, NJ: Prentice-Hall, 1980).

38 Emile Durkheim, *The Elementary Forms of Religious Life*, trans. Karen E. Fields (New York: Free Press, 1912 [1995]).

39 Erving Goffman, "Where the Action Is," in *Interaction Ritual: Essays on Face-to-Face Behavior* (New York: Anchor Books, 1967).

40 For example, Michael Atkinson, "Triathlon, Suffering, and Exciting Significance," *Leisure Studies* 27 (2008); Michele K. Donnelly, "'Take the Slam and Get Back Up' Hardcore Candy and the Politics of Representation in Girls' and Women's Skateboarding and Snowboarding Television," in *Youth Culture and Sport: Identity, Power, and Politics*, eds. Michael D. Giardina and Michele K. Donnelly (New York: Routledge, 2008); Kyle Kusz, "BMX, Extreme Sports, and the White Male Backlash," in *To the Extreme: Alternative Sports Inside and Out*, eds. Robert E. Rinehart and Synthia Sydnor (Albany, NY: State University of New York Press, 2003); Kevin Young, Philip White, and William McTeer, "Body Talk: Males Athletes Reflect on Sport, Injury, and Pain," *Sociology of Sport Journal* 11 (1994). Traceurs do, occasionally, engage in talk that glorifies danger. Sometimes they will also hype the rush they get from taking risks—even describing themselves as "adrenaline junkies." However, this type of discourse is thoroughly tempered by the much more ubiquitous discussions of safety and responsibility.

41 Lyng, "Edgework"; also see Hunter, "Divers' Accounts of Normal Risk"; Jason Laurendeau, "'He Didn't Go in Doing a Skydive': Sustaining the Illusion of Control in an Edgework Activity," *Sociological Perspectives* 49 (2006); Daniel R. Wolf, *The Rebels: A Brotherhood of Outlaw Bikers* (Toronto: University of Toronto Press, 1991).

42 Similarly, Sarah Moore and Adam Burgess discuss what they call risk rituals— "behavioral adaptations to perceived risks or uncertainties that become embedded in daily practices." Sarah E. H. Moore and Adam Burgess, " Risk Rituals?" *Journal of Risk Research* 14 (2011), 114. Further, Moore and Burgess argue that with risk rituals, actually reducing exposure to peril becomes secondary to performing the actions themselves. For example, instead of limiting their binge drinking behaviors and attendance at alcohol-fueled parties (activities highly correlated with sexual assault), many college women focus on protecting their drinks from being spiked (which research shows to be a extremely uncommon crime). Such rituals, however, provide an effective means for psychologically coping with uncertainty—without adversely interfering with other social imperatives.

43 Victor W. Turner, "Betwixt and Between: The Liminal Period in 'Rites de Passage'" in *The Forest of Symbols: Aspects of the Ndembu Ritual* (Ithaca, NY: Cornell University Press, 1964 [1967]).

44 Jeffrey C. Alexander, "Cultural Pragmatics: Social Performance Between Ritual and Strategy," *Sociological Theory* 22 (2004); Roy A. Rappaport, *Rituals and Religion in the Making of Humanity* (New York: Cambridge University Press, 1999).

45 The distinction between rites and rituals is often muddled in the literature. The term "rite" is usually discussed in reference to specific types of activities (e.g., rites of passage). The term "ritual" is usually used to describe the more general process of prescribed, reoccurring collective activities. See especially Alexander, "Cultural Pragmatics"; Randall Collins, *Interaction Ritual Chains* (Princeton NJ: Princeton University Press, 2004); Rappaport, *Rituals and Religion in the Making of Humanity*. For this chapter, the value in distinguishing rites and rituals is in analytically separating individual practices (i.e., risky stunts) from the collectively enacted, communicative performances that provide the meaningful framework for them (i.e., symbolic appeals to safety). Rites (whether performed in isolation or in a group) denote membership and faith, but the significance of such acts is forged in rituals (which are always performed communally). Thus, as I am using the terms,

rites and rituals are interdependent. Rituals are composed of rites, but the social meaning of rites is generated in rituals.

46 There is considerable debate within the exercise and sports science literature (as well as in the mainstream media) about the efficacy of warming up and stretching, as well as about the best protocols to follow. However, in a review of existing research, Krista Woods and her co-researchers demonstrate the value of mild muscle exertion and stretching prior to intense athletic activity in reducing injury and improving athletic performance. Krista Woods, Phillip Bishop, and Eric Jones, "Warm-up and Stretching in the Prevention of Muscular Injury," *Sports Medicine* 37 (2007). Most important for the purposes of my argument (regardless of what future research might determine about the value of stretching and warming up before strenuous exercise), traceurs uniformly claimed such protocols were beneficial to their health.

47 To further clarify my use of rite and ritual: conditioning/stretching alone would be a rite (i.e., an act of membership and faith to the notion of responsible training). When done in a group, conditioning/stretching become a ritual. Unless a traceur is talking to himself, talk of progression is always a ritual. While rites of risk are often performed communally, the prescribed modes for carrying out the action—Victor Turner's definition of ritual—are about calling forth symbolic forms of safety. See Turner, "Betwixt and Between." Thus, I refer to risk taking as a rite, and appeals to symbolic safety as a ritual. Further, as the data show, traceurs' performances of safety are meant to communicate the significance of those symbols to others. This is the essential component of both Jeffrey Alexander's and Roy Rappaport's definitions of ritual. See Alexander, "Cultural Pragmatics"; Rappaport, *Rituals and Religion in the Making of Humanity*.

48 An instructive counterexample was Mintal's canned speech to me at my first jam. Despite common sense and incidents I had already witnessed (e.g., Counsel tearing his ACL just hours before), Mintal assured me that no one had *ever* been injured at a jam in Chicago. Similarly, upon reading the article on which chapter three is based, a traceur from New York wrote me a series of emails expressing her concern over my findings. Much like Mintal, this traceur insisted that real practitioners do not take risks. "If you were taught and trained properly you would realize that the risk of bodily harm is insignificant most of the time. You are taught how to assess risk, deal with uncertainty, and make appropriate decisions in accordance to your abilities and limitations. And eventually you realise your movements are NOT risky because you have the abilities to complete them—and you back off when you don't." Additionally, this traceur informed me, "True practitioners [. . .] discourage and disallow any dangerous behavior." Referencing the same article, Julie Angel intimates that the traceurs in my study were a small minority within the global community and that "a silent majority" within the discipline eschews any hint of the bravado I describe. Julie Angel, "Manhood Parkour, a Quick Response to 'Parkour, Masculinity, and the City' by Jeffrey L. Kidder," JulieAngel.com (2013), accessed September 2, 2015, http://julieangel.com/quickresponse/. These critiques of my findings no doubt represent the way some traceurs would *like* parkour to be practiced (or at least how they would like parkour to be viewed from the outside). However, my interactions with traceurs from around the United States, along with extensive study of parkour materials from around the globe, make it perfectly clear that the risky stunts discussed in this book are ubiquitous within the discipline. Further, the flamboyance with which these stunts are performed is also

commonplace. These things are true, even if the way in which I describe them is considered taboo by some in the parkour community.

49 As case in point, like the other traceurs discussed in this book, I let the person designated as "Arnold" in the text read the excerpts he appeared in. Understandably, he was not happy about how he was portrayed. When confronted with this unflattering looking-glass self, Arnold responded by attempting to symbolically realign his previous actions. "You don't give me credit for the fact that I've trained every weekend in the gym for the past ten years [. . .]." Likewise, my depiction of his roof jump ignored his "preparing for the jump" and that he "knew he had it." In other words, while in day-to-day training Arnold routinely violated ritual protocols, it was important to his identity to present a sacred self through the ideals of safety. His effort involved the same tropes as that of other traceurs: gym training, progression, risk assessment, etc. One is reminded here of Elijah Anderson's observation that everyone at Jelly's barroom wanted to be considered a "regular," irrespective of how much they might violate the regular's norms. See Elijah Anderson, "Jelly's Place: An Ethnographic Memoir," *Symbolic Interaction* 26 (2002).

50 David Le Breton, "Playing Symbolically with Death in Extreme Sports," *Body & Society* 6 (2000): 1.

51 Clifford Geertz, "Deep Play: Notes on the Balinese Cockfight," *Daedalus* 101 (1972).

Conclusion

1 Mike Christie, *Jump London* [film] (London: Channel 4, 2003). This film can be watched on YouTube, accessed March 1, 2011, https://www.youtube.com/watch?v=l8fSXGP9wvQ.

2 Graham Murray, "France: The Riots and the Republic," *Race & Class* 47 (2006).

3 Quoted in Alec Wilkinson, "No Obstacles: Navigating the World by Leaps and Bounds," *The New Yorker*, April 16 (2007).

4 Z-Boys refers to the original riders for the Zephyr Skate Team. They are widely credited with inspiring the contemporary skateboard subculture. They integrated the sport with aggressive, surf-influenced movements, and they cultivated a brash, anti-establishment attitude in their public presentations. The Z-Boys are perhaps most famous for illegally skating in drained backyard pools. See Stacy Peralta, *Dogtown and Z-Boys* [film], Culver City, CA: Sony Pictures (2001).

5 Henri Lefebvre, *The Production of Space*, trans. Donald Nicholson-Smith (Cambridge, MA: Blackwell 1974 [1991]).

6 See Iain Borden, *Skateboarding, Space, and the City: Architecture and the Body* (New York: Berg, 2001); Francisco Vivoni, "Waxing Ledges: Built Environments, Alternative Sustainability, and the Chicago Skateboarding Scene," *Local Environment* 18 (2013); Jeff Ferrell, *Crimes of Style: Urban Graffiti and the Politics of Criminality* (Boston: Northeastern University Press, 1996); Nancy Macdonald, *The Graffiti Subculture: Youth, Masculinity, and Identity in London and New York* (New York: Palgrave Macmillan, 2001).

7 Borden, *Skateboarding, Space, and the City.*

8 Anthony Giddens, *The Constitution of Society: Outline to the Theory of Structuration* (Berkeley: University of California Press, 1984).

9   Mihaly Csikszentmihalyi, *Beyond Boredom and Anxiety* (San Francisco: Jossey-Bass Publishers, 1975).

10 Clifford Geertz, "Religion as a Cultural System," in *The Interpretation of Cultures: Selected Essays* (New York: Basics Books, 1973), 112. I address the connection between play, rituals, and flow elsewhere. See Jeffrey L. Kidder, *Urban Flow: Bike Messengers and the City* (Ithaca, NY: Cornell University Press, 2011).

11 Arjun Appadurai, "Global Ethnoscapes: Notes and Queries for a Transnational Anthropology," in *Modernity at Large: Cultural Dimensions of Globalization* (Minneapolis: University of Minnesota Press, 1993 [1996]).

12 Many videos attempt to give an aura of authenticity by including bloopers and failed efforts, but these supposed glimpses into the backstage are themselves only approximations of reality.

13 Daniel J. Boorstin, *The Image: A Guide to Pseudo-Events in America* (New York: Harper & Row, 1961).

14 Michael Schwalbe, "Identity Stakes, Manhood Acts, and the Dynamics of Accountability," *Studies in Symbolic Interaction* 28 (2005).

15 Macdonald, *The Graffiti Subculture.*

16 Stephen Lyng, "Edgework: A Social Psychological Analysis of Voluntary Risk Taking," *American Journal of Sociology* 95 (1990).

17 Erving Goffman, "Where the Action Is," in *Interaction Rituals: Essays on Face-to-Face Behavior* (New York: Anchor Books, 1967).

18 William H. Whyte, *City: Rediscovering the Center* (New York: Doubleday, 1988).

19 A bokken is a wooden sword used in martial arts training. Few of the Chicago traceurs had any formal training in martial arts, but, just as they learned about parkour online, many watched various YouTube tutorials on fighting. Most felt an elective affinity between parkour and the movements found in martial arts. For some, this interest merged with the hopes of one day being able to transfer their parkour skills into a career as a stuntman (which usually requires an ability to mock fight). In fact, several older Chicago traceurs had done just that, and many young traceurs planned to follow in their footsteps.

20 Deb Kadin, "Overlooked Cummings Square in River Forest Slated for 2015 Upgrades," OakPark.com, July 3, 2014, accessed October 7, 2015, http://www.oakpark.com/News/Articles/7-3-2014/Overlooked-Cummings-Square-in-River-Forest-slated-for-2015-upgrades/.

21 Michel de Certeau, *The Practice of Everyday Life*, trans. Steven Rendall (Berkeley: University of California Press, 1984).

22 Sophie Fuggle, "Le Parkour: Reading or Writing the City?" in *Rhythms: Essays in French Literature, Thought, and Culture*, eds. Elizabeth Lindley and Laura McMahon, (Bern, Switzerland: Peter Lang, 2008), 162.

23 See Ulrich Beck, *World Risk Society* (Malden, MA: Polity Press); Ronen Shamir, "The Age of Responsibilization: On Market-Embedded Morality," *Economy & Society* 37 (2008).

24 Clifford Geertz, "Deep Play: Notes on the Balinese Cockfight," *Daedalus* 101 (1972).

25 See especially Ocean Howell, "Skatepark as Neoliberal Playground: Urban Governance, Recreation Space, and the Cultivation of Personal Responsibility," *Space & Culture* 11 (2008); Leslie Heywood, "Producing Girls: Empire, Sport, and the Neoliberal Body," *Physical Culture, Power, and the Body*, eds. Jennifer Hargreaves and Patricia Vertinsky (New York: Routledge, 2007).

Appendix A Brief Note on Data and Method

1   See especially Richard K. Nelson, *Hunters on the Northern Ice* (Chicago, University of Chicago, 1969); Loïc Wacquant, "For a Sociology of Flesh and Blood," *Qualitative Sociology* 38 (2015); also see Loïc Wacquant, *Body and Soul: Notebooks of an Apprentice Boxer* (New York: Oxford University Press, 2004).

2   See especially Michèle Lamont and Ann Swidler, "Methodological Pluralism and the Possibilities and Limits of Interviewing," *Qualitative Sociology* 37 (2014); Shamus Khan and Colin Jerolmack, "Saying Meritocracy and Doing Privilege" *Sociological Quarterly* 54 (2013).

3   Anselm Strauss et al., *Psychiatric Ideologies and Institutions* (New York: Free Press, 1964).

4   Michael Alosi's film, *Point B*, can be accessed online: http://www.pointbmovie.com/Watch.html; information about Kaspar Schröder's film, *My Playground* can be found at: http://www.kasparworks.com/shop-movies/.

5   A LexisNexis search of "parkour," "l'art du déplacement," and "Yamakasi" yields no English-language articles before 2000. *The Independent* published a short article on the Yamakasi in 2000: Astrid Mayer, "The Broader Picture: Mind the Gap," March 26. Over the next two years, at least eighteen more articles on parkour were published. After 2003, when the term "freerunning" was introduced, the variations "freerunning" and "free running" were added to the search criteria. These terms bring up thousands of hits, but many articles are duplicates, only tangentially connected to the discipline, or totally unrelated (e.g., "free running" brings up articles about feral animals and dog parks).

6   Julie Angel, *Ciné Parkour* (self-published, 2011).

7   Lofland et al., *Analyzing Social Settings: A Guide to Qualitative Observation and Analysis* (Belmont, CA: Wadsworth/Thompson Learning, 2006).

8   For example, see Ruth Horowitz, "Remaining an Outsider: Membership as a Threat to Research Rapport," *Urban Life* 14 (1986); Sandra Meike Bucerius, "Becoming a 'Trusted Outsider': Gender, Ethnicity, and Inequality in Ethnographic Research," *Journal of Contemporary Ethnography* 42 (2013). To this end, Michael Agar writes of the ethnographer, "Eventually, people come to accept you for what you are—a strange person who asks dumb questions." Michael Agar, *The Professional Stranger: An Informal Introduction to Ethnography* (New York: Academic Press, 1980), 60.

Appendix B On the Parkour Terminology Used in This Book

1   Anselm L. Strauss, "A Social World Perspective," *Studies in Symbolic Interaction* 1 (1978).

2   It is not my intent in this book to get into a debate about subcultural theory. However, following Andy Bennett, parkour might best be conceived as a form of "neo-tribe"—temporary (but often reoccurring) associations between people based on affective ties. Andy Bennett, "Subcultures or Neo-Tribes? Rethinking the Relationship Between Youth, Style, and Musical Taste," *Sociology* 33 (1999); also see Michel Maffesoli, *The Time of the Tribes: The Decline of Individualism in Mass Society* (Thousand Oaks: Sage, 1996). Paul Gilchrist and Belinda Wheaton also make this observation about traceurs. Paul Gilchrist and Belinda Wheaton, "New Media Technologies in Lifestyle Sport" in *Digital Media Sport: Technology, Power, and Culture in the Network Society*, eds. Brett Hutchinson and David Rowe (New York: Routledge, 2013).

Bibliography

Aalbers, Manuel B. "Neoliberalism Is Dead . . . Long Live Neoliberalism!," *International Journal of Urban & Regional Research* 37 (2013): 1083–1090.

Agar, Michael. *The Professional Stranger: An Informal Introduction to Ethnography*. Studies in Anthropology. New York: Academic Press, 1980.

Alexander, Jeffrey C. "Cultural Pragmatics: Social Performance between Ritual and Strategy." *Sociological Theory* 22 (2004): 527–573.

Allan, Kenneth. *The Meaning of Culture: Moving the Postmodern Critique Forward*. Westport, CT: Praeger, 1998.

Ameel, Lieven, and Sirpa Tani. "Everyday Aesthetics in Action: Parkour Eyes and the Beauty of Concrete Walls." *Emotions, Space, & Society* 5 (2012): 164–173.

———. "Parkour: Creating Loose Spaces?" *Geografiska Annaler: Series B, Human Geography* 94 (2012): 17–30.

Anderson, Elijah. "The Iconic Ghetto." *ANNALS of the American Academy of Political & Social Science* 642 (2012): 8–24.

———. "Jelly's Place: An Ethnographic Memoir." *Symbolic Interaction* 26 (2003): 217–237.

Angel, Julie. *Ciné Parkour*. Self-published book, 2011.

Appadurai, Arjun. "Global Ethnoscapes: Notes and Queries for a Transnational Anthropology." In *Modernity at Large: Cultural Dimensions of Globalization*, 48–65. Minneapolis: University of Minnesota Press, 1993 [1996].

Archer, Neil. "Virtual Poaching and Altered Space: Reading Parkour in French Visual Culture." *Modern & Contemporary France* 18 (2010): 93–107.

Atencio, Matthew, Becky Beal, and Charlene Wilson. "The Distinction of Risk: Urban Skateboarding, Street Habitus and the Construction of Hierarchical Gender Relations." *Qualitative Research in Sport & Exercise* 1 (2009): 3–20.

Atkinson, Michael. "Fell Running and Voluptuous Panic: On Caillois and Post-Sport Physical Culture." *American Journal of Play* 4 (2011): 100–120.

———. "Parkour, Anarcho-Environmentalism, and Poiesis." *Journal of Sport & Social Issues* 32 (2009): 169–194.

———. "Triathlon, Suffering and Exciting Significance." *Leisure Studies* 27 (2008): 165–180.

Atkinson, Michael, and Kevin Young. *Deviance and Social Control in Sport*. Champaign, IL: Human Kinetics, 2008.

Balibar, Étienne. "Uprisings in the *Banlieues*." *Constellations* 14 (2007): 47–71.

Barthes, Roland. *Elements of Semiology*. Translated by Annette Lavers and Colin Smith. New York: Hill and Wang, 1964 [1967].

Baudrillard, Jean. *Simulacra and Simulation*. Translated by Shelia Faria Glaser. Ann Arbor: University of Michigan Press, 1981 [1994].

———. *Symbolic Exchange and Death*. Translated by Iain Hamilton Grant. Thousand Oaks: Sage Publications, 1976 [1993].

Bauman, Zygmunt. *Intimations of Postmodernity*. New York: Routledge, 1992.

Baumgartner, M. P. *The Moral Order of a Suburb*. New York: Oxford University Press, 1988.

Bavinton, Nathaniel. "From Obstacle to Opportunity: Parkour, Leisure, and the Reinterpretation of Constraints." *Annals of Leisure Research* 10 (2007): 391–412.

Beal, Becky. "Disqualifying the Official: An Exploration of Social Resistance through the Subculture of Skateboarding." *Sociology of Sport Journal* 12 (1995): 252–267.

Beal, Becky, and Charlene Wilson. "'Chicks Dig Scars': Commercialisation and the Transformation of Skateboard Identities." In *Understanding Lifestyle Sports: Consumption, Identity, and Difference*, edited by Belinda Wheaton, 31–54. New York: Routledge, 2004.

Beck, Ulrich. *The Brave New World of Work*. Malden, MA: Polity Press, 2000.

———. *World Risk Society*. Malden, MA: Polity Press, 1999.

Beck, Ulrich, Wolfgang Bonss, and Christoph Lau. "The Theory of Reflexive Modernization: Problematic, Hypotheses and Research Programme." *Theory, Culture & Society* 20 (2003): 1–33.

Beisser, Arnold R. *The Madness in Sports: Psychosocial Observations on Sports*. New York: Appleton-Century-Crofts, 1967.

Benjamin, Walter. *The Arcades Project*. Translated by Howard Eiland and Kevin McLaughlin. Cambridge, MA: Belknap Press, 1982 [1999].

Bennett, Andy. "Subcultures or Neo-Tribes? Rethinking the Relationship between Youth, Style, and Musical Taste." *Sociology* 33 (1999): 599–617.

Boorstin, Daniel J. *The Image: A Guide to Pseudo-Events in America*. New York: Harper & Row, 1961.

Booth, Douglas. "Expression Sessions: Surfing, Style, and Prestige." In *To the Extreme: Alternative Sports, Inside and Out*, edited by Robert E. Rinehart and Synthia Sydnor, 315–333. Albany, NY: State University of New York Press, 2003.

———. "Paradoxes of Material Culture: The Political Economy of Surfing." In *The Political Economy of Sport*, edited by John Nauright and Kimberly S. Schimmel, 104–125. New York: Palgrave Macmillan, 2005.

———. "Surfing: From One (Cultural) Extreme to Another." In *Understanding Lifestyle Sports: Consumption, Identity, and Difference*, edited by Belinda Wheaton, 94–109. New York: Routledge, 2004.

Borden, Iain. *Skateboarding, Space and the City: Architecture and the Body*. New York: Berg, 2001.

Borer, Michael Ian. "Important Places and Their Public Faces: Understanding Fenway Park as a Public Symbol." *Journal of Popular Culture* 39 (2006): 205–224.

boyd, danah. *It's Complicated: The Social Lives of Networked Teens*. New Haven: Yale University Press, 2014.

Breivik, Gunnar. "Trends in Adventure Sports in a Post-Modern Society." *Sport in Society* 13 (2010): 260–273.

Browne, David. *Amped: How Big Air, Big Dollars, and a New Generation Took Sports to the Extreme*. New York: Bloomsbury, 2004.

Bucerius, Sandra Meike. "Becoming a 'Trusted Outsider': Gender, Ethnicity, and Inequality in Ethnographic Research." *Journal of Contemporary Ethnography* 42 (2013): 690–721.

Butler, Judith. *Gender Trouble: Feminism and the Subversion of Identity*. New York: Routledge, 1990.

Cairncross, Frances. *The Death of Distance: How the Communications Revolution Is Changing Our Lives*. 2nd ed. Boston: Harvard Business School Press, 2001.

Carrigan, Tim, Raewyn Connell, and John Lee. "Toward a New Sociology of Masculinity." *Theory & Society* 14 (1985): 551–604.

Carter, Thomas F. *In Foreign Fields: The Politics and Experiences of Transnational Sport Migration*. Anthropology, Culture and Society. New York: Pluto, 2011.

Castells, Manuel. *Communication Power*. New York: Oxford University Press, 2009.

———. *The Rise of the Network Society*. Information Age. Malden, MA: Blackwell Publishers, 1996.

Centeno, Miguel A., and Joseph N. Cohen. "The Arc of Neoliberalism." *Annual Review of Sociology* 38 (2012): 317–340.

Certeau, Michel de. *The Practice of Everyday Life*. Translated by Steven Rendall. Berkeley: University of California Press, 1984.

Chow, Broderick D. V. "Parkour and the Critique of Ideology: Turn-Vaulting the Fortresses of the City." *Journal of Dance & Somatic Practices* 2 (2012): 143–154.

Clegg, Jennifer L., and Ted M. Butryn. "An Existential Phenomenological Examination of Parkour and Freerunning." *Qualitative Research in Sport, Exercise & Health* 4 (2012): 320–340.

Clemmitt, Maria. "Extreme Sports: Are They Too Dangerous?" *CQ Researcher* 19 (2009): 297–320.

Coakley, Jay. "Ideology Doesn't Just Happen: Sports and Neoliberalism." *ALESDE Revista* 1 (2011): 67–84.

Collins, Jessica L., and Barry Wellman. "Small Town in the Internet Society: Chapleau Is No Longer an Island." *American Behavioral Scientist* 53 (2010): 1344–1366.

Collins, Randall. *Interaction Ritual Chains*. Princeton, NJ: Princeton University Press, 2004.

Connell, Raewyn. *Masculinities*. Berkeley: University of California Press, 1995.

———. *The Men and the Boys*. Berkeley: University of California Press, 2000.

Corte, Ugo. "A Refinement of Collaborative Circles Theory: Resource Mobilization and Innovation in an Emerging Sport." *Social Psychology Quarterly* 76 (2013): 25–51.

Cresswell, Tim. *Place: A Short Introduction*. Malden, MA: Blackwell, 2004.

Csikszentmihalyi, Mihaly. *Beyond Boredom and Anxiety*. San Francisco: Jossey-Bass Publishers, 1975.

Da Rocha, Jaime Aparecido, Juan Carlos Pérez Morales, George Schayer Sabino, Bento João Arbeu, Diogo Carvalho Felício, Bruno Pena Couto, Marcos Daniel M. Drummond, and Leszek A. Szmuchrowski. "Prevalence and Risk Factors of Musculoskeletal Injuries in Parkour." *Archives of Budo Science of Martial Arts and Extreme Sports* 10 (2014): 39–42.

Daskalaki, Maria, Alexandra Stara, and Miguel Imas. "The 'Parkour Organization': Inhabitation of Corporate Spaces." *Culture & Organizations* 14 (2008): 49–64.

Daskalaki, Maria, and Oli Mould. "Beyond Urban Subcultures: Urban Subversions as Rhizomatic Social Formations." *International Journal of Urban & Regional Research* 37 (2013): 1–18.

Debord, Guy. *The Society of the Spectacle*. Translated by Donald Nicholson-Smith. New York: Zone Books, 1967 [1994].

Dikec, Mustafa. *Badlands of the Republic: Space, Politics and Urban Policy*. Rgs-Ibg Book Series. Malden, MA: Blackwell, 2007.

Dogtown and Z-Boys. Dir. Stacy Peralta. Sony Pictures, 2001. Film.

Donnelly, Michele K. "'Take the Slam and Get Back Up': Hardcore Candy and the Politics of Representation in Girls' and Women's Skateboarding and Snowboarding Television." In *Youth Culture and Sport: Identity, Power, and Politics*, edited by Michael D. Giardina and Michele K. Donnelly, 127–143. New York: Routledge, 2008.

Donnelly, Peter, and Trevor Williams. "Subcultural Production, Reproduction, and Transformation in Climbing." *International Review for the Sociology of Sport* 20 (1985): 3–16.

Donnelly, Peter, and Kevin Young. "The Construction and Confirmation of Identity in Sport Subcultures." *Sociology of Sport Journal* 5 (1988): 223–240.

Douglas, Mary. *Risk Acceptability According to the Social Sciences*. New York: Russell Sage Foundation, 1985.

Douglas, Mary, and Aaron B. Wildavsky. *Risk and Culture: An Essay on the Selection of Technical and Environmental Dangers*. Berkeley: University of California Press, 1982.

Dowd, James J. "An Act Made Perfect in Habit: The Self in the Postmodern Age." *Current Perspectives in Social Theory* 16 (1996): 237–263.

———. "Social Psychology in a Postmodern Age: A Discipline without a Subject." *American Sociologist* 22 (1991): 188–209.

Dozier, Raine. "Beards, Breasts, and Bodies: Doing Sex in a Gendered World." *Gender & Society* 19 (2005): 297–306.

Duany, Andrés, Elizabeth Plater-Zyberk, and Jeff Speck. *Suburban Nation: The Rise of Sprawl and the Decline of the American Dream*. New York: North Point Press, 2000.

Duneier, Mitchell. *Sidewalk*. New York: Farrar, Straus and Giroux, 1999.

Dunning, Eric. "The Dynamics of Modern Sport: Notes on Achievement-Striving and the Social Significance of Sport." In *The Quest for Excitement: Sport and Leisure in the Civilizing Process*, edited by Norbert Elias and Eric Dunning, 205–223. New York: Basil Blackwell, 1986.

Durkheim, Emile. *The Elementary Forms of Religious Life*. Translated by Karen E. Fields. New York: Free Press, 1912 [1995].

Edwardes, Dan. *The Parkour and Freerunning Handbook*. New York: HarperCollins, 2009.

Edwards, Bob, and Ugo Corte. "Commercialization and Lifestyle Sport: Lessons from 20 Years of Freestyle Bmx in 'Pro-Town, USA.'" *Sport in Society* 13 (2010): 1135–1151.

Elias, Norbert. "Introduction." In *The Quest for Excitement: Sport and Leisure in the Civilizing Process*, edited by Norbert Elias and Eric Dunning, 19–62. New York: Basil Blackwell, 1986.

———. *What Is Sociology?* Translated by Stephen Mennell and Grace Morrissey. New York: Columbia University Press, 1970 [1978].

Erickson, Bruce. "Recreational Activism: Politics, Nature, and the Rise of Neoliberalism." *Leisure Studies* 30 (2011): 477–494.

Evers, Clifton. "Men Who Surf." *Cultural Studies Review* 10 (2004): 27–41.

Fainstein, Susan S. "The Changing World Economy and Urban Restructuring." In *Leadership and Urban Regeneration*, edited by Dennis Judd and Michael Parkinson, 31–47. Thousand Oaks, CA: Sage Publications, 1990.

Fasteau, Marc Feigen. *The Male Machine*. New York: McGraw-Hill, 1974.

Ferrell, Jeff. *Crimes of Style: Urban Graffiti and the Politics of Criminality.* Boston: Northeastern University Press, 1996.

Force, William Ryan. "Consumption Styles and the Fluid Complexity of Punk Authenticity." *Symbolic Interaction* 32 (2009): 289–309.

Fuggle, Sophie. "Discourses of Subversion: The Ethics and Aesthetics of Capoeira and Parkour." *Dance Research* 26 (2008): 204–222.

———. "Le Parkour: Reading or Writing the City?" In *Rhythms: Essays in French Literature, Though, and Culture*, edited by Elizabeth Lindley and Laura McMahon, 159–170. Bern, Switzerland: Peter Lang, 2008.

Gammon, Earl. "The Psycho- and Sociogenesis of Neoliberalism." *Critical Sociology* 39 (2012): 511–528.

Gans, Herbert J. "Planning for People not Buildings." *Environment & Planning* 1 (1969): 33–46.

Garrett, Bradley L. "Cracking the Paris Carriers: Corporal Terror and Illicit Encounter under the City of Light." *ACME: An international e-journal for critical geographies* 10 (2011): 269–277.

Geertz, Clifford. "Deep Play: Notes on the Balinese Cockfight." *Daedalus* 101 (1972): 1–37.

———. "Religion as a Cultural System." In *Interpretation of Cultures: Selected Essays*, 87–125. New York: Basic Books, 1966 [1973].

Generation Yamakasi. Dir. Mark Daniels. France2 TV, 2005. Film.

Gergen, Kenneth J. *The Saturated Self: Dilemmas of Identity in Contemporary Life.* New York: Basic Books, 1991.

Geyh, Paula. "Urban Free Flow: A Poetics of Parkour." *M/C Journal* 9 (2006). Accessed December 31, 2011, http://journal.media-culture.org.au/0607/06-geyh.php.

Gibson, James J. *The Ecological Approach to Visual Perception.* Boston: Houghton Mifflin Company, 1979.

Giddens, Anthony. *The Consequences of Modernity.* Stanford, CA: Stanford University Press, 1990.

———. *The Constitution of Society: Outline of the Theory of Structuration.* Berkeley: University of California Press, 1984.

———. *Modernity and Self-Identity: Self and Society in the Late Modern Age.* Stanford, CA: Stanford University Press, 1991.

———. "Risk and Responsibility." *Modern Law Review* 62 (1999): 1–10.

Gieryn, Thomas F. "A Space for Place in Sociology." *Annual Review of Sociology* 26 (2000): 463–496.

Gilchrist, Paul, and Belinda Wheaton. "Lifestyle Sport, Public Policy, and Youth Engagement: Examining the Emergence of Parkour." *International Journal of Sport Policy & Politics* 3 (2011): 109–131.

———. "New Media Technologies in Lifestyle Sport." In *Digital Media Sport: Technology, Power, and Culture in the Network Society*, edited by Brett Hutchins and David Rowe, 169–185. New York: Routledge, 2013.

Giroux, Henry A. "Neoliberalism and the Death of the Social State: Remembering Walter Benjamin's Angel of History." *Social Identities* 17 (2011): 587–601.

Goffman, Erving. "Where the Action Is." In *Interaction Ritual: Essays on Face-to-Face Behavior*, 149–270. New York: Anchor Books, 1967.

Gregory, Derek. *Geographical Imaginations.* Cambridge, MA: Blackwell, 1994.

Guss, Nathan. "Parkour and the Multitude: Politics of a Dangerous Art." *French Cultural Studies* 22 (2011): 73–85.

Hacker, Jacob S. *The Great Risk Shift: The Assault on American Jobs, Families, Health Care, and Retirement and How You Can Fight Back*. New York: Oxford University Press, 2006.

Hackworth, Jason R. *The Neoliberal City: Governance, Ideology, and Development in American Urbanism*. Ithaca, NY: Cornell University Press, 2007.

Hampton, Keith, and Barry Wellman. "Neighboring in Netville: How the Internet Supports Community and Social Capital in a Wired Suburb." *City & Community* 2 (2003): 277–311.

Harvey, David. *A Brief History of Neoliberalism*. New York: Oxford University Press, 2005.

———. *The Condition of Postmodernity: An Enquiry into the Origins of Cultural Change*. Cambridge, MA: Blackwell, 1990.

———. "Space as a Keyword." In *David Harvey: A Critical Reader*, edited by Noel Castree and Derek Gregory, 270–293. Malden, MA: Blackwell, 2006.

Heino, Rebecca. "What's So Punk About Snowboarding." *Journal of Sport & Social Issues* 24 (2000): 176–191.

Heywood, Ian. "Urgent Dreams: Climbing, Rationalization, and Ambivalence." *Leisure Studies* 13 (1994): 179–194.

Heywood, Leslie. "Producing Girls: Empire, Sport, and the Neoliberal Body." In *Physical Culture, Power, and the Body*, edited by Jennifer Hargreaves and Patricia Vertinsky, 101–120. New York: Routledge, 2007.

Holyfield, Lori. "Manufacturing Adventure: The Buying and Selling of Emotions." *Journal of Contemporary Ethnography* 28 (1999): 3–32.

Holyfield, Lori, and Gary Alan Fine. "Adventure as Character Work: The Collective Taming of Fear." *Symbolic Interaction* 20 (1997): 343–363.

Horowitz, Ruth. "Remaining an Outsider: Membership as a Threat to Research Rapport." *Urban Life* 14 (1986): 409–430.

Howell, Ocean. "Skatepark as Neoliberal Playground: Urban Governance, Recreation Space, and the Cultivation of Personal Responsibility." *Space & Culture* 11 (2008): 475–496.

Huizinga, J. *Homo Ludens: A Study of the Play-Element in Culture*. Translated by R.F.C. Hull. Boston: Routledge & Kegan Paul, 1944 [1949].

Humphreys, Duncan. "Selling Out Snowboarding." In *To the Extreme: Alternative Sports Inside and Out*, edited by Robert E. Rinehart and Synthia Sydnor, 407–428. Albany, NY: State University of New York Press, 2003.

Hunt, Jennifer C. "Divers' Accounts of Normal Risk." *Symbolic Interaction* 18 (1995): 439–462.

Ito, Mizuko, Sonja Baumer, Matteo Bittanti, danah boyd, Rachel Cody, Becky Herr-Stephenson, Heather A. Horst, Patricia G. Lange, Dilan Mahendran, Katynka Z. Martínez, C. J. Pascoe, Dan Perkel, Laura Robinson, Christo Sims, and Lisa Tripp. *Hanging Out, Messing Around, and Geeking Out: Kids Living and Learning with New Media*. Cambridge, MA: MIT Press, 2010.

Jacobs, Jane. *The Death and Life of Great American Cities*. New York: Random House, 1961.

Jameson, Fredric. "Postmodernism, or the Cultural Logic of Late Capitalism." *New Left Review* 146 (1984): 53–92.

Johnson, Allan G. *The Gender Knot: Unraveling Our Patriarchal Legacy, Revised and Updated*. Philadelphia: Temple University Press, 2005.

Jones, Phil. "Performing the City: A Body and a Bicycle Take on Birmingham, UK." *Social & Cultural Geography* 6 (2005): 813–830.

Jones, Rodney H. "Sport and Re/creation: What Skateboarding Can Teach Us about Learning." *Sport, Education & Society* 16 (2011): 593–611.

Jump London. Dir. Mike Christie. Channel 4, 2003. Film.

Kalleberg, Arne L. *Good Jobs, Bad Jobs: The Rise of Polarized and Precarious Employment Systems in the United States, 1970s to 2000s.* New York: Russell Sage Foundation, 2011.

Kaplan, Janice. *Women and Sports.* New York: Viking Press, 1979.

Kay, Joanne, and Suzanne Laberge. "Mapping the Field of 'AR': Adventure Racing and Bourdieu's Concept of Field." *Sociology of Sport Journal* 19 (2002): 25–46.

Kelly, Deirdre M., Shauna Pomerantz, and Dawn H. Currie. "'You Can Break So Many More Rules': The Identity Work and Play of Becoming Skater Girls." In *Youth Culture and Sport: Identity, Power, and Politics*, edited by Michael D. Giardina and Michele K. Donnelly, 113–125. New York: Routledge, 2008.

Khan, Shamus, and Colin Jerolmack. "Saying Meritocracy and Doing Privilege." *Sociological Quarterly* 54 (2013): 9–19.

Kidder, Jeffrey L. *Urban Flow: Bike Messengers and the City.* Ithaca, NY: Cornell University Press, 2011.

Kiewa, Jackie. "Traditional Climbing: Metaphor of Resistance or Metanarrative of Oppression?" *Leisure Studies* 21 (2002): 145–161.

Kimmel, Michael S. "The Cult of Masculinity: American Social Character and the Legacy of the Cowboy." In *The History of Men: Essays in the History of American and British Masculinities*, 91–104. New York: State University of New York Press, 1987 [2005].

———. "Consuming Manhood: The Feminization of American Culture and the Recreation of the Male Body, 1820–1920." In *The History of Men: Essays in the History of American and British Masculinities*, 7–36. New York: State University of New York Press, 1993 [2005].

Kusz, Kyle. "BMX, Extreme Sports, and the White Male Backlash." In *To the Extreme: Alternative Sports, Inside and Out*, edited by Robert E. Rinehart and Synthia Sydnor, 153–175. Albany, NY: State University of New York Press, 2003.

———. "Extreme America: The Cultural Politics of Extreme Sports in 1990s America." In *Understanding Lifestyle Sports: Consumption, Identity, and Difference*, edited by Belinda Wheaton, 197–213. New York: Routledge, 2004.

Lamb, Matthew D. "Misuses of the Monument: The Art of Parkour and the Discursive Limits of Disciplinary Architecture." *Journal of Urban Cultural Studies* 1 (2014): 107–126.

Lamont, Michèle, and Ann Swidler. "Methodological Pluralism and the Possibilities and Limits of Interviewing." *Qualitative Sociology* 37 (2014): 153–171.

Laurendeau, Jason. "'Gendered Risk Regimes': A Theoretical Consideration of Edgework and Gender." *Sociology of Sport Journal* 25 (2008): 293–309.

———. "'He Didn't Go in Doing a Skydive': Sustaining the Illusion of Control in an Edgework Activity." *Sociological Perspectives* 49 (2006): 583–605.

Laurendeau, Jason, and Nancy Sharara. "'Women Could Be Every Bit as Good as Guys': Reproductive and Resistant Agency in Two 'Action' Sports." *Journal of Sport & Social Issues* 32 (2008): 24–47.

Le Breton, David. "Playing Symbolically with Death in Extreme Sports." *Body & Society* 6 (2000): 1–11.

Lefebvre, Henri. *The Production of Space.* Translated by Donald Nicholson-Smith. Cambridge, MA: Blackwell, 1974 [1991].

Leonard, David J. "To the White Extreme in the Mainstream: Manhood and White Youth Culture in a Virtual Sports World." In *Youth Culture and Sport: Identity, Power, and Politics*, edited by Michael D. Giardina and Michele K. Donnelly, 91–111. New York: Routledge, 2008.

Lewis, Neil. "The Climbing Body, Nature, and the Experience of Modernity." *Body & Society* 6 (2000): 58–80.

Lofland, John, David A. Snow, Leon Anderson, and Lyn H. Lofland. *Analyzing Social Settings: A Guide to Qualitative Observation and Analysis.* Belmont, CA: Wadsworth/ Thomson Learning, 2006.

Lofland, Lyn H. *The Public Realm: Exploring the City's Quintessential Social Territory.* Hawthorne, NY: Aldine de Gruyter, 1998.

Lyman, Stanford M., and Marvin B. Scott. *A Sociology of the Absurd.* New York: Appleton-Century-Crofts, 1970.

Lyng, Stephen. "Edgework, Risk, and Uncertainty." In *Social Theories of Risk and Uncertainty: An Introduction,* edited by Jens O. Zinn, 106–137. Malden, MA: Blackwell Publishers, 2008.

———. "Edgework: A Social Psychological Analysis of Voluntary Risk Taking." *American Journal of Sociology* 95 (1990): 851–886.

Lyng, Stephen G., and David A. Snow. "Vocabularies of Motive and High-Risk Behavior: The Case of Skydiving." *Advances in Group Processes* 3 (1986): 157–179.

Lyotard, Jean-François. *The Postmodern Condition: A Report on Knowledge.* Translated by Geoff Bennington and Brian Massumi. Minneapolis: University of Minnesota Press, 1984.

Mörtenböck, Peter. "Free Running and the Hugged City." *Thresholds* 30 (2005): 12–18.

Macdonald, Nancy. *Graffiti Subculture: Youth, Masculinity and Identity in London and New York.* New York: Palgrave Macmillan, 2001.

Maffesoli, Michel. *The Time of the Tribes: The Decline of Individualism in Mass Society.* Translated by Don Smith. Thousand Oaks, CA: Sage, 1988 [1996].

Marshall, Bill. "Running across the Rooves of Empire: Parkour and the Postcolonial City." *Modern & Contemporary France* 18 (2010): 157–173.

Merleau-Ponty, Maurice. *Phenomenology of Perception.* Translated by Colin Smith. New York: Routledge, 1945 [2002].

Merrifield, Andy. *Henri Lefebvre: A Critical Introduction.* New York: Routledge, 2006.

Messner, Michael A. "Riding with the Spur Posse." In *Sex, Violence, and Power in Sports: Rethinking Masculinity,* edited by Michael A. Messner and Donald F. Sabo, 66–70. Freedom, CA: The Crossing Press, 1993 [1994].

———. *Taking the Field: Women, Men, and Sports.* Sport and Culture Series. Minneapolis: University of Minnesota Press, 2002.

———. "When Bodies Are Weapons: Masculinity and Violence in Sport." *International Review for the Sociology of Sport* 25 (1990): 203–218.

Midol, Nancy, and Gérard Broyer. "Toward an Anthropological Analysis of New Sport Cultures: The Case of Whiz Sports in France." *Sociology of Sport Journal* 12 (1995): 204–212.

Mills, C. Wright. "Situated Actions and Vocabularies of Motive." *American Sociological Review* 5 (1940): 904–913.

Mitchell, Richard G. *Dancing at Armageddon: Survivalism and Chaos in Modern Times.* Chicago: University of Chicago Press, 2002.

———. *Mountain Experience: The Psychology and Sociology of Adventure.* Chicago: University of Chicago Press, 1983.

Moore, Sarah E.H. and Adam Burgess. "Risk Rituals?" *Journal of Risk Research* 14 (2011): 111–124.

Mould, Oli. "Parkour, Activism, and Young People." In *Space, Place and Environment,* edited by Karen Nairn, Peter Kraftl and Tracey Skelton, 1–19. Singapore: Springer Singapore, 2015.

———. "Parkour, the City, the Event." *Environment and Planning D: Society & Space* 27 (2009): 738–750.

Murray, Graham. "France: The Riots and the Republic." *Race & Class* 47 (2006): 26–45.

My Playground. Dir. Kaspar Astrup Schröder. Kasparworks, 2010. Film.

Nelson, Richard K. *Hunters of the Northern Ice*. Chicago: University of Chicago Press, 1969.

Newman, Joshua I. "'A Detour through 'NASCAR Nation': Ethnographic Articulations of a Neoliberal Sporting Spectacle." *International Review for the Sociology of Sport* 42 (2007): 289–308.

Newman, Joshua I., and Michael. D. Giardina. "Neoliberalism's Last Lap? NASCAR Nation and the Cultural Politics of Sport." *American Behavioral Scientist* 53 (2010): 1511–1529.

Nie, Norman H. "Sociability, Interpersonal Relations, and the Internet: Reconciling Conflicting Findings." *American Behavioral Scientist* 45 (2001): 420–435.

O'Grady, Alice. "Tracing the City—Parkour Training, Play and the Practice of Collaborative Learning." *Theatre, Dance & Performance Training* 3 (2012): 145–162.

Ortuzar, Jimena. "Parkour or L'Art du Déplacement: A Kinetic Urban Utopia." *The Drama Review* 53 (2009): 54–66.

Pascoe, C. J. *Dude, You're a Fag: Masculinity and Sexuality in High School*. Berkeley: University of California Press, 2007.

Pattillo, Mary E. *Black on the Block: The Politics of Race and Class in the City*. Chicago: University of Chicago Press, 2007.

Pike, Elizabeth C. J. "Injury." In *Berkshire Encyclopedia of Extreme Sports*, edited by Douglas Booth and Holly Thorpe. Great Barrington, MA: Berkshire Publishing Group, 2007.

Point B. Dir. Michael Alosi. Creative Commons, 2009. Film.

Pred, Allan. *Place, Practice, and Structure: Social and Spatial Transformation in Southern Sweden, 1750–1850*. Totowa, N.J.: Barnes & Noble, 1986.

Pronger, Brian. "Post-Sport: Transgressing Boundaries in Physical Culture." In *Sports and Postmodern Times*, edited by Geneviève Rail, 277–298. Albany, NY: State University of New York Press, 1998.

Rappaport, Roy A. *Rituals and Religion in the Making of Humanity*. New York: Cambridge University Press, 1999.

Rheingold, Howard. *The Virtual Community: Homesteading on the Electronic Frontier*. Reading, MA: Addison-Wesley Publishing, 1993.

Rinehart, Robert E. "Dropping into Sight: Commodification and Co-Optation of In-Line Skating." In *To the Extreme: Alternative Sports, Inside and Out*, edited by Robert E. Rinehart and Synthia Sydnor, 27–51. Albany, NY: State University of New York Press, 2003.

———. "Emerging Arriving Sport: Alternatives to Formal Sports." In *Handbook of Sports Studies* edited by Jay Coakley and Eric Dunning, 504–519. Thousand Oaks, CA: Sage Publications, 2000.

———. "Exploiting a New Generation: Corporate Branding and the Co-Option of Action Sports." In *Youth Culture and Sport: Identity, Power, and Politics*, edited by Michael D. Giardina and Michele K. Donnelly, 71–89. New York: Routledge, 2008.

———. "Inside of the Outside: Pecking Orders within Alternative Sports at ESPN's 1995 'the Extreme Games.'" *Journal of Sport & Social Issues* 22 (1998): 398–415.

———. *Players All: Performances in Contemporary Sport*. Bloomington, IN: Indiana University Press, 1998.

Robins, Kevin. "Cyberspace and the World We Live In." *Body & Society* 1 (1995): 135–155.

Robinson, Victoria. *Everyday Masculinities and Extreme Sport: Male Identity and Rock Climbing*. New York: Berg, 2008.

Sabo, Donald F. "Best Years of My Life." In *Jock: Sports and Male Identity*, edited by Donald F. Sabo and Ross Runfola, 74–78. Englewood Cliffs, NJ: Prentice-Hall, 1980.

Sampson, Robert J. *Great American City: Chicago and the Enduring Neighborhood Effect.* Chicago: University of Chicago Press, 2012.

Saville, Stephen John. "Playing with Fear: Parkour and the Mobility of Emotion." *Social & Cultural Geography* 9 (2008): 891–914.

Scheff, Thomas J. *Goffman Unbound!: A New Paradigm for Social Science.* Boulder, CO: Paradigm Publishers, 2006.

Schrock, Douglas, and Michael Schwalbe. "Men, Masculinity, and Manhood Acts." *Annual Review of Sociology* 35 (2009): 277–295.

Schwalbe, Michael. "Identity Stakes, Manhood Acts, and the Dynamics of Accountability." *Studies in Symbolic Interaction* 28 (2005): 65–81.

Sedgwick, Eve Kosopsky. "Gosh Boy George, You Must Be Awfully Secure in Your Masculinity!" In *Constructing Masculinity*, edited by Maurice Berger, Brian Wallis and Simon Watson, 11–20. New York: Routledge, 1995.

Sennett, Richard. *The Uses of Disorder: Personal Identity and City Life.* New York: Knopf, 1970.

Shamir, Ronen. "The Age of Responsibilization: On Market-Embedded Morality." *Economy & Society* 37 (2008): 1–19.

Silbey, Susan S. "Taming Prometheus: Talk About Safety and Culture." *Annual Review of Sociology* 35 (2009): 341–369.

Silverman, Maxim. *Deconstructing the Nation: Immigration, Racism, and Citizenship in Modern France.* New York: Routledge, 1992.

Silverstein, Paul A., and Chantal Tetreault. "Postcolonial Urban Apartheid." *Riots in France* (2006). Accessed February 16, 2015, http://riotsfrance.ssrc.org/Silverstein_Tetreault/.

Simmel, Georg. "The Adventurer." Translated by Donald N. Levine. In *On Individuality and Social Forms: Selected Writings*, edited by Donald N. Levine, 187–198. Chicago: University of Chicago Press, 1911 [1971].

Simon, Jonathan. "Taking Risks: Extreme Sports and the Embrace of Risk in Advanced Liberal Societies." In *Embracing Risk: The Changing Culture of Insurance and Responsibility*, edited by Tom Baker and Jonathan Simon, 177–208. Chicago: University of Chicago Press, 2002.

Small, Mario Luis. *Villa Victoria: The Transformation of Social Capital in a Boston Barrio.* Chicago: University Of Chicago Press, 2004.

Snyder, Gregory J. "The City and the Subculture Career: Professional Street Skateboarding in LA." *Ethnography* 13 (2012): 306–329.

Soja, Edward W. "The Socio-Spatial Dialectic." In *Postmodern Geographies: The Reassertion of Space in Critical Social Theory*, 76–93. New York: Verso, 1980 [1989].

Sontag, Susan. *On Photography.* New York: Farrar, Straus and Giroux, 1977.

Stapleton, Scott, and Susan Terrio. "Le Parkour: Urban Street Culture and the Commoditization of Male Youth Expression." *International Migration* 50 (2010): 18–27.

Stoddart, Mark C. "Constructing Masculinized Sportscapes: Skiing, Gender, and Nature in British Columbia, Canada." *International Review for the Sociology of Sport* 46 (2010): 108–124.

Stranger, Mark. *Surfing Life: Surface, Substructure, and the Commodification of the Sublime.* Farnham, UK: Ashgate, 2011.

Strauss, Anselm L. "A Social World Perspective." *Studies in Symbolic Interaction* 1 (1978): 119–128.

Strauss, Anselm L., Leonard Schatzman, Rue Bucher, Danuta Erlich, and Melvin Sabshin. *Psychiatric Ideologies and Institutions*. New York: Free Press of Glencoe, 1964.

Stryker, Sheldon. "Identity Salience and Role Performance: The Relevance of Symbolic Interaction Theory for Family Research." *Journal of Marriage & the Family* 30 (1968): 558–564.

Thompson, David. "Jump City: Parkour and the Traces." *South Atlantic Quarterly* 107 (2008): 251–263.

Thorpe, Holly. *Snowboarding Bodies in Theory and Practice*. New York: Palgrave Macmillan, 2011.

Thorpe, Holly, and Nida Ahmad. "Youth, Action Sports, and Political Agency in the Middle East: Lessons from a Grassroots Parkour Group in Gaza." *International Review for the Sociology of Sport* 50 (2015): 678–704.

Thorpe, Holly, and Belinda Wheaton. "'Generation X Games,' Action Sports, and the Olympic Movement: Understanding the Cultural Politics of Incorporation." *Sociology* 45 (2011): 830–847.

Turkle, Sherry. *Alone Together: Why We Expect More from Technology and Less from Each Other*. New York: Basic Books, 2011.

———. *Life on the Screen: Identity in the Age of the Internet*. New York: Simon & Schuster, 1995.

Turner, Victor W. "Betwixt and Between: The Liminal Period in 'Rites De Passage.'" In *The Forest of Symbols: Aspects of the Ndembu Ritual*, 93–111. Ithaca, NY: Cornell University Press, 1964 [1967].

Vaccaro, Christian. A., Douglas. P. Schrock, and Janice. M. McCabe. "Managing Emotional Manhood: Fighting and Fostering Fear in Mixed Martial Arts." *Social Psychology Quarterly* 74 (2011): 414–437.

Vester, Heinz-Günter. "Adventure as a Form of Leisure." *Leisure Studies* 6 (1987): 237–249.

Vivoni, Francisco. "Waxing Ledges: Built Environments, Alternative Sustainability, and the Chicago Skateboarding Scene." *Local Environment* 18 (2013): 340–353.

Wacquant, Loïc. *Body and Soul: Notebooks of an Apprentice Boxer*. New York: Oxford University Press, 2004.

———. "For a Sociology of Flesh and Blood." *Qualitative Sociology* 38 (2015): 1–11.

———. "Marginality, Ethnicity and Penality in the Neo-Liberal City: An Analytic Cartography." *Ethnic & Racial Studies* 37 (2014): 1687–1711.

———. *Urban Outcasts: A Comparative Sociology of Advanced Marginality*. Malden, MA: Polity Press, 2008.

Waitt, Gordon. "'Killing Waves': Surfing, Space, and Gender." *Social & Cultural Geography* 9 (2008): 75–94.

Waitt, Gordon, and Andrew Warren. "'Talking Shit over a Brew after a Good Session with Your Mates': Surfing, Space and Masculinity." *Australian Geographer* 39 (2008): 353–365.

Walker, Rob. *Buying In: The Secret Dialogue between What We Buy and Who We Are*. New York: Random House, 2008.

Wanderer, Jules J. "Simmel's Forms of Experiencing: The Adventure as Symbolic Work." *Symbolic Interaction* 10 (1987): 21–28.

Wellman, Barry. "The Three Ages of Internet Studies: Ten, Five and Zero Years Ago." *New Media & Society* 6 (2004): 123–129.

West, Amanda, and Linda Allin. "Chancing Your Arm: The Meaning of Risk in Rock Climbing." *Sport in Society* 13 (2010): 1234–1248.

West, Candace, and Don H. Zimmerman. "Doing Gender." *Gender & Society* 1 (1987): 125–151.

Wheaton, Belinda. *The Cultural Politics of Lifestyle Sports*. New York: Routledge, 2013.

———. "Introduction: Mapping the Lifestyle Sport-Scape." In *Understanding Lifestyle Sports: Consumption, Identity, and Difference*, edited by Belinda Wheaton, 1–28. New York: Routledge, 2004.

———. "'Just Do It': Consumption, Commitment, and Identity in the Windsurfing Subculture." *Sociology of Sport Journal* 17 (2000): 254–274.

———. "Selling Out?: The Commercialisation and Globalisation of Lifestyle Sport." In *The Global Politics of Sport: The Role of Global Institutions in Sport*, edited by Lincoln Allison, 140–61. New York: Routledge, 2005.

Wheaton, Belinda, and Becky Beal. "'Keeping It Real': Subcultural Media and the Discourse of Authenticity in Alternative Sports." *International Review for the Sociology of Sport* 38 (2003): 155–176.

Whyte, William H. *City: Rediscovering the Center*. New York: Doubleday, 1988.

Williams, J. Patrick. *Subcultural Theory: Traditions and Concepts*. Malden, MA: Polity Press, 2011.

Wilson, William Julius. *The Truly Disadvantaged: The Inner City, the Underclass, and Public Policy*. Chicago: University of Chicago Press, 1987.

———. *When Work Disappears: The World of the New Urban Poor*. New York: Knopf, 1996.

Wolf, Daniel R. *The Rebels: A Brotherhood of Outlaw Bikers*. Toronto: University of Toronto Press, 1991.

Woods, Krista, Phillip Bishop, and Eric Jones. "Warm-up and Stretching in the Prevention of Muscular Injury." *Sports Medicine* 37 (2007): 1089–1099.

Young, Kevin, Philip White, and William McTeer. "Body Talk: Male Athletes Reflect on Sport, Injury, and Pain." *Sociology of Sport Journal* 11 (1994): 175–194.

Index

About the Author

JEFFREY L. KIDDER is an associate professor of sociology at Northern Illinois University.